LABVIEW
POWER PROGRAMMING

OTHER McGRAW-HILL BOOKS OF INTEREST

LabVIEW
Power
Programming

Gary W. Johnson

McGraw-Hill
New York • San Francisco • Washington, D.C. • Auckland • Bogotá
Caracas • Lisbon • London • Madrid • Mexico City • Milan
Montreal • New Delhi • San Juan • Singapore
Sydney • Tokyo • Toronto

Library of Congress Cataloging-in-Publication Data

Johnson, Gary W., date.
    LabVIEW power programming / Gary W. Johnson.
       p.   cm.
    Includes index.
    ISBN 0-07-913666-4
    1. LabVIEW. 2. Scientific apparatus and instruments—Computer
simulation. 3. Computer graphics. I. Title.
Q185.J644 1998
006—dc21
                                            98-18295
                                                  CIP

McGraw-Hill

*A Division of The **McGraw·Hill** Companies*

1 2 3 4 5 6 7 8 9 0 DOC/DOC 9 0 3 2 1 0 9 8

P/N 032943-5
Part of ISBN 0-07-913666-4

*The sponsoring editor for this book was Steve Chapman and the production supervisor
was Sherri Souffrance. It was set in Vendome by North Market Street Graphics.*

Printed and bound by R. R. Donnelley & Sons Company.

McGraw-Hill books are available at special quantity discounts to use as premiums and sales promotions, or for use in corporate training programs. For more information, please write to Director of Special Sales, McGraw-Hill, 11 West 19th Street, New York, NY 10011. Or contact your local bookstore.

 This book is printed on recycled, acid-free paper containing a minimum
of 50% recycled, de-inked fiber.

CONTENTS

V

Contents

Contents

Contents

FOREWORD

This book represents the culmination of over 10 years of work—from intense brainstorming sessions in 1984 and 1985 to development on the *fat Mac* in 1985 and 1986 to the release of LabVIEW 1 in 1986. As the pioneers will attest, the early product was only effective for small-scale problems, in context with the computing power available at that time, in a dominantly text-based programming world.

We were looking for an alternative to Basic for controlling GPIB instruments. But LabVIEW is a new kind of language—a graphical programming language that has brought the power of the computer to the scientist and the engineer in a powerful new metaphor that is natural to the user, not the machine. As such, it has expanded the community of computer "programmers."

Today, almost 15 years later, computers are 50 times faster, with 50 times as much memory and hundreds of times as much disk space. Systems are portable, networked, and Internetworked.

And the modern LabVIEW has now reached maturity as well. Thousands of users on all six continents work with the program every day, in large, complex, real-time and mission-critical applications. In the modern world, with graphical user interfaces now commonplace, LabVIEW has become the programming language of choice for the systems engineer and the scientific community.

This achievement comes from teamwork—of the dedicated development staff at National Instruments, of hardworking and patient users at a wide variety of educational, research, and industrial organizations, and especially of the Alliance program members. The application specialists of the Alliance (started in 1987 as the LabVIEW Consultants Group) have become the true experts in the effective development of successful systems. And, not surprisingly, many of the chapters of this book have been authored by Alliance members.

In my view, LabVIEW has advanced the state of software development in three key areas: graphical programming, user interface design, and development environment. I recall user group meetings where we attempted to teach structured user interface design under the guise of the *open when called* checkbox on a subVI. The VI front panel makes user interface development very easy for everyone—the novice and the experienced developer alike. The graphical programming approach to design and debugging has brought the power of programming to the scientific user, who is neither ready for nor interested in Hyper-C+++ or whatever. Technicians, engineers, and scientists can now develop complex systems without advanced degrees in computer science. But, interestingly, those same CS experts find LabVIEW more effective for many system development applications as well.

Application diversity is fascinating. One customer started using Lab-VIEW for testing in a manufacturing environment, then expanded the system to run the entire manufacturing operation, a very elaborate database application. One user collects manufacturing quality data every few seconds, and keeps the data for years, on-line. The database query, statistical analysis, user interface, and information display systems are all built in LabVIEW.

So, we've come a long way over ten years, from Basic for instruments to real-time measurements in interplanetary space. And the fun is just beginning!

—JACK MACCRISKEN
AUSTIN, TEXAS
JANUARY 1, 1998

INTRODUCTION

Graphical programming as embodied in LabVIEW has undergone explosive growth in popularity and diversity of application since its inception in 1987. Much of this growth is due to the nearly unchallenged productivity boost that LabVIEW provides, as demonstrated by programmers in all fields of science and engineering. Whereas conventional textual languages often leave us wallowing in syntactical quagmires, LabVIEW frees us to concentrate on the problem, moving rapidly to a solution with high-level tools that are actually fun to use. With each new LabVIEW release, and with the proliferation of high-performance personal computers with standardized interfaces, we move to ever higher levels of capability and ease of use.

LabVIEW is a product of National Instruments Corp. (Austin, TX) and has been available since 1987. Programs developed in LabVIEW are portable among several platforms: PCs running all versions of Microsoft Windows, Macintoshes, Sun SPARCStations, HP PA/RISC workstations, and Concurrent PowerMAX systems. A nearly unlimited range of instrumentation I/O interfaces (such as GPIB, VXI, plug-in data acquisition boards, and serial ports) is fully supported, as are several networking and interapplication communication protocols. A related product, BridgeVIEW, is based on the same graphical language—G—with extra features for industrial process control applications. Everything in this book applies to BridgeVIEW as well as LabVIEW.

Many of us now consider LabVIEW an indispensable tool—as important as a multimeter, microscope, or calculator. Much of my recent success as an instrumentation engineer is attributable to LabVIEW in combination with various I/O devices, particularly plug-in boards. This is truly a new way of doing business in instrumentation, and the payoffs are significant in terms of performance, cost savings, and reduced effort. Proof of these claims, and some of the techniques by which success is achieved, are contained herein.

This book is primarily intended for experienced LabVIEW users in all fields, as well as those in academia who have an interest in graphical programming concepts and applications. For a general introduction to LabVIEW with a focus on common applications in instrumentation, you may want to obtain a copy of my previous book, *LabVIEW Graphical Programming*, available from McGraw-Hill. Also, National Instruments offers a wide variety of educational materials including live training courses, videos, and printed matter covering LabVIEW and many of their instrumentation products. Call (800) 433-3488 or (512) 794-0100 for information regarding LabVIEW and other National Instruments products.

With its increasing versatility and so many application areas, I believe we have reached the point at which no one person can be a universal LabVIEW guru. For this reason, I have invited (dare I say coerced?) an international panel of LabVIEW experts to contribute their words of wisdom in areas ranging from computer science to math to networking.

The opening shot is fired by Ed Baroth and Chris Hartsough of the NASA Jet Propulsion Laboratory in Chap. 1, "LabVIEW Enables the Interactive Communication Process." Their thesis is that LabVIEW lets the customer and software developer work together as a team in a much more effective manner than traditional programming languages. This intense interaction and involvement—and fun!—leads to exceptional productivity in software development. Read how these authors implement a strategy of *programming while you help,* and see why the Measurement Technology Center at the Jet Propulsion Laboratory is such an outstanding organization.

Computer scientists have been paying more attention to LabVIEW as it grows in popularity. Its graphical nature necessitates some study of how to map traditional approaches into the G language paradigm, and this is where the next three chapters come in. In Chap. 2, "Data Structures," Joe Damico of Sandia National Laboratories begins our journey with a discussion of stacks, queues, linked lists, trees, and graphs, and shows us how they're implemented in G. Continuing in Chap. 3, "Algorithms," Joe dissects some of the well-known searching and sorting algorithms and supplies their LabVIEW counterparts. By modifying his VIs, you can create your own optimized search or sort algorithm, tuned to your data's structure and size.

Joe Damico branches into virtual hardware in Chap. 4, "Boolean Machine Architectures," where he emulates basic logic functions, shifters, latches, and flip-flops. He then assembles these fundamental elements into the core elements of a digital computer: an arithmetic logic unit, and a central processing unit. This chapter is of particular interest to those who wish to learn about or simulate the workings of a CPU.

Joe's final chapter, "Cryptography," is an accessible overview of a complex topic where you'll find some interesting and useful LabVIEW cryptographic machines. He covers several well-known algorithms, including the Caesar Cipher, the One-Time Pad system, and public key encryption. See if LabVIEW can outwit the international spies!

Lothar Wenzel is an applied mathematician with an affinity toward LabVIEW as a teaching aid as well as a problem-solving tool. To you and me, he's a math professor with his feet planted firmly in reality. In Chap. 6, "LabVIEW in Mathematics," he starts us on an inspiring trip through the workings of the G Math Toolkit, of which he is the primary author. You'll see equation solving, curve fitting, fractals, optimization, and encryption, all implemented and displayed graphically. G is a novel alternative to conventional mathematical notation, and most people find it intuitive and quite instructive.

Lothar continues with a mathematical viewpoint in Chap. 7, "LabVIEW as a Simulation Tool." We look at interesting situations like artificial life, heat conduction, tomography, acoustics, and the Laplace equation as applied to soap films. Only the last few examples require the G Math Toolkit, proving again that the built-in features of LabVIEW are sufficient for serious simulation.

The Lothar Wenzel trilogy is completed in Chap. 8, "Digital Signal Processing." This chapter shows how the G Math Toolkit extends the DSP capabilities of the standard LabVIEW package to tackle some state-of-the art problems. Many of the examples are founded on the fractional Fourier transform and its modern relatives such as the chirp-z algorithm, Walsh-Hadamard transforms, and wavelet transforms. This also leads us to a discussion of joint time-frequency analysis, the Gibbs phenomenon, and the construction of optimal FIR filters.

Turning to more of the nuts and bolts of advanced LabVIEW applications, Brad Hedstrom of Advanced Measurements discusses "ActiveX and Application Control" in Chap. 9. ActiveX (formerly called OLE Automation) is a Microsoft Windows mechanism that allows applications to manipulate each other using a specific protocol. LabVIEW 5 can function as both an OLE client and a server, which lets you extend and intermix the capabilities of LabVIEW with those of other applications in a relatively painless way. As an example, Brad shows you how to use the Microsoft Access database as a report generator for a LabVIEW-based automated test application. Another new feature of LabVIEW 5 is the Application Control VIs, which permit you to programmatically invoke methods and change properties of VIs. An example shows how to automatically generate LabVIEW documentation with this new toolbox. Source code is included on the CD-ROM.

Perhaps the most flexible kind of networking is TCP/IP, and Brad Hedstrom explains its usage in Chap. 10, "Networking with TCP/IP." He covers two applications (with source code on the CD-ROM) that handle a wide variety of situations. The first is a fast-response, unidirectional system for high-speed data transfer. The other is a bidirectional client/server application that supports multiple clients with great flexibility—very useful in remote control of laboratory experiments.

Ed Baroth of JPL returns in Chap. 11, "Data Acquisition from Space via the Internet," to demonstrate the real importance and practicality of using the Internet and LabVIEW for remote data acquisition. You'll see the details of how researchers monitored the recent Mars Sojourner Rover, and another sophisticated experiment on the space shuttle, the Brilliant Eyes Ten-Kelvin Sorption Cryocooler Experiment (BETSCE), which demonstrated the feasibility of chemisorption cryocooler technology in space. If you have any doubts about the viability of LabVIEW in mission-critical systems, read this chapter.

Chapter 12, "Advanced LabVIEW Applications for Space Missions," is another adventure in space with the JPL team focusing on the Galileo mission to Jupiter in 1995. LabVIEW was an integral part of the telemetry system development, providing simulation and analysis of complex data streams. These elaborate applications require easy configuration, flexible architectures, and an effective user interface for the display of data and communications error flags. During these projects, some measurements were made comparing LabVIEW productivity with conventional C coding. I don't need to tell you the outcome. And at the end of the chapter, there's a surprise regarding the future of LabVIEW in real-time, high-reliability applications.

If you develop advanced applications in LabVIEW, you need a working knowledge of professional software development techniques; this is the subject of Chap. 13, "Software Engineering Primer." Gregg Fowler of National Instruments originally wrote the text of this chapter for the G Professional Developers Toolkit, and we've updated it for this book. Learn about software life cycle models, prototyping and design techniques, scheduling, and project tracking.

Writing software that meets verifiable quality standards is a challenge in all programming languages, including LabVIEW. In Chap. 14, "LabVIEW Software Quality Assurance Guide and Toolkit," Gary Johnson covers the process of managing the LabVIEW development process with an eye toward meeting ISO 9000 requirements. Topics include planning and designing your project, coding standards, and testing. A toolkit comprising a set of quality management documents is included on the CD-ROM to make the process easier, especially your first time through.

In Chap. 15, "LabVIEW Code Extensions," CIN wizard Brian Paquette of SensArray Corporation discusses the world of Code Interface Nodes, the Call Library Function, and other methods of linking external code modules to LabVIEW. Brian goes beyond the LabVIEW manuals to give you insight into *when* and *why* you might want to use these techniques, and he points out a number of tricks and pitfalls.

Our final chapter, "LabVIEW and Serial Interfaces," was written by George Wells of JPL. Most of us know that serial interfacing is a nontrivial exercise, though it sure seems easy at first glance. George has spent many years interfacing computers and instruments with RS-232 and other serial connections, and his wisdom finally appears on paper. He'll walk you through the basics of RS-232 connections, establishing communications, and debugging in difficult situations.

 \path_ name\file

The accompanying CD-ROM includes sample LabVIEW code and utilities referenced in many chapters. The Appendix lists the general contents of the CD-ROM and gives instructions regarding software installation and compatibility. Throughout this book, you will see a CD-ROM icon in the margin (as shown here), with the file system path to the item of interest.

There are many topics that are as yet uncovered in this book or any other. Given the broad diversity of LabVIEW applications, I have no doubt that library shelves will continue to fill with wondrous LabVIEW topics for many years to come. Stay connected to the World Wide Web, especially the National Instruments site, www.natinst.com, and watch for announcements of new products, new features, new resources, and new adventures in LabVIEW.

—GARY W. JOHNSON
LIVERMORE, CA

ACKNOWLEDGMENTS

Compiling a book such as this is a lot of work for the editor, but it's even more work for the contributors. They are busy people, in high demand because of their proven expertise with LabVIEW and in other areas. I came to know these authors through a variety of channels, particularly user group meetings and the info-labview mailgroup on the Internet. Their credentials are, individually and collectively, remarkable. It is a great personal honor to have made their acquaintance and to have obtained their valuable written insights into the many complex topics that are LabVIEW today.

Thanks to those who took the time to review one or more chapters:

Larry Desonier, Sandia National Laboratories

Ron Frye, Lawrence Livermore National Laboratory

John Goldsmith, Sandia National Laboratories

Leo Mara, Sandia National Laboratories

Murali Parthasarathy, National Instruments

Jeff Parker, SensArray Corp.

Stepan Riha, National Instruments

Ian Riley, Brill Engineering Limited

Jason Dunham, Software for Industrial Systems

Special thanks go to my wife, Katharine, who created the original illustrations for this book and attended to the details associated with the hundreds of screen images. I especially appreciate her patience with me while I spent countless evenings and weekends in front of the computer.

Finally, thanks to my editor at McGraw-Hill, Steve Chapman, for supporting this project, and to the LabVIEW developers at National Instruments for creating such a cool product.

LabVIEW Enables the Interactive Communication Process

Ed Baroth, Ph.D., and Chris Hartsough, M.S.

Measurement Technology Center (MTC), Jet Propulsion Laboratory, California Institute of Technology

Introduction

This is a book about LabVIEW *power,* LabVIEW programming. Perhaps you are reading this before you purchase this copy, perhaps not. In any event, *power* is a word bandied about a great deal these days. What does it mean? If you see a book on *Power Dressing* (in the business section, not cooking section), what do you expect? I would expect to see a book that exposes the subtleties of costume explained/exposed and just what effect each element or style will likely have on the others. From such a book you would expect to learn how to dress to preload others into expecting you to appear as a marketing expert, university professor, entertainer, klutz, or what have you. Not only would such a book tell you how to achieve an effect, it is also a catalogue of the effects that are available. In short, it is an advanced instruction book about a social tool. The book you are reading will analogously provide you with advanced instruction in the use of a technical tool: LabVIEW. There is a risk inherent in most *power* books: they describe the tool effectively but don't describe what you can do. You can be "all dressed up with nowhere to go."

This chapter will tell you where to go (in the most positive sense!). Developing proficiency is challenging and fun, and that may be enough. But if you wish to make a maximum contribution to your organization, there is more. In fact, there are actually two *mores.* The first is a model of system development and deployment based on communications and the second is about ascending from the abilities of a journeyman to those of a LabVIEW master.

LabVIEW as a general-purpose programming language is a good deal. Not a great deal, but a good deal. If what you are doing is simply developing programs from specifications or requirements delivered by a client or a customer—a needs provider—LabVIEW will be somewhat faster than conventional text-based languages. That's important. With the tools and knowledge you gain from this book there will be two advances: your ability to do smart things will be increased, and you will gain knowledge that allows you to do more smart things. That's also important. What you will be missing is the improved *communication power* available from the graphical programming paradigm. It is this paradigm that enables the truly huge productivity gains that are possible with the use of LabVIEW.

The Power of Communication

In conventional development where the program developer is not working on his or her own problem—that is, in development for a customer—conventional wisdom has events proceeding in several distinct and abutted stages (Fig. 1.1). First, the needs provider prepares requirements. If you are lucky, these are written; if you are very lucky, they mostly hold together. If you are unlucky, they are delivered in a more or less disjointed conversation, one time through, and fast. On really bad days you are not given the time to even prepare written notes of the conversation: "Don't bother with all that red-tape paperwork, you know what we need; build it!" (But guarantee it works and don't go over budget!)

Then the developer goes off and codes the thing and does a unit test (maybe). The customer will then tell you what is wrong. This is also known as failing the acceptance test. There are many variations on this theme. A *code walk-through* can be added, or you can start with rapid prototyping or any number of steps that fall under the heading of software engineering. Volumes and volumes have been written telling us how to do it right. Some are useful; all are expensive in the use of your time. What all of these techniques aim at is, at least from one point of view, to have a predictable translation of requirements from the language of the customer into the language of the computer. In short, **communications**.

The word *communication* comes from the same root as communion, or co-union: causing the union of the representations of two ideas from two locations. Predictably, problems are introduced through the translation of the ideas into the computer world. What would happen if we could avoid the translation? What if the needs provider and the computer could use the same language to represent the needs? Magic is what would happen. And magic is what happens with LabVIEW, under the right circumstances. In fact, we have demonstrated that development in LabVIEW can be 4 to 10 times more productive than development in conventional, textual languages. How do we do this? We wish it were as simple as a one-word answer—a word like *LabVIEW*—but it's not. To determine why it's not, we must delve into this communications business a bit.

IMPORTANCE OF COMMUNICATIONS How is communications important? With the faster pace of business and increased global competition, a new way of delivering specifications interactively is becoming more common and companies are scrambling for a better method to handle the process. There simply is not time to prepare long, complicated specifications and requirements documents before work can begin. Bet-

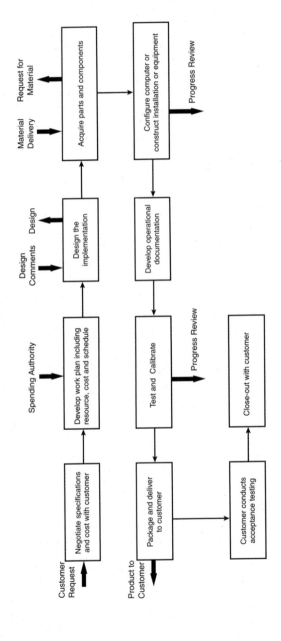

Figure 1.1

The traditional model for programming involves a long sequence of events, generally spanning long periods of time. Customer-developer communication is generally not real-time.

ter and increased communications is the key factor in shortening development time while maintaining quality and keeping risk manageable.

When we humans are developing any formal statement, for example a law, a policy statement, a procedure, or the like, there are at least two stages. First, the group working on the statement typically kicks around ideas and tries out various approaches. Wording is drafted for key ideas for an outline or structure before the result—usually a document—is developed. (Exploratory activities such as this usually occur even if the "group" is an individual.) Second, the crafting of a formal statement is undertaken. The activities that make up this formalization of content are not just wordsmithing or polishing style. Often, in the preparation of the formal expression, conflicts surface, ideas are refined, and the integrity of the entire document is developed, tested, and refined. Very rarely does a formal statement in any medium just "fall out of the authors' minds" ready to go to press.

LabVIEW VERSUS TEXTUAL LANGUAGES With LabVIEW it is possible for the formal language to be the **diagram**, which often replaces more formal specifications. The customer, developer, and computer participate in the formal expression of the idea, need, or requirement. This is essentially the same process that occurs in any joint writing project. In fact, the traditional development steps of discovery of requirements, design, code, unit test, and acceptance test can be collapsed into a single conversation. In approximately the time it takes to write a formal requirements document, the system can be built!

Why, you might reasonably ask, has this not been done with textual languages? The answer is both as simple and as complex as why people generally won't sit around watching and kibitzing while another person writes a memo. Oddly, we will sit, generally squirming, while a moderator writes on flip charts. What probably lies at the core of this behavior is information rate. When the input information rate that we experience falls below some threshold, we stop having a conversation. If you try a simple experiment you can see just how important the rate of information flow really is. Have a discussion with someone on a topic of mutual interest, only put a long pause between each word you speak. Force the other person to wait thirty seconds after you have spoken before they can begin to respond. (An American classic is Bob and Ray's *Slow Talkers of America* bit.) This is guaranteed to drive the other person crazy. Most people would rather check their toes for hangnails than communicate in this form.

With textual languages, there is so much that is meaningless to the uninitiated (look at C syntax, for example) that, coupled with the slowness of writing the code, there is no real hope that a conversation can be maintained. This is not to say that communications cannot take place; it's just that they take place as monologues, not as conversation. In a very real way, formal requirements documents are monologues, and the resulting communications, critiques, and requests for clarification or amplification are responding monologues. Because all of the communication is formal, the speed at which it can take place is much slower than that of a live conversation.

A conversational exchange is just more time-efficient, especially if there is an undisputed arbiter as to the meaning of each statement. In our case the computer is the arbiter. Why LabVIEW? Actually the key is the graphical nature of the language. There is some formal research and much practical observation that leads to the conclusion that we humans think in pictures of some sort. When writing, you in effect describe the diagram or picture you have formed in your mind. As you read, the author intends that you develop from the words the same (or essentially the same) graphic he or she had in mind when the words were set down. Using graphics directly as a formal syntax can eliminate whole steps—stages, in fact—in the communication process.

ESTABLISHING COMMUNICATIONS So where does that leave us? With any luck, in a conversation. If an environment can be established where the customer, developer, and computer can be in one conversation, then we can collapse the process as described in the preceding paragraph. How? Well, the customer and the developer (you) have a preliminary discussion—the computer couldn't care less—and, when it's appropriate, formally record the material in the LabVIEW syntax. The user interface is a formality that is negotiated in the conversation. (This part is now an industry standard: Visual <anything> from Microsoft and all the folks that inspired them or were inspired by them provide similar facilities.)

Next, the real power of LabVIEW comes into action. The semantics—what has been discussed and what happens—can be immediately recorded and tested. Here is the opening shot in the real power of Lab-VIEW power programming: *The customer will happily help the developer draw the diagram.* Customers will participate in the conversation, if not as authors, then as editors. The computer now plays its part, first in checking syntax (a broken *Run* arrow) and then in semantics. It's as if the paper won't let you construct improper grammar and then immediately reflects exactly what you said—instant feedback testing.

This is becoming more common in other programs, for example Microsoft Word and its on-line grammar checker, but there is a fundamental difference between that and LabVIEW. You, as the author, have the final say in how the words appear on the page in a Word document. If you want to use bad grammar, punctuation, or spelling, it's your choice. LabVIEW, however, has the final word in deciding how the VIs are wired. You can certainly decide what icons appear on the page and how they are wired. On the other hand, you cannot wire up an icon in an invalid manner. The broken wires will not let you make *syntactical errors*. But if you add when you should subtract, LabVIEW will not correct this *logical error*.

This interactivity separates graphical from textual programming. The customer, though not formally trained in LabVIEW, still participates in the process of developing the diagram. Together with the programmer, customers see the flow of information appearing on the page. They make corrections and additions. They, in real time, refine the choices and outcomes. Both customers and programmer make immediate decisions concerning the user interface interactively at the computer. This simply cannot occur in textual languages. And it is that fact that enables the increased productivity (Fig. 1.2).

Try it out with friends. Pretend you have to develop a program for them, perhaps something financial for home or a scorekeeping program for Little League. Ask them to write specifications down on paper and go away and program. When they refuse to do that, then ask to do it together on the computer using LabVIEW. See if they don't think this is fun.

Actually the mechanism is a bit more subtle. The diagram is an abstract expression of the process. When we wire A and B into a ▷ object, we are not forced to explicitly specify the outcome for all possible values of A and B—that is the power of arithmetic. With complex situations, the degree of certainty we have with arithmetic is not present. What we do is to work a few examples. We realize—literally make real— an outcome. This *rapid prototyping* moves the expression of our process into a more concrete domain. Usually we check the *boundary conditions:* what will happen for the smallest and largest legal input values (and for ones a little smaller and a little bigger). Then we check the correctness of the results for a few selected input values. Since this can all be done in a conversation, the productivity is enormous.

Another term bandied about a great deal these days is *seamless integration*. What is it, other than an increase in productivity due to less formal barriers between stages of a task or project? The increase in productivity from LabVIEW comes from the interactive approach to software development. If there really is a seamless integration and a conversational model for development, just what does the developer bring to the party?

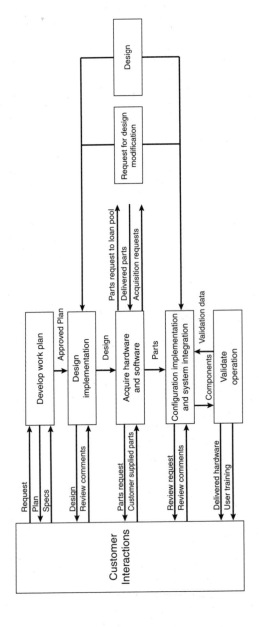

Figure 1.2
LabVIEW turns software development into a live conversation among the customer, programmer, and computer. Exceptional productivity results.

Role of the Developer

Why do we need a developer? For several things, actually. Even if there are no seams in the integration process, there may be wrinkles, and the developer brings the iron. There are several useful things, and one critical one, that the developer brings.

- *Formal language skills.* In publishing terms, the developer is the author of the diagram, and the customer is the editor. From experience, we have found that customers can read and edit the diagram as it is being produced long before they could realistically create a diagram (program) on their own. That represents a productivity gain.

- *Development and operations environment knowledge.* For the foreseeable future, there will be an operating system underlying the graphical environment and its needs must be tended to. When the program is running, there are other operating systems issues that must likewise be attended. Better the customer not have to worry about these issues.

- *Data integrity and/or database expertise.* Measurement and control in the modern setting implies data logging and historical records in some form. While the customer is generally responsible for prescribing the nature of the information to record, developers should hold themselves responsible for the details of this part of the system.

- *Guiding the conversation for development.* The developer is in the best position to understand what has not been specified (the computer knows too; it's just a bit rude). The responsibility of managing the conversation for completeness is the developer's.

STRUCTURE   *Structure,* or architecture, is the most critical contribution of the developer toward the overall success of the project! There are several areas that need structure. Clearly the program needs some. *Spaghetti* is a structure, or lack thereof, that has earned a bad name in the software world. It deserves it. (A different form of pasta design has a following in the UNIX world: shell scripts.) If the problem is small, and the life of the software is on the order of 30 days, just throwing it together and then throwing it away (!) is not necessarily a bad idea. If the problem has any size or life span, then structure is needed. There is plenty of choice in basic architectural design as discussed in the world of software engineering:

- HIPO (Hierarchical Input Process Output)
- Data-driven

- Event-driven
- Decision tables
- Structured design
- Data flow
- Object-oriented
- More—lots more...

It's beyond the scope of this chapter to delve into these, or any other, design structures and their methods. Some of the structural notions in the list are out of vogue just now. Some deserve to be. What we have found is that these methods all have their limitations and strengths. The important thing here is that the system will get a structure, and the key questions are: "Will the structure be designed or defaulted?" and "Will the structure support or hinder the processes of system development, system operation, and system maintenance?" If the developer does not know what these architecture techniques are, it will be hard for him or her to select the ones that are best. For better or worse, it will be the developer who spans the full spectrum of conversations and it will be the developer who has the only opportunity to supply system structure.

What else needs structuring? The diagram itself. The structure of the drawing itself is critical to the conversation. The structure of the conversation has already been noted. What we are emphasizing is perhaps an element of design, where *design* is meant in a broader context than engineers are accustomed to applying to their own work.

Journeyman to Master

You can be a whiz at LabVIEW programming (know *how* to wire the icons), but if you do not know *when* to use *what* icon, you will not be able to translate the customer's desires into reality. Everyone who uses Lab-VIEW has access to the same VIs. All the icons are available all the time. How do you learn when to use which one? How do you satisfy the customer? That is really the only goal—to satisfy the customer. Not to write a killer app or to provide fantastic graphics or neat diagrams. Those are means to an end, not ends in themselves.

National Instruments provides training classes, of course. These are valuable, no question about it, but is that all there is to becoming a systems integrator? National Instruments has always made it quite clear that it is a tool developer, not a systems integrator. Integration is left up to the systems integrators. National Instruments cannot teach you to become a systems integrator because it is not one itself.

As a tool creator, NI teaches you how to use the tool. The analogy we've often used involves learning to drive. NI teaches you how to start the car, how to make a turn, and so forth, much like a driving school. NI teaches you how to physically make the car move, turn, and stop, but not really how to drive. If you think you know how to drive simply because you took some driving lessons, please stay off the L.A. freeways. Anyone can tell you there is a big difference between *learning* how to drive and really *knowing* how to drive. This book is intended to teach you how to really drive LabVIEW around the block. That's the difference.

Of course that difference is experience, for which there is simply no substitute. But how can you make the most of your experience? Communication. The developer is the translator between the customer and the computer. Do not expect the customer to know, understand, or be able to enunciate his or her ideas clearly without assistance on your part. Unless they know LabVIEW directly, customers have no idea what the software is even capable of doing. You are the person who pulls ideas from the customer and turns those ideas into code the computer can understand. But you can't go anywhere without specific help and direction from the customer.

And the conversation just doesn't happen by itself. You, as the developer, must draw the information out of the customer. You must be persistent and assertive. We know that most of us engineers, scientists, and computer jocks tend to be introverts, but customers are looking at us to direct the conversation. Do not be afraid to ask questions frequently and repeatedly, if necessary, to really understand what the customer thinks he or she wants. Do not be afraid to suggest alternatives, simplifications, or compromises if these will save time (and money). By doing so you will, at a minimum, make the customer definitive about his or her ideas. And you will be surprised how flexible customers become when you tell them that the specific approach they want will take a day to code and with a minor simplification it can be done in a half hour. Remember, not *repair* but *repeat* business is the proof of customer satisfaction. It's one way to tell journeymen (or journeywomen) from masters.

Another way requires a musical analogy. At first you have to practice simply making a chord on a guitar. Beginners are most concerned with physically *how* to play the chords. Then, after you've mastered the chords and how many different ways there are to play them, the real challenge of *when* to play the chords appears. If you've ever seen a jazz chart, they frequently include just the melody line and chords for each measure. Sometimes the same chord is shown for four or even eight measures. But if you've ever heard jazz, you know that the same chord is rarely played for two beats, let alone two measures. Where do the other chords come from? How do you know what to play? It's the knowing when to play what chord that separates the journeyman musician from the master. Just as it's knowing when to use what icon in LabVIEW.

Other ways to separate a master from a journeyman are present in their respective overall views of the language. Journeymen are concerned with individual icons, new ones for specific purposes, and different ways to use the existing ones. Masters want to move the language itself in new directions, into new fields. Masters also consider the big picture when creating VIs. Is this VI just for this particular task, or if I just put additional work into it, will it become more of a general library tool that I can use again and again?

Remembering the big picture is always important. It's part of the communication. Ask yourself some questions: What big picture or program is this small VI a part of? How does it relate to the whole project? Once the customer has the capability that this VI provides, what is he or she likely to ask for next? For example, if you are creating a data acquisition VI, what is the customer using for data analysis? A spreadsheet? Custom analysis? Did you ask? Remember, many people do not think LabVIEW does data analysis, just data acquisition. It's up to you to suggest possibilities. They usually become opportunities—for repeat business.

Another area of separation between journeyman and master involves the role of the developer in a team setting. In the past, because the process of development was a series of discrete steps, people usually performed their tasks alone or with people of similar technical background. The move is now toward creating teams of people with diverse backgrounds to accomplish tasks interactively. It's all part of improving communication as products are designed, built, and tested. The area of designing spacecraft involves considering the ground support and testing of the spacecraft as it's being designed, not as an afterthought. Here again the master understands the big picture of how and where LabVIEW might be used to reduce the overall cost of subsystem- and system-level testing, while the journeyman is narrowly focused on data acquisition. The journeyman is there to *support* the team, but the master is an *integral part* of the team. The difference may be one of perception, of willingness to contribute ideas, or even of willingness to listen.

Summary

The most important advantage the Measurement Technology Center has found in using graphical programming is the communication among the customer, developer, and hardware that visual programming enables. Without the visual component, the communication is not present.

The visual component is the ability to graphically communicate the state of execution of a system to the customer. This capability of seeing what the "code" is doing directly is of inestimable value. The graphical description of the system without the animation would be not much more than a CASE tool with a code generator; with the animation, the boundaries between requirements, design, development, and test appear to collapse. Seamless movement from one activity focus to another makes the development different in kind, not degree. This is because we can sustain the communication among the customer, developer, and computer. If there are substantial time lags in changing tools (e.g., conventional debuggers or third-party applications), the conversational environment breaks down.

Having additional capability (data analysis, visualization, database access, etc.) in the same iconic format extends the language and increases the communication. This expands the possibilities into other engineering disciplines. Access to other (non-LabVIEW) tools is, of course, better than nothing. But if the language used to control the third-party tool is different from the host language, the advantage is severely diminished. It would be as if you took your car in for repair and had to describe engine problems in English, suspension in French, braking in German, and so on. It's better than not getting your car repaired, but far from ideal.

Given where we are—where we train specialists who limit themselves to formal computer language skills—and given where we need to be—where developers are pivotal members of the entire process—we need education. We need to provide education in thinking processes in addition to specific skills. This is a path less traveled but not uncharted. We need to educate ourselves in structure, expression, and conversation. As suppliers, we need to provide tools that promote expression and conversation across technical disciplines. This path leads to increased productivity and an overall improvement of the process by redefining the user base.

Postscript

Another way to differentiate people who really use LabVIEW from those who simply know people who use LabVIEW is the spelling. Real Lab-VIEW programmers know how LabVIEW is spelled. They even know that LabVIEW is an acronym for Laboratory Virtual Instrument Engineering Workbench. People who spell LabVIEW as *LabView* are people who know people who use LabVIEW, but do not use it themselves. These are people like upper management, program or project managers, and so on. Never hire someone who spells it *LabView* to do any real programming for you. Such people are only good at making reports and viewgraphs.

Bibliography

Edmund Baroth, "How the Internet Changes Data Acquisition—Using BETSCE as an Example," *Evaluation Engineering*, February 1997, pp. S1–S9.

Edmund Baroth and C. Hartsough, "Experience Report: Visual Programming in the Real World," in Margaret Burnett, Adele Goldberg, and Ted Lewis (eds.), *Visual Object Oriented Programming*, Manning Publications, Greenwich, CT, 1995.

Edmund Baroth and C. Hartsough, "Visual Programming as a Means of Communication in the Measurement System Development Process," *SciTech Journal*, vol. 5, no. 5, pp. 17–20, 1995.

Data Structures

Joseph P. Damico

Sandia National Laboratories, Livermore, CA

Data structures are a fundamental aspect of software development. Lab-VIEW presents many predefined data types and structures to the programmer. The simple or *atomic* data types include Boolean, integer, and floating point. We consider these types to be atomic since they have no smaller parts. A data structure differs from an atomic type because it can be decomposed into smaller parts, which may be atomic types or other data structures. Typical LabVIEW data structures include arrays, clusters, strings, and graphs. The LabVIEW cluster is the same as the structure (*struct*) in C or the record in Pascal. Data structures include definitions for data and related operations. A well-designed data structure can greatly simplify a complicated algorithm. Several common data structures include stacks, queues, linked lists, trees, and graphs. This chapter describes these data structures and presents their LabVIEW implementations, which form the foundations for the sorting and searching algorithms discussed in the next chapter, "Algorithms."

A good data structure has several important characteristics. **Encapsulation** prevents users from accessing protected data. A familiar example of encapsulation comes from LabVIEW's array data type. While we can read the array size, we cannot modify it directly. We modify it only when we append to the array or otherwise resize it. **Information hiding** keeps programmers from seeing internal data in a structure. Hiding internal data keeps VI diagrams cleaner. The linked list example presented in this chapter hides internal data from the external interface. **Implementation independence** allows the programmer to use different internal implementations while keeping the same external interface. **Abstraction** lets the programmer concentrate on the problem at hand rather than the minute details of the data structure. For example, when we copy one Lab-VIEW array to another, we don't worry about how the data is copied, what type of loop is used, or any other details; we consider the array copy operation in simplified, abstract terms.

Stacks

\data_
structures\Int
Stack.vi

A stack behaves as a last in, first out (LIFO) data structure. The last item placed on the stack will be the first one removed from it. The user of a stack only has access to the top of the stack—all contents are accessed from there. A stack is a simple data structure. In LabVIEW it is an array where inserts and deletes are done from only one end—the top of stack. A stack has a very simple interface: The **push** operation places items on the stack, and the **pop** operation removes items from the stack. Figure 2.1 shows the VI diagram for an integer stack. The *initialize* operation creates an empty array and sets the *size* shift register variable to 0. The *push* operation prepends *element* to the array and increments the size. *Pop* indexes out the 0th array element, then resizes the array to remove it, and decrements *size*. These simple array operations enforce the stack's LIFO behavior. You could add other operations if needed, such as "is the stack empty?"

You can adapt the stack VI to any data type by taking advantage of **typedefs**. Typdefs are created by editing any front-panel control with the **Control Editor** and make it easy to define and maintain data structures. In this VI, you would use the same typedef for the *element* control and indicator. Then, if you want to change the data type, just edit the typedef with the Control Editor, and you're ready to run. Use typedefs liberally in your LabVIEW development process whenever you define a data structure.

The allocation and deallocation of array space during these stack operations creates some unnecessary overhead. The stack used in the Quicksort VI (discussed in the next chapter, "Algorithms") reduces the allocation overhead with more intelligent array management. This exemplifies implementation independence. The stack's external interface doesn't change, so the programmer can choose either implementation without changing any other code.

The programmer using the stacks and queues defined here has no access to the internal array. The stack data structure allows users to access

Figure 2.1
A LabVIEW stack implementation for integers.

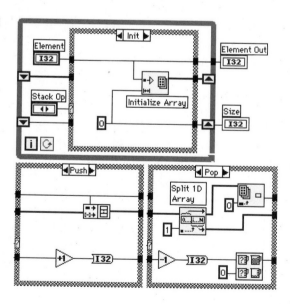

the top of the stack for pushes and pops and to initialize the array. But other than that, the user cannot sort the array, replace elements, or otherwise change the data (and upset the logical LIFO structure!). This demonstrates the role of encapsulation within a data structure. Encapsulation ensures the integrity of the data structure by limiting access to the internal data.

Users benefit from implementation independence, too. The calling VI does not care how the stack is implemented as long as it provides an efficient LIFO structure.

The LIFO behavior of a stack pops data items off of the stack in the reverse order of how they were pushed on. A string or any list of data items can be reversed by pushing the elements on the stack and then popping them off element by element. Stacks manage the calling chain for procedure and function calls in a procedural language and provide a way to make recursive calls in LabVIEW. Several algorithms presented in this book use the Stack VI.

Queues

\data_
structures\Int
Queue.vi

\data_
structures\Int
Priority Queue.vi

The first in, first out (FIFO) queue data structure, shown in Fig. 2.2, closely resembles the stack. The difference is the **enqueue** operation, where the new data element is appended to the array. The **dequeue** operation, like the stack pop, removes the data element from the first array element and then resizes the array. The FIFO structure outputs data in the order it was placed in the queue.

The FIFO queue is the most familiar example, but other types of queues are commonly used too. **Priority** queues can be implemented by adding some logic to the enqueue operation. The new element can be inserted into the array at a point determined by the defined priority scheme. The Integer Queue VI can be made into a priority queue that returns the largest integer in the queue (this also sorts the internal array in descending order). The enqueue logic for the **Integer Priority Queue VI** appears in Fig. 2.3. The Priority Enqueue loops through the array searching for the insertion point for the new element, then inserts the element. The rest of the queue internal logic works as is, and the external interface does not change either.

The stack and queue data structures provide foundations for many important algorithms. In the next chapter, "Algorithms," the stack structure is used in the Quicksort algorithm as well as the tree and graph tra-

Data Structures

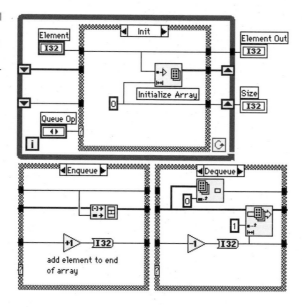

Figure 2.2
The Integer Queue VI diagram.

versal algorithms. The queue is used by the Breadth First search algorithm, discussed later in the section on graphs. The VI diagrams for these algorithms show how these simple data structures can greatly reduce the complexity of an algorithm. The Quicksort algorithm shows how recursion can be implemented in a LabVIEW VI by using explicit stacking and the stack data structure.

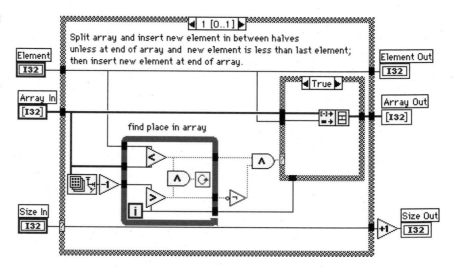

Figure 2.3
Enqueue logic for the Integer Priority Queue VI.

Memory Pointers

LabVIEW provides a range of data types from Boolean to complex clusters of data. One data type that LabVIEW lacks is the **memory pointer**, which allows indirect memory references. A memory pointer variable contains the *location* of a variable rather than its value. Programs access the memory pointer to find a variable's location and then read the value from that location. In the C language, many common data structures such as linked lists and trees are built using pointers, which provides great flexibility for the programmer. However, the flexibility comes with a cost: Pointer references lead to a significant number of errors that can be very difficult to find and fix. Pointer manipulation code can be difficult to read and can hide malicious operations (for instance, accessing another program's memory space). The Java programming language does not include pointers for these reasons, nor does LabVIEW. Despite these problems, many algorithms and data structures use pointers because of their efficiency.

The lack of pointers does not prevent LabVIEW programmers from developing and using data structures. Instead of using pointers, the LabVIEW programmer can create robust array-based data structures by intelligently indexing the array. Typically, you access an element in array A with a simple index operation like $A[1]$ or $A[i + 2]$. The pointer-based data structures discussed here add a slight wrinkle to array accesses. The index value for the access comes from the same array, or possibly some other array. These index operations look like $A[A[i]]$ or $A[B[i + 2]]$, where A and B are both arrays and i is a scalar value. A useful example would be an arbitrary reordering (sorting) of array A according to an array of indices $B[i]$. While the elements of array A are sequentially ordered in memory, any logical ordering of the array data is then possible without maintaining multiple copies of array A. The particular logical ordering depends on the data structure, but all rely on manipulation of array indices to provide the desired behavior.

Linked Lists

Linked lists are a fundamental data structure and are widely used in many different algorithms. A typical linked list consists of a group of **nodes** that contain data as well as one or more **links** to other nodes. The links in a linked list are **pointers** to other list nodes. With a linked list, you can add, remove, or reorder list elements without any changes to or sorting of the data list. Only the list of link pointers need be changed. This can provide dramatic speed improvements by avoiding memory shuffling.

The nature of pointers is important in understanding linked lists. A pointer is an indirect reference to the location of a data element. Figure 2.4 shows a diagram of an example linked list. In this diagram, the list *head* points to the first element in the list. This element contains *data* and a *next* pointer to the next list element. To access the list elements, the list is traversed starting at the list head and moving through the nodes sequentially. The *next* pointer from the last node does not point to a valid node, so the traversal ends there. This final, invalid node is often referred to as a *nil* pointer.

The LabVIEW linked list implementation presented here encapsulates the list in a VI. The *data* and *next* pointers for a list node can be placed in a cluster to more closely resemble the model presented above. However, the *bundle* and *unbundle* operations add overhead to the algorithm. The linked list data structure used here stores the *data* and *next* pointers in separate arrays. The *data* array contains the data nodes and the *links* array contains the *next* pointers for the nodes. The type of element in the *data* array depends on the application and is encapsulated in a cluster. The indices logically link the arrays: The data element stored at *data* array location i has its *next* pointer stored at *links* array location i. A *links* array element with a value of −1 indicates an invalid, or nil, *next* pointer.

Figure 2.5 shows the VI diagram for a LabVIEW linked list. The *Initialize* case shows how the key elements of the data structure are initialized. The VI initializes the *data* array with *size* elements, each with the value passed in through the *data* control. The VI stores this array in a shift register. The shift register variable *head* points to the first element in the list. Its initial value of −1 indicates an empty list. The *links* array contains the *next* pointers that link the list together. This array is initialized so that the

\data_ structures\ Linked List.vi

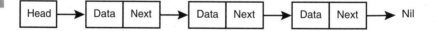

Figure 2.4
Model for a linked list. The final *next* pointer on the right does not point to a valid location; it is commonly refered to as a *nil* pointer.

last element (*size* –1) points to its predecessor (*size* –2), which points to its predecessor (*size* –3), and so on until the 0th element, which points to –1 (nil), indicating the end of the list. These values set up a list of all free nodes. The shift register variable *free* points to the last *links* array element. So, starting from *free,* one can traverse the entire list of free nodes by following the links stored in the *links* array.

Figure 2.6 shows a logical diagram of the initial state of this linked list when initialized for a five-element list. *Head* has been initialized to –1 to indicate an empty list. The *data* array elements have an initial value of 0. The shift register variable *free* has a value of 4, which points it to index 4 of the *links* array. *Links*[4] points to *links*[3], which points to *links*[2], and so on until *links*[0], which points to –1 and terminates the list.

The linked list data structure contains two lists. The list pointed to by *head* contains the list elements, and the list pointed to by *free* contains the unused nodes. Both lists use the *links* array to link their nodes. The *free* list allows the reuse of list nodes. The user knows nothing about the *free* list. This illustrates information hiding in a data structure.

Other important operations on the linked list presented here include insert node, delete node, and find node.

Insertion into the list involves finding a node in which to store the data and then linking it into the list [Fig. 2.7(*a*)]. Figure 2.7(*b*) shows the arrays after the first element has been inserted into the list. The first *free* list node is used to store the new element. If the *free* list is empty (*free* = –1), then no insert is performed and *error* is set true. This list scheme

Figure 2.5

Initializing the linked list.

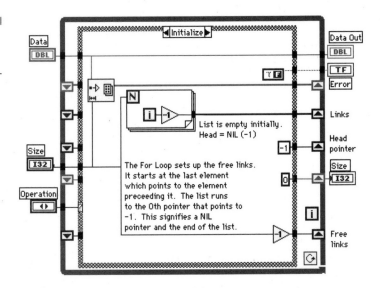

Figure 2.6
Initial state of the
data list and link list
in the Linked List VI.

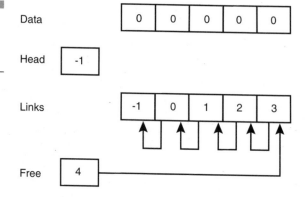

inserts elements at the front of the list so the new node's index is copied
to *head*. The new node must then be linked to the rest of the list, so the
old value of *head* is copied to the *links* array at the new node's index. Note
that this maintains the proper list termination when the first node is
inserted, since the old value of *head* (–1) becomes the next link from the
only node.

There are valid reasons for simply inserting new data at the front of
the list. The inserts take a constant amount of time regardless of the list

Figure 2.7
(a) Conceptual dia-
gram for linked list
insertion; (b) state of
the list after the first
element has been
inserted.

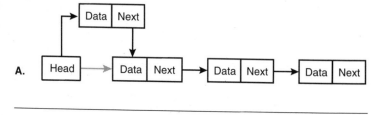

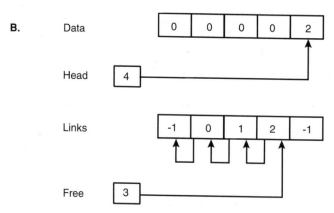

length. Accesses to list elements occur in spurts, so often an insert is followed by one or more finds for that element. A list scheme that inserts and deletes from the front of the list creates a stack. Lists for other purposes will enforce other insert and delete logic. A sorted list finds the proper list location based on the desired ordering and inserts the new element there. No matter what the insertion scheme, the same logic applies: find the location and link the new element in by pointing to it and pointing from it to the rest of the list. Figure 2.8 shows the frame of the LabVIEW diagram in the Linked List VI that implements the insertion logic discussed.

Deleting a list node involves removing the link to it and linking the nodes that followed back into the list. In general, the node that pointed to the deleted node points to the node that the deleted node had pointed to. To delete the first element in the list, take its *next* pointer and copy it to the list head. To delete the last node, copy its next pointer (−1 again) into the new last node, the list node that had pointed to it.

Figure 2.9 shows a deletion from the conceptual list and the before and after conditions of the data structure. In the data structure diagram, the *data* array element containing 2 is deleted. This node was at the front of the list, so the deletion involves the list *head.* After the deletion, the list *head* points to what had been the second list node. The conceptual diagram does not show the handling of the deleted node. If the deleted node is not kept in some list, then that memory is lost. This is one source of memory "leaks"—which often lead to crashes—in an application. In the C

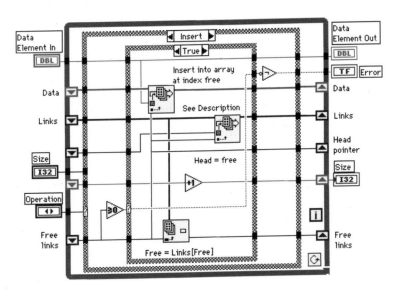

Figure 2.8
Linked list insertion diagram.

Data Structures

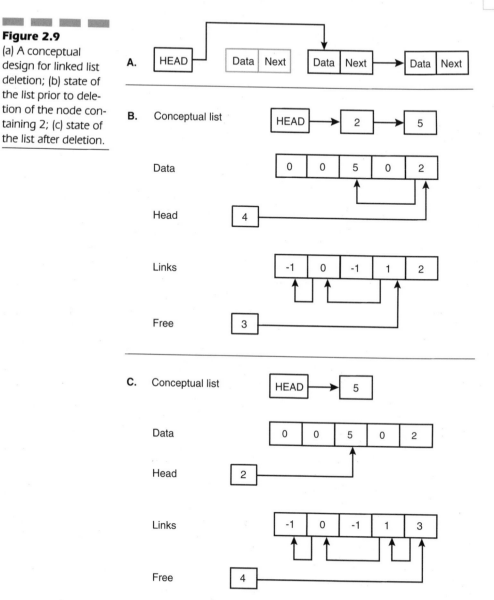

Figure 2.9
(a) A conceptual design for linked list deletion; (b) state of the list prior to deletion of the node containing 2; (c) state of the list after deletion.

language, this memory location can be deallocated. The LabVIEW implementation keeps the unused nodes in the *free* list. This eliminates allocation and deallocation calls and their memory management overhead. The deleted node is placed at the front of the *free* list and points to the previous head of the *free* list. Note that the *data* array is not modified; this is not necessary since the *data* array element will not be accessed by any future list operations until a new value is inserted there.

Figure 2.10
This frame of the
Linked List VI per-
forms the deletion
operation.

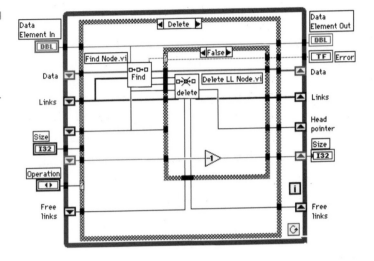

Figure 2.10 shows the Linked List VI's delete operation. This list implementation deletes by node value: It searches the *data* array for a matching value and deletes it if found. Note that there may be duplicate nodes in the list; this operation deletes the first one found.

The diagram of the **Delete LL Node VI** is shown in Fig. 2.11. This VI takes the deleted node, the node prior to it, the *free* list head, and the list *head* as inputs. If the node is equal to the *head,* then the node is the first list element. In this case, the following node is "promoted" to the list head by indexing it out of the *links* array and passing it to *head.* The newly deleted node is placed at the front of the *free* list by passing its index to *free.* The rest of the *free* list is linked to the new first element by replacing that element's next link value with the old value of *free.* The case of a

Figure 2.11
Diagram of the
Delete Linked List
Node VI.

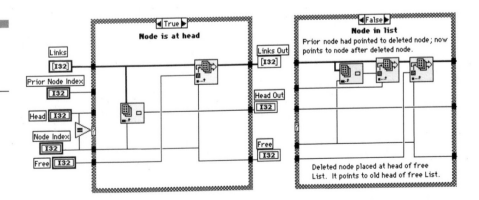

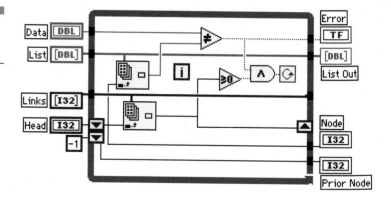

Figure 2.12
Diagram of the
Linked List Find VI.

node somewhere in the list is slightly more complicated. The prior node's next link is replaced with the deleted node's next link. The deleted node is placed at the front of the *free* list, and the rest of the *free* array is linked from it as in the first case.

The diagram of the **Linked List Find VI** is shown in Fig. 2.12. This VI demonstrates how a list search differs from a sequential search on the data array. A sequential array search indexes sequentially through the array, while the list search uses more intelligent indexing based on the indices stored in the *links* array. This VI starts at the list head and goes node to node through the list until a node that matches the *data* search key is found or the end of the list is reached. The value of *head* is passed through a shift register into the loop. The value from this shift register is the index into the *data* array. A data element is indexed out and compared to the search key, *data*. The *head* shift register value also indexes the next list node index from the *links* array and determines the next node in the list. The previous node is also tracked using a second shift register element. This value is important for properly deleting nodes from the list. If no match is found after the list is traversed, then an error is returned.

The Multi-List

\data_
structure\Multi
List.vi

The linked list discussed so far encapsulates two linked lists: the *data* and the *free* lists. This structure can be expanded to hold multiple lists. A **multi-list** (list of lists) structure requires only two more arrays (Fig. 2.13). A list *head* array provides any number of lists, and a *size* array keeps track of their sizes. One *free* list keeps track of the spare nodes. A structure ini-

Figure 2.13
A multi-list, or list of lists, is a very flexible data structure.

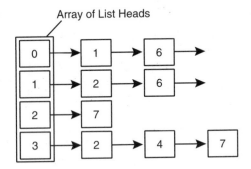

tialization command initializes all *head* array elements and the *free* list. Single lists can be initialized too. The list is copied to the *free* list. The other commands from the standard Linked List VI work as is. The *head* value passed out of the case is inserted back into the *head* array. The diagram for the Multi-List VI appears in Fig. 2.14.

Three arrays encapsulated in the multi-list store any number of lists. This simple data structure provides a foundation for other important data structures and algorithms. This multi-list data structure works with graph and hashed lookup algorithms. The section on graphs describes how a multi-list can represent a graph. Chapter 3, "Algorithms," presents a multi-list—based hash table that enables very fast searches.

Figure 2.14
Diagram for the Multi-List VI.

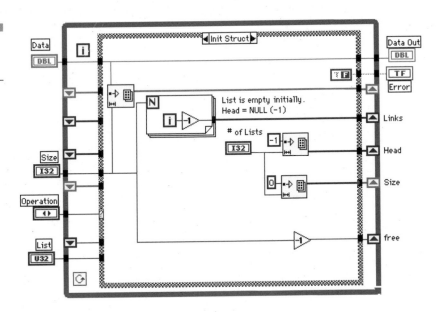

Trees

Tree data structures sprout up in a wide variety of computer programs. Trees are often used to describe hierarchies, like file systems, and LabVIEW's VI Hierarchy display. A hierarchy implies an ordering of elements. The top element in a hierarchy is linked (directly or indirectly) to all elements below. Elements lower in the hierarchy have elements above them and possibly elements below. In the tree structure, the top element is called the **root node**. The root node contains data and pointers to its **children** nodes. These children can in turn be root nodes to subtrees below them. At the bottom of the tree (these trees grow from the root down) are the **leaf nodes** that have no children. The **depth** of a node is the number of links between it and the root node. The depth of a tree is the number of links between the root node and the farthest leaf node.

A **binary** tree consists of a root node and no more than two subtrees, or child nodes. This recursive definition applies to the subtrees, too. The two subtrees are often referred to as the left and right subtrees. The **binary search tree** (BST) has a special characteristic: All nodes stored in the left subtree contain smaller data elements than the parent node, and all nodes in the right subtree contain data elements that are greater than or equal to the parent node's data. This characteristic of the BST is enforced through insert and delete operations. The BST shown in Fig. 2.15 stores integer values. The root node stores the value 5. Its left child contains the value 2, and this child node is the root node for a subtree. The subtree has no right child, which implies that there is no node in the sub-

Figure 2.15
A binary search tree.

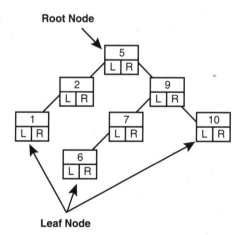

tree greater than or equal to 2. The right child of the tree's root node is a larger subtree whose own root node stores the value 9.

A BST storing n data elements will have an average depth of $\log_2 n$, since n elements can be halved at most $\log_2 n$ times. The worst-case depth is n when the tree degenerates into a linked list. All BSTs tend to keep a minimal depth near $\log_2 n$. A BST search starts at the root node and branches through the tree until a match is found or a leaf node is reached. Thus, a BST search takes no more than $\log_2 n$ comparisons on average. This characteristic makes the binary search tree well suited for applications requiring rapid searching.

An implementation for a LabVIEW BST data structure, the **Binary Search Tree VI**, appears in Fig. 2.16. This data structure uses implied pointer indices to store the tree in an array. The root node is always at index 0. The left child node is stored at index 1, and the right child node is stored at index 2. In general, if a node is stored at index i, its left child will be found at index $2i+1$ and its right child will be found at index $2i+2$. The *used* array keeps track of which array elements store tree nodes.

The BST structure is maintained with a very simple insert algorithm. The algorithm starts at the root node, moves through the tree according to the BST branching rules, and inserts the new data at the first unused node found. Size comparisons determine the path through the tree. If the new node is less than the tree node, the search moves to the left child. If the new node is greater than or equal to the tree node, the search moves to the right child.

The first node inserted into the structure is the root node. In Fig. 2.13, 5 would have been the first node inserted. Any nodes inserted after that are compared to the root node. If they are less than the root node, then they move to the left subtree; if they are greater than or equal to the root node, they move to the right subtree. The insert search continues, moving through subtrees until it reaches an unused node, where it inserts the new node.

Searching in a BST closely resembles the insert algorithm. The **BST Find VI** appears in Fig. 2.17. The search begins at the root node. If the root node is equal to the search key, then the search is over. If the key is less than the root node, then the left subtree is searched. If the key is greater than the root, then the right subtree is searched. The successful search branches through the subtrees until the key is matched. Unsuccessful searches run until they reach an unused node.

\data_ structures\ **Binary Search Tree.vi**

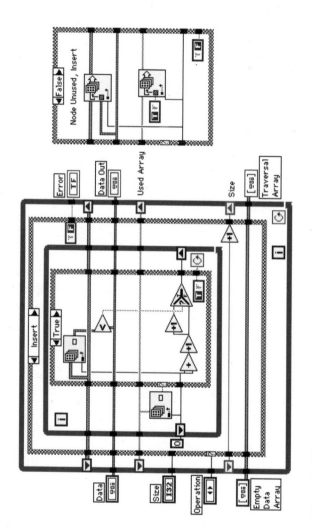

Figure 2.16
A LabVIEW implementation of the binary search tree data structure.

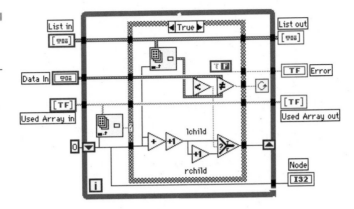

Figure 2.17
Diagram of the BST Find VI.

\data_
**structures\Tree
Traversal.vi**

Tree Traversals

The contents of a tree structure can be returned with a **tree traversal**. There are three common tree traversal algorithms: **preorder**, **inorder**, and **postorder**. In computer science texts, tree traversal algorithms are commonly expressed recursively. To implement these algorithms in Lab-VIEW, the recursion must be managed implicitly within a traversal VI rather than explicitly through recursive VI calls, since those are illegal. Our old friend, the Stack VI, enables the self-managed recursion. The **Tree Traversal VI** appears in Fig. 2.18.

The preorder traversal visits the root node before visiting the child nodes (left child, then right child). The inorder traversal visits the left child, then the parent, then the right child. The postorder traversal visits the left child, the right child, and then the parent. The inorder traversal returns the tree contents in sorted order.

Since a tree grows randomly on the basis of the insert order of the nodes, it is possible that array elements will be unused. For example, three elements can be inserted into a tree in six different orders. If the elements are 0, 1, and 2, the possible orderings are (0,1,2), (0,2,1), (1,0,2), (1,2,0), (2,0,1), and (2,1,0). The first ordering uses the array elements 0, 2, and 5, since these elements use only the right subtrees. Elements 1, 3, and 4 are not used. The orderings (1,0,2) and (1,2,0) use only locations 0, 1, and 2. While some insertion orders waste no space, most leave gaps of unused elements in the array. For large data sets, or certain insertion orderings, huge arrays are needed to properly store the data. Many of the array elements will not be used, either. This limits the usefulness of this BST implementation to

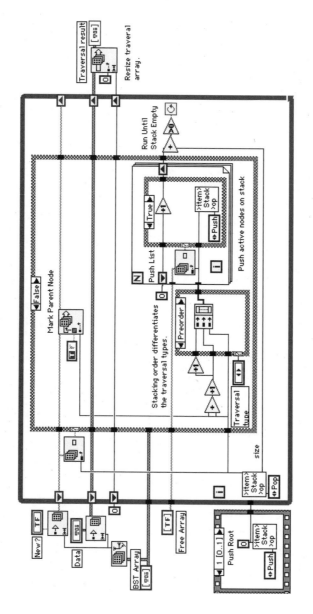

Figure 2.18
Diagram of the Tree Traversal VI.

33

an academic example. More space-efficient BST implementations are possible but are not discussed here.

A linked list is an alternative and efficient solution in this case. Rather than using the fixed indexing for left $(2i + 1)$ and right $(2i + 2)$ child nodes, we add new nodes to the end of the data array and use one link array to store indices of left children and a second array to store indices of right children.

Graphs

The **graph** data structure might cause confusion in LabVIEW, where graphs are defined data types—XY Graphs and such. Another way to envision the graphs described here is as networks or interconnected elements. A graph consists of a set of **nodes**, or vertices, and a set of **edges** that connect the nodes. For example, in a computer network, the computers are nodes, and their interconnections are the edges. For a set of n nodes, there can be up to n^2 edges (in this case, every node is connected to every other node, forming a **complete** graph). If A and B are nodes, then AB and BA are possible edges. The edge AB means that B is adjacent to A, or reachable from A. Graphs are defined as being *directed* or *undirected*. In an **undirected graph**, the edges allow two-way travel, so edge AB implies edge BA. In a **directed graph**, or digraph, the edges allow one-way travel: The edge AB allows B to be reached from A, but does not allow A to be reached from B. Edges in a directed graph are denoted with arrows indicating the direction of travel on the edge. A **path** is a sequence of nodes connected by edges. A **cycle** is a path with a repeated node. In diagram form, directed graphs use arrows to denote edge directions.

Graphs represent many different phenomena, from computer networks to urban traffic. In operating systems, they model concurrent processes. Graphs can also show the calling relationships between functions and procedures in a computer program.

Computer representations of graphs involve **adjacency lists** or **adjacency matrices**. In both cases the adjacency structure stores each node's neighbors. Figure 2.19 displays a directed graph and its corresponding adjacency matrix and adjacency list. Note the bidirectional edge between nodes 0 and 6. All other nodes allow only unidirectional travel.

The adjacency list contains the adjacent nodes for each node. To find out which nodes are adjacent to a node, the list is traversed. The adjacency matrix for a graph with n nodes is an n by n array of entries. Nodes are

Figure 2.19

Three representations of a directed graph. (a) the directed graph diagram; (b) the corresponding adjacency matrix; (c) its adjacency list.

A. Directed Graph Diagram

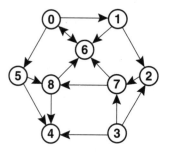

C Adjacency List for diagram

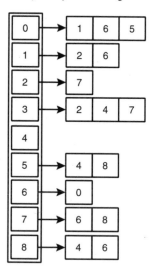

B. Adjacency Matrix for diagram

		End Node								
		0	1	2	3	4	5	6	7	8
	0		X				X	X		
	1			X				X		
Start Node	2								X	
	3			X		X			X	
	4									
	5					X				X
	6	X								
	7							X		X
	8					X		X		

numbered 0 to *n* – 1. If node *k* is reachable from node *j*, then the array element m[*j,k*] is set to 1 to indicate a valid edge. All other entries are set to some default value indicating no connection between the nodes. In a **weighted graph** the adjacency matrix contains the relative cost of each edge.

Figure 2.20 shows the LabVIEW implementation of a graph data structure, the **Graph VI**. This VI uses an adjacency matrix to store the graph structure and creates a directed graph with variable edge weights. An edge weight of –1 indicates no connection. The *Initialize* case of the VI creates a two-dimensional adjacency matrix. The *# of Nodes* control determines the matrix dimensions. After the adjacency matrix is initialized, the matrix is populated with the *Add Edge* command. In the *Add Edge* case, the edge running from node 1 to node 2 is added to the adjacency matrix. The VI tests the node values to ensure that they are within range and then tests to make sure that the new edge doesn't already exist. If the nodes are that valid, and the edge does not exist, the new edge is added to the adjacency matrix. The *Delete Edge* command tests for legal node values and for the presence of the delete edge candidate. A weight of –1

\data_
structures\
Graph.vi

Figure 2.20
Diagram of an adja-
cency matrix-based
Graph VI.

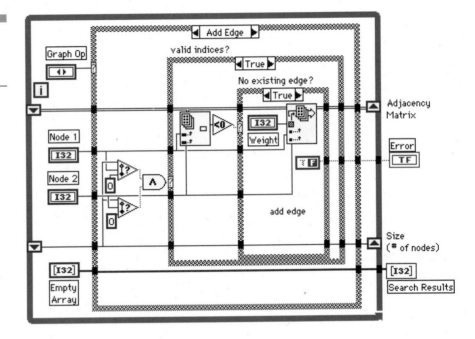

is inserted into the adjacency matrix to delete the edge. Other commands allow two different graph traversals.

Graph traversal is a fundamental aspect of graph algorithms. Two common traversals are breadth-first and depth-first searches. In the **breadth-first search** (BFS), an arbitrary node is selected as the starting point. All of its adjacent, or neighbor, nodes are visited, then all of the neighbors' neighbors are visited, and so on. In the **depth-first search** (DFS), the start node is visited, then one of its neighbors, then one of its neighbor's neighbors, and so on. The other neighbors of the start node are not visited until all nodes reachable from the first neighbor have been visited. In both types of traversals, the operations performed when a node is visited depend on the application and the data stored in the node. The traversal algorithms presented here merely append the visited nodes to an array.

The BFS and DFS traversals use the same basic algorithm with different data structures. The BFS uses a queue, while the DFS uses a stack. In the **Breadth First Search VI**, shown in Fig. 2.21, the start node is enqueued to "prime the pump" (or queue) for the first loop iteration. The first iteration of the loop dequeues the start node, indexes its adjacency list, and loops through the adjacency list enqueueing all unmarked nodes adjacent to the start node. The main loop runs until nothing remains on the queue. The next iteration dequeues one of the start node's neighbors and

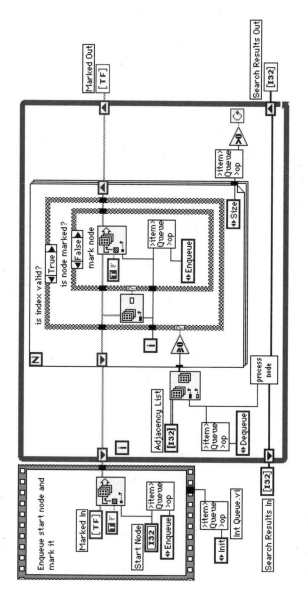

Figure 2.21
Breadth-first search algorithm.

processes its adjacency list. The queue's FIFO structure ensures that the search visits all of the start node's neighbors before any of its neighbors' neighbors. Thus all nodes with path length of 1 from the start node are processed before any nodes within a path length of 2 from the start node. For this reason, the BFS will find the shortest path between the start node and any other reachable node. The marked array indicates whether a node has been processed and enqueued. If so, it is not enqueued again, because each node is processed only once. When the algorithm finishes, any nodes unreachable from the start node will remain unmarked.

 \data_ structures\ **Depth First Search.vi**

The DFS algorithm, shown in Figure 2.22, closely resembles the BFS but requires a more complex stack and a slightly more complicated routine to push nodes on the stack. The stack data element consists of a cluster of the node and the next adjacency list node index to be processed. To initialize the algorithm, the start node and adjacency list node 0 are clustered and pushed on the stack. The first loop iteration pops this cluster back off the stack and indexes out the start node's adjacency list. The adjacency list processing continues until the first neighbor node is found. At this point, the algorithm stops processing the start node's neighbors and follows the newly found node to its neighbors. The algorithm pushes a cluster containing the start node and position in the adjacency list onto the stack. This serves as a bookmark to remember the current position. When the search has exhausted all deeper nodes below this neighbor, the algorithm pops this cluster off the stack and resumes the DFS search on the start node's remaining neighbors.

After setting the bookmark, the algorithm pushes the neighbor node on the stack and exits the inner loop. The next pass of the main loop will pop the neighbor node off the stack, process its adjacency list for a neighbor, and then push both back on the stack. The stack's LIFO structure allows the farthest neighbors from the start node to be processed before the closest neighbors.

The DFS algorithm presented here demonstrates self-managed recursion in LabVIEW. The nodes and adjacency list nodes stored on the stack form a subset of the data that would be present on the run time stack of an explicit recursive algorithm.

Summary

This chapter has presented several fundamental data structures. Stacks and queues provide important behaviors that are used by many algo-

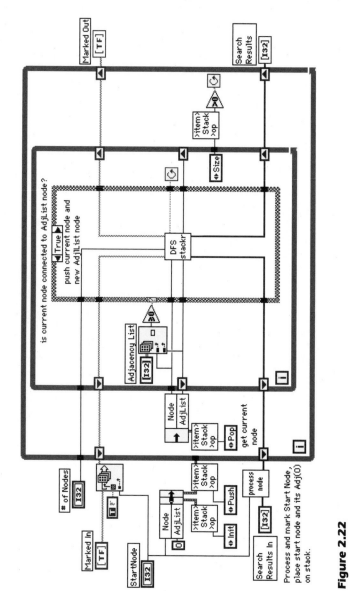

Figure 2.22
Diagram of the Depth First Search VI.

rithms, including the tree and graph traversals discussed here. The simple stack enables the use of recursive algorithms in LabVIEW. Linked lists are another fundamental data structure and are easily implemented in Lab-VIEW. The linking concept is fundamental to the design of trees, where a root node points to subtrees. The binary search tree data structure provides rapid inserts, deletes, and searches. It also provides a sorted output using the inorder traversal. Finally, the graph data structure represents a set of objects and their interconnections. These basic data structures provide building blocks for many important algorithms.

Algorithms

Joseph P. Damico
Sandia National Laboratories, Livermore, CA

Because G is a true programming language, LabVIEW programmers can and should apply the elements of computer science. This chapter presents a brief introduction to one of those elements: the analysis of computer algorithms and the accompanying metrics and notations. Several common types of problems will be discussed and several algorithms for each problem type will be presented and analyzed.

An **algorithm** is a well-defined sequence of steps that is guaranteed to terminate with a correct solution. Multiple algorithms may be available to solve a given problem, but one may have advantages over another. The size and nature of the input often determine the most effective algorithm. Convenient data structures and limitations on time and space can also favor one algorithm over another. Real-time systems require algorithms that are more efficient in their use of time. To choose the best algorithm, a programmer needs some metrics to evaluate the possible choices.

Analysis of Algorithms

Algorithms for a given problem can be evaluated and compared to determine the best solution. Common operations in the different algorithms can be identified and counted to evaluate the algorithms fairly. An algorithm performs many operations on its input but some fundamental operation(s) take up the bulk of the run time. The fundamental operation in a sorting routine can be the comparisons between elements or the swapping of elements, since an array cannot be sorted without comparing all elements and possibly moving some of them. For searching algorithms, the fundamental operation is comparison between elements.

Differences between computers, operating systems, and machine state can complicate the analysis of algorithms. But the number of fundamental operations is the same regardless of the machine, operating system, or other variables. This allows the analysis performed on one machine to be applied to another.

LabVIEW's **Profile Window** provides several ways to compare similar algorithms. If the fundamental operation is encoded as a subVI, the Profile Window counts the number of fundamental operations as the number of calls to the subVI. The Profile Window also provides relatively accurate run time measurements for the VIs. Using the same input for all algorithms, we can compare performance by counting fundamental operations or comparing run times. These techniques can determine the average performance of an algorithm.

The relative performance of the possible algorithms varies widely with the size and structure of the input. An algorithm that performs well with a small input may not be the best choice for a much larger input. For a small input array or list, the choice of sorting or searching algorithm may not be clear, but for large inputs, the choice of algorithm can greatly affect the time needed to complete the task. The structure of the input also affects performance. For instance, the binary search requires a sorted input list in order to run correctly. Meanwhile, the Quicksort algorithm performs worst with an already-sorted input. Knowledge of data size and structure can help determine the best algorithm for a given application.

Growth Rates of Algorithms

The growth of an algorithm's run time as the input size increases is a fundamental metric for comparing algorithms. The run time growth rates for algorithms can be compared and classified with a common notation. One of the most common classifications is the Big-Oh notation, $O(f)$, which is the set of functions that grow no faster than f. A function g is in $O(f)$ if there are some constants c_1 and c_2 such that

$$c_1 g(n) \leq c_2 f(n)$$

as n approaches infinity.

If a function g is in $O(f)$, then its run time is bounded by some constant multiplied by function $f(n)$. The differences between algorithms may make one algorithm run faster for smaller inputs, but the Big-Oh notation applies to the performance of the algorithm as the size of the input approaches infinity.

There are several standard ranges used to classify and compare algorithms. In increasing order they are 1, $\log_2 n$, n, $n\log_2 n$, n^2, n^3, 2^n, and $n!$, where n is the number of inputs or data items. These functions provide well-characterized bounds for the algorithm run times. For example, sort algorithms range from $O(n\log_2 n)$ to $O(n^2)$.

Several important types of algorithms appear repeatedly in computer programs. Searching for a value involves comparing multiple elements of an array or list to find matches with a search key. Sorting an array or list places the elements in a defined order. We'll look at searching and sorting in detail next.

Search Algorithms

Search algorithms appear in any number of applications and have received a great deal of attention from computer scientists. There are many ways to find a list element that matches a given search key (or to determine that there are no matches).

Sequential Search

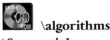

\algorithms
\Sequential
Search.vi

The sequential search works by starting at one end of the list and stepping sequentially through the list until either a match is found or the other end of the list is reached (Fig. 3.1). For an *n*-element list, where each element has an equal probability of matching the key, the sequential search will have to compare an average of *n*/2 elements before finding a match. The worst-case performance occurs when no matching elements are in the list. Here the algorithm performs *n* comparisons as it tests every list element.

Binary Search

\algorithms
\Binary Search.vi

The sequential search works for any array. But if the input is a sorted array, the binary search provides vastly better performance. The diagram for the binary search algorithm appears in Fig. 3.2. This algorithm assumes the input array is sorted in ascending order but can be easily modified to search an array sorted in descending order. This algorithm's G language implementation provides a simple, intuitive, readable diagram. The algorithm uses basic low-level operations like comparison, increment, decrement, and shift.

This algorithm revolves around the indices that bound the unsearched portion of the input array. The upper and lower index wires bracket the computation that yields the middle index. The middle index becomes a fulcrum that provides the leverage to eliminate one half of the remaining array.

Figure 3.1
The sequential search is simple but a relatively poor performer.

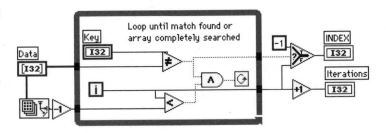

Figure 3.2
Diagram of the
Binary Search VI.

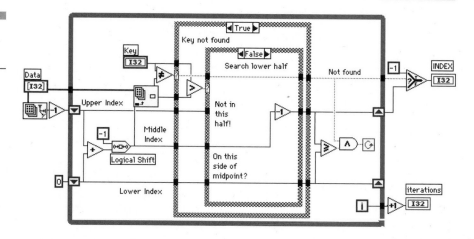

The upper index bound is initialized to the last array element and the lower index bound is initialized to 0. The algorithm splits the unsearched array into two halves by finding the index at the midpoint between the bounds. Adding the bounds indices and dividing by 2 (using a right logical shift) produces the floor of one half of the indices' sum.[1] The array element at the computed midpoint is compared to the search key. If they match, the search is over, so the Boolean representing *not found* is set false. If they do not match, then they are compared to see which is greater. If the key is greater, and then the matching element cannot be between the midpoint index and the lower bound, so the midpoint is incremented and becomes the new lower bound. If the key is not greater, then the matching element cannot be between the midpoint and the upper index, so the midpoint is decremented and becomes the new upper bound. The loop continues running as long as the lower bound is not greater than the upper bound and the match is not found. When the loop terminates, if the Boolean value *not found* is false, then the index in the upper bound is fed to the *index* output. Otherwise, a value of –1 is fed to the *Index* output to indicate that the key was not found.

The binary search algorithm provides the same $O(\log_2 n)$ performance as the binary search tree, discussed later. In the binary search, the information from each comparison eliminates half of the remaining unsearched list (the sequential search eliminates $1/m$ of the remaining m unsearched elements). By reducing the list by half on each iteration, the

---

[1]It's interesting to note that the act of dividing by 2 with a right logical shift can be implemented as a single CPU instruction and typically takes a single clock cycle in the CPU. An alternative method is to use the Quotient and Remainder (integer division) node, but a quick benchmark test indicates that this is 60% slower than the logical shift.

binary search algorithm will complete the search in at most $\log_2 n$ comparisons. The binary search requires a sorted list, which requires $O(n\log_2 n)$ operations to sort the list. Despite this additional cost, the binary search algorithm will speed up algorithms that frequently search a given array, since the array can be sorted a single time at the beginning.

Comparing the performance of the sequential search with the binary search reveals some interesting observations. The sequential search dutifully inspects each array element for a match, while the binary search concentrates on finding in which half of the unsearched array the match might be found. The sequential search closely matches the description of the problem and seems to be an intuitive solution. But the binary search offers incredibly better performance. The worst-case performance of the binary search is on the order of $\log_2 n$, which is better than the average performance of the sequential search. Thus, for an array of 2^{32} elements, the binary search will require no more than 32 iterations, while the sequential search will require an average of 2 billion (2^{31}) iterations—4 billion (2^{32}) iterations in the worst case!

Other Search Techniques

Several other techniques are used for searching and fast lookup. One technique uses a data structure, the **binary search tree**, to provide rapid searches. Another technique uses **hashing** and hash tables to enable rapid lookups.

BINARY SEARCH TREE   The binary search tree (BST) data structure enables a search logic similar to that of the binary search algorithm. The root of the BST is an approximate median value for the tree contents. This is similar to the computed index median used in the binary search. The search path through the tree depends on the comparison between the root data element and the search key. If the key is greater than the element, the search goes to the right subtree; if the key is less, then the search goes to the left subtree. Each branch selection in the tree traversal eliminates the other half of the tree, so the BST halves the uncertainty with each iteration, just like the binary search. When a matching key is found, the search ends successfully. If a tree leaf is reached without a match, the search fails. In either case, the search will require an average of $\log_2 n$ comparisons, since that is the tree's average depth.

The BST and binary search algorithm offer similar search performance, but one may be the better choice depending on the application. The BST is well suited for a dynamic array where elements are added and deleted often. Insertions take an average of $\log_2 n$ comparisons to find the insert location, and deletions take an average of $\log_2 n$ comparisons to find the element and $\log_2 n$ to find a replacement. The binary search algorithm requires a sorted list, so each insert and delete requires resorting, which is at best an $O(n\log_2 n)$-order operation. If the list is static, the sort overhead of the binary search may be tolerable.

HASHING   Another widely used search technique is hashing with chaining. This technique provides a mechanism for computing the expected location of the key and thus limits the amount of searching required. Hash algorithms range from simple truncation, digit selection, and modulo operations to complex cryptographic algorithms. Hash functions should produce a random distribution of values for the expected set of input keys. The hash algorithm takes the search key and rapidly computes a number that determines the key's storage location. In future searches, a matching key will produce the same hash value that points to the location of the stored key. Hash functions are one-way; you cannot determine which string generated a given hash value.

\algorithms \Hash Function.vi

The hash algorithm used in this example appears in Fig. 3.3. It converts the input string into a byte array, then indexes through the array, processing each element. The choice of a hash function is somewhat arbitrary. This function multiplies the new element times a relatively large prime number, and then left-shifts the product zero to three times and accumulates the result in a shift register. The number of shifts depends on the iteration count value $\boxed{\text{i}}$. This ensures that similar strings, like *cat* and *tac*, generate different hash values. The multiplication and shift operations ensure that the hash values spread into the upper end of their range and possibly overflow.[2] The output is an unsigned 32-bit integer. This function maps all strings into one of more than 4 billion possible hash values. Hash functions can be compared by evaluating the hash value distribution produced for similar inputs.

[2]LabVIEW, like most other computer languages, uses standard integer math where the value rolls over from its maximum to its minimum upon overflow. For an unsigned 32-bit integer, the maximum value is $2^{32} - 1$ or 4,294,967,295. Add 1, and the value rolls over to 0.

Figure 3.3
Diagram of the Hash Function VI.

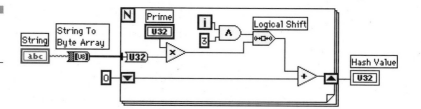

The elements in a hashed lookup algorithm can be stored in an array where the hash function computes the storage index. This solution can lead to problems: A *collision* occurs when two different keys produce the same hash value. This can be handled by allowing the hash table to contain multiple elements at a given location through the use of **external chaining**. A linked list structure provides a good mechanism for chaining, since the number of keys that hash to a given location can be difficult to determine. In this scheme, the hash table is an array of list pointers to the first elements of the linked lists. Once a key is associated with one of the linked lists containing several items, then a simple sequential search is performed on this list.

Figure 3.4 shows a simple hash table with chaining. The hash table is an array of five linked lists. The hash function in this example returns the key modulo to the table size. So, for key = 6, the hash function returns a value of 1, which determines which linked list the key would be stored or found in. A search for key = 21 would also hash to linked list 1 but fail after traversing the list without finding a match.

Figure 3.5 shows a LabVIEW implementation of a hash table with chaining algorithm. This VI uses the multi-list data structure presented in the Chap. 2, "Data Structures." The multi-list data structure enables a simple but fast implementation. The input is hashed to determine the list where the data element belongs. The Multi-List VI encapsulates the lists and related functions, while the Hash Table With Chaining VI simply calls it to store, delete, and search for list data.

The hash table lookup algorithm provides $O(1)$ performance and outperforms the built-in LabVIEW search as well as binary search algorithms for large inputs. The variable size of the hash table allows the data struc-

\algorithms \Hash Table With Chaining.vi

Figure 3.4
Hash table with chaining.

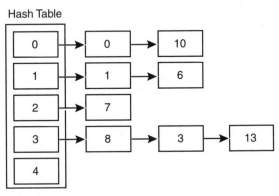

Hash Table

Table Size = 5
H(key) = key mod 5

Figure 3.5
Diagram of the
Hash Table With
Chaining VI.

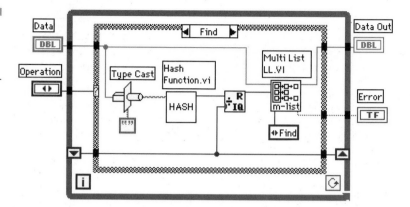

ture to be tuned with varying input sizes. With a large enough hash table, each chain will contain only several elements to search through. Insert and delete operations on the data structure are also $O(1)$. This data structure illustrates how additional memory for the larger hash table can greatly speed up an algorithm. This algorithm is well suited to applications with frequent inserts, deletes, and lookups and is commonly used for symbol tables in compilers.

Hashing scatters the array elements randomly throughout the hash table, while the binary search requires that the array be already sorted. The table's randomized storage scheme obscures any relationships present in the data. If any relationships, such as sort order, need to be preserved during use of the hash table, another data structure can store the original data at the cost of more memory.

Analysis of Search Algorithms

The hash table and binary search algorithm both outperform LabVIEW's **Search 1D Array** function for larger inputs. It should be noted that the Binary Search VI works with a sorted array of double precision floating point numbers, while LabVIEW's function provides polymorphic inputs that accept any type of array, sorted or unsorted. These additional features have their performance costs. Despite the fact that the LabVIEW function is highly optimized and executes synchronously, the VI-encoded algorithms provide better performance for large inputs. The binary search algorithm shows how additional knowledge of an algorithm's inputs (i.e., a sorted array) can provide better performance. The binary search tree incorporates the binary search strategy into a data structure that offers performance similar to that of the binary search. The hash table algorithm shows how a randomized storage scheme reduces search times from $O(n)$ to $O(1)$. The hash table also demonstrates a time-space trade-off: The run time can be reduced at the expense of more memory for a larger hash table.

Sort Algorithms

Sorting appears in a wide range of algorithms. The binary search algorithm demonstrates how the structure of a sorted array significantly speeds up searching. The large number of sorting algorithms indicates the great deal of research that has been performed on this topic. This section presents two sorting algorithms and evaluates their performance relative to LabVIEW's Sort 1D Array function.

An array can be sorted in two possible orders: ascending or descending. The primary sort key is the data element used in the comparisons that lead to the ordering. While secondary sort keys are possible, they are not supported by LabVIEW's Sort 1D Array function. The Sort 1D Array function sorts an array of clusters by using the 0th cluster element as the only sort key. Sorting based on other cluster elements is not possible because this requires custom logic for every possible cluster. The sorting VIs presented in this section can be easily modified to support sorting with multiple keys and still provide better performance than the Sort 1D Array function.

Sorting requires that every element of the input array be placed in the output array according to the sort order. This seems to imply that each array element must be compared with every other element, so each of the n elements must be compared with the other $n - 1$ elements to sort the list. This produces an $O(n^2)$ algorithm, which is a common average performance for many sorting algorithms like the Insertion Sort presented here. The popular Quicksort algorithm offers $O(n\log_2 n)$ average performance. Figure 3.6 shows that the difference between an $O(n\log_2 n)$ and an $O(n^2)$ algorithm becomes painfully obvious as the size of the input array grows.

The Insertion Sort Algorithm

The logic behind the insertion sort algorithm is simple and easily understood. Figure 3.7 shows several steps in the algorithm.

Figure 3.6
This run time study shows the divergence in performance between Quicksort and the slower insertion sort algorithms.

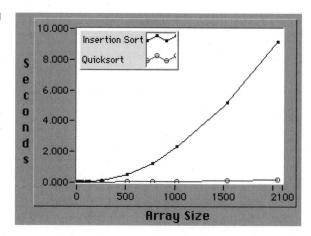

The algorithm divides the array into sorted and unsorted portions, as shown in Fig. 3.7(a). Initially, the first element is considered sorted, and the rest of the array is unsorted. This is a valid assumption because any one-element array can be considered sorted in any order. The next unsorted element is compared to the sorted elements. Any larger sorted elements are moved "up" one location, leaving an open location behind. This continues until an element smaller than x is reached. The value of x is then stored in the open location. In Fig. 3.7(c), element 6 is moved to the right, leaving a free location. Element 5 is soon moved into that hole. The value of x is stored in the free location left by 5 when x is compared to 1 and found to be greater. The algorithm then increases the size of the sorted portion by 1, and repeats the operation on the next unsorted element.

Figure 3.7
Steps in the insertion sort algorithm.

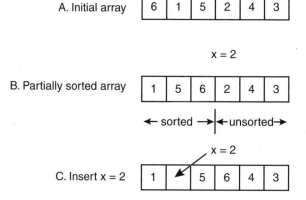

Figure 3.8 shows the diagram for an ascending-order **Insertion Sort VI**. The outer For Loop runs $n - 1$ times for an n-element array. The algorithm assumes that each array element up to and including the current value of the For Loop's iteration counter (i) is sorted. In the first iteration of the For Loop, array element 0 is assumed to be sorted. Array element $i + 1$, labeled x in the diagram, is indexed and then inserted into its proper place in the sorted subarray. To find the proper place for x, the inner While Loop scans through the sorted sublist running from the For Loop's current i value down to 0. Subtracting the While Loop's i value from the For Loop's i value provides the decreasing series of index values, labeled j in the diagram. The elements indexed from the sorted subarray are compared to x. If x is smaller than the element, then the element is moved to the next higher index. When an element smaller than x is found or the computed index goes negative, the While Loop terminates. When the While Loop has terminated, x is stored in the array at location $j + 1$.

An important LabVIEW programming technique is visible in Fig. 3.8. Because the input and output arrays (unsorted and sorted lists) are guaranteed to be the same size, you can avoid data duplication and its attendant memory management overhead by using shift registers and the **Replace Array Element** function as shown. Less efficient methods use shift registers in conjunction with the **Build Array** function, which always creates duplicate memory buffers.

Informal analysis shows that the outer For Loop runs $(n - 1)$ times. The inner While Loop runs from the outer For Loop's i value back to 0. This operation is $O(n)$, too. The insertion sort algorithm therefore provides $O(n^2)$ performance.

Insertion sort provides decent performance for an $O(n^2)$ algorithm. The example in Fig. 3.7 shows how the element $x = 2$ moved two locations to reach its place in the sorted array. The ability to move an element across multiple array locations allows the insertion sort to outperform other

Figure 3.8
Diagram of the Insertion Sort VI.

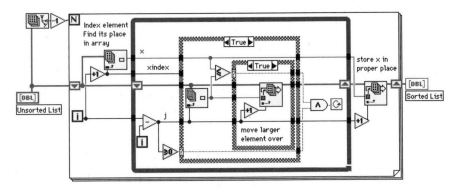

$O(n^2)$ algorithms, like bubble sort, that move elements one location at a time across the whole array.

Quicksort

The Quicksort algorithm uses a divide-and-conquer strategy to sort an array. The input array is arranged so that the small keys precede the large keys. The array is split between the small and large keys, and these two subarrays are then sorted in the same way.

RECURSIVE ALGORITHMS   In a language like C, the Quicksort function would call itself with a **recursive** call. A recursive function simply calls itself just as it would call another function. All recursive algorithms have two parts: an **anchor** that terminates the recursion, and the recursive call itself. Without an anchor, the recursion would continue like an infinite loop; this is a common problem with recursive algorithms.

The *n*-factorial (*n*!) function is a classic example of a recursive algorithm. The pseudo-code for this algorithm looks like this:

```
function n_factorial (Integer n)

{

if (n = 0) then

        return (1)        // this is the recursive anchor

else

        return (n * n_factorial (n-1) )// this is the recursive call

}
```

The *n_factorial* function demonstrates how a recursive algorithm can drastically change the look of an algorithm. A nonrecursive solution would loop from *n* to 1 and keep a running product of the loop counter. The recursive algorithm hides the iteration in the recursive calls. There will be as many recursive calls as loop iterations. The return values store the running product. The recursive function lets the compiler and run time stack handle the iteration and passing of return values. While their appearances are drastically different, the recursive algorithm works like a nonrecursive one.

The current version of LabVIEW does not allow a VI to call itself. This lack of support for recursion does not prevent the use of recursive algorithms like Quicksort. A simple **stack**-based algorithm can manage the recursive calls in the VI. When a C function calls itself recursively, the calling instance of the function is placed on the run time stack, and a new instance is stacked above it. The original calling procedure will not be popped off of the stack to resume running until the new instance of the procedure and all procedures called by it have terminated. In the C program, the compiler handles the run time stack operations for the programmer. The LabVIEW solution for a recursive algorithm creates a stack data structure and lets the VI manage it.

This chapter presents several recursive algorithms, all implemented with the user-constructed stack technique. Our first example is the **Quicksort VI** (Fig. 3.9). The diagram displays the typical form of a recursive VI, using a stack subVI. The VI first initializes the stack, then pushes the first instance of the problem onto it. A While Loop runs until the stack is empty. The stack data structure varies with the problem. For Quicksort, the stack contains a cluster of the first and last indices of the subarray to be sorted.

The **Split VI** (Fig. 3.10) does the bulk of the Quicksort algorithm's work. Its operation is demonstrated in the **Visual Split Demo VI**. The split algorithm starts by indexing the splitpoint value from the subarray at the first index. It compares the splitpoint value to all subarray elements from index first + 1 to last. When a smaller element is found, the splitpoint index is incremented, and the element at the new location is swapped with the smaller element. The terms *splitpoint value* and *splitpoint index* may cause some confusion. The splitpoint value is indexed out before the For Loop begins executing, but the splitpoint index is incremented as elements are swapped. After the For Loop terminates, the elements at the first index and splitpoint are swapped. Thus, all subarray elements at

\algorithms \Quicksort.vi

\algorithms \Visual Split Demo.vi

Figure 3.9
Diagram for the Quicksort VI.

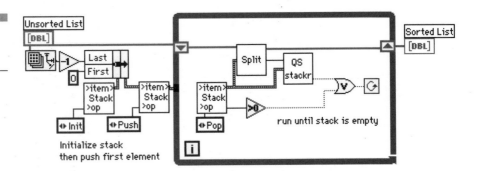

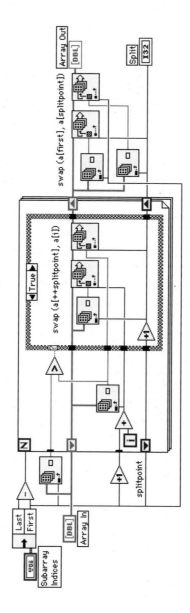

Figure 3.10
Diagram of the Split VI, used by the Quicksort VI.

55

locations smaller than the splitpoint index are less than the splitpoint value and all elements at higher locations are greater than or equal to the splitpoint value.

Another subVI called by Quicksort, the **QS Stack Handler VI**, pushes the new subarray data structures onto the stack. It checks the subarray indices to prevent any one-element subarrays from being stacked, since they are already sorted. This saves significant stack overhead, since the algorithm reduces all subarrays to this size.

The algorithm does not try to order the keys beyond grouping them into large and small keys. The smallest key always ends up in the group of smaller keys and thus migrates to the low end of the list. For simplicity, imagine that the Split routine always divides the keys into two equally sized halves. After the first Split iteration, the smallest key will be in the half that was smaller than the splitpoint. When that half is split again, the smallest key will be in the lowest quarter of all keys. As the algorithm progresses, the list is broken into smaller groups and the smallest key can be found in the lowest eighth, sixteenth, and so on. This continues until the smallest key is in a group containing only two keys—the smallest and the next smallest. The algorithm may need to swap the locations of these two elements, but after that this portion of the list is sorted. The algorithm then proceeds to arrange the keys in the other groups that it placed on the stack. Quicksort's continual splitting of subarrays between large and small keys eventually sorts the subarrays.

Quicksort has one of the best average performances among all sorting algorithms. In fact, Quicksort's average performance approaches the theoretical limit for algorithms that sort by comparing keys. An informal analysis for a random input shows the performance is $O(n\log_2 n)$. The Split function is called $\log_2 n$ times for an n-element input array since n can be halved $\log_2 n$ times. Each call to Split performs $(n-1)$ comparisons for an n-element input array; this is $O(n)$. Surprisingly, Quicksort performs worst when the input is already sorted. In this case, Split will partition the array into a one-element array and an $n-1$-element array. This leads to $O(n^2)$ performance, since Split will be called n times.

There are numerous improvements to Quicksort. The Split VI ideally splits the input array in half. In order for this to happen, the splitpoint value must be the median of the input. Since this Split function implementation uses the first element of the subarray as a one-point approximation of the median, the split ratio between the two subarrays can vary widely. A better median value could be selected from the first five elements of the subarray, or from the first, middle, and last elements.

Quicksort works best on large arrays, and does not process small arrays very efficiently. As the input is increasingly subdivided, the algorithm processes smaller subarrays. At some small input size Quicksort is not the most efficient algorithm. So using another algorithm, like insertion sort, to sort the small lists can improve the overall performance, as can be seen in Fig. 3.11.

\algorithms
\Quicksort
Hybrid.vi

A hybrid sort algorithm that uses both Quicksort and insertion sort performs better than Quicksort alone. The VI diagram appears in Fig. 3.12. The **Quicksort Hybrid VI** provides a variable *switch size* that allows tuning of the algorithm for variably sized inputs.

Timing tests of the Quicksort Hybrid VI reveal some interesting anomalies. Since Fig. 3.11 shows that insertion sort outperforms Quick-

Figure 3.11
This run time comparison between the insertion sort and Quicksort algorithms shows performance trade-offs based on array size.

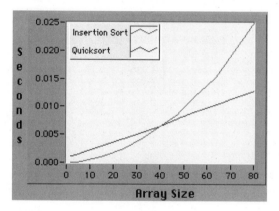

Figure 3.12
Diagram of the Quicksort Hybrid VI.

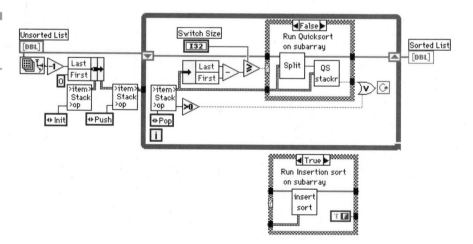

sort for arrays smaller than 40 elements, we would expect to choose 40 as the switch value. Figure 3.13 shows that an optimal switch value when processing large arrays is actually near 2000 elements. This performance variation may be due to subtleties in the way LabVIEW manages memory, or to execution scheduling, or to something else. Without intimate knowledge of the inner workings of LabVIEW, we cannot be certain.

Figure 3.14 shows that the Quicksort Hybrid VI performs favorably against LabVIEW's Sort 1D Array function. To achieve this performance, the Quicksort Hybrid VI was set to run with subroutine priority, much like the synchronous execution of the LabVIEW function. The Quicksort Hybrid offers an easily modifiable sort routine that extends sorting capability beyond the Sort 1D Array function.

Figure 3.13
With the Quicksort Hybrid VI, various settings for the crossover point (switch values) yield interesting changes in performance.

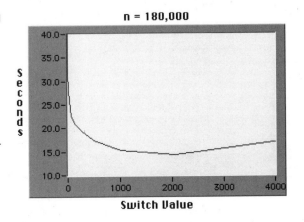

Figure 3.14
Run time comparison of the Quicksort Hybrid VI versus the built-in LabVIEW function, Sort 1D Array.

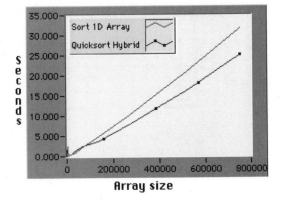

Summary

Many algorithms exist for the common problems of searching and sorting. While LabVIEW offers built-in sort and search functions with adequate performance, it is possible to write VIs that provide better performance and more flexibility. The choice of algorithm depends on the size and nature of the input, since the relative performance of algorithms varies significantly with these factors. Here, we've looked at several sort and search VIs that can be modified to meet specific needs. These VIs demonstrate once again that any algorithm can be coded in LabVIEW.

The performance of these algorithms depends on *in-place* use of arrays, where memory already allocated is reused without any memory management activity. Any extra memory allocation or type *coercion dots* can significantly degrade their performance. Keep this in mind if your modified versions do not perform as well.

A common remedy for a slow program is to get a faster processor. As quickly as the technology evolves, we don't have to wait long for the next greatest processor. However, another approach promises the potential for much faster performance with existing hardware. Choosing a more efficient algorithm (for example, Quicksort over insertion sort) can reduce the run times far more effectively than the incremental 20 percent speed improvements we get with each new processor. Find an algorithm cookbook and develop your own VIs when the existing VIs or built-in functions don't meet your needs. The rewards can be significant.

CHAPTER

Boolean Machine Architectures

Joseph P. Damico

Sandia National Laboratories, Livermore, CA

LabVIEW's basic Boolean functions (AND, OR, NOT, etc.) have the same behavior and schematic symbols as their hardware equivalents. These software functions can be combined to emulate many digital logic components and circuits. This chapter discusses several basic digital components and the VIs that emulate them. Many of the VIs can be coded using other LabVIEW structures and functions, but the emphasis is on emulating circuits with schematically equivalent software diagrams.

The NAND, NOR, and NOT gates are the primitive circuits used to build modern computers. The NOT, or inverter, can be fabricated with a single transistor if you use the simple (but obsolete) resistor-transistor logic (RTL) circuit. Two transistors in series can form a NAND gate. Two transistors in parallel can form a NOR gate. While we think of the AND and OR as the fundamental logic components, they are more commonly built from the NAND and NOR gates with inverters on their outputs. The NOT, NAND, and NOR gates combine in many ways to build higher-level circuits and components. Corresponding software functions combine to build emulations of higher-level logical operations.

Basic Logic Functions

A Boolean function with n inputs has at most 2^n distinct input states. These states and the corresponding outputs can be described with a **truth table**. A truth table typically lists the input states in (base 2) numerical order. Table 4.1 displays the truth tables for the basic Boolean functions provided in LabVIEW.

$\overline{A}$ represents NOT (A) in the truth table and throughout this chapter. The NOT function logically inverts the input: The output is true for a false input and false for a true input. The AND function forms an exclusive operation: the output is true only when both inputs are true. The OR function provides an inclusive function: the output is true when at least

TABLE 4.1

Truth Table for
Basic Logic
Functions

A	B	$\overline{A}$	A AND B	A OR B	A XOR B
0	0	1	0	0	0
0	1	1	0	1	1
1	0	0	0	1	1
1	1	0	1	1	0

one input is true. The XOR (exclusive OR) is true when only one of the inputs is true. Other basic logic functions involve negating the inputs or outputs of these functions.

The three basic logic functions can be combined in an infinite number of ways. **De Morgan's Law** provides methods to simplify logic designs by reducing the number of gates required to build circuits. The law takes two forms:

$$\overline{(\text{A AND B})} = \overline{\text{A}} \text{ OR } \overline{\text{B}}$$

$$\overline{(\text{A OR B})} = \overline{\text{A}} \text{ AND } \overline{\text{B}}$$

\Boolean Arch\DeMorgans Law.vi

The simplifying power of the law comes from the fact that the negated AND gate (or NAND) replaces two inverters and an OR gate. The equivalence of these functions can be proven with truth table analysis or by running the **De Morgan's Law VI** shown in Fig. 4.1.

The exclusive characteristic of the AND gate allows one input to **enable** or **disable** another input. With a false enable input, the AND output goes false regardless of the other input's state. If the enable input is true, then the AND output depends on the value of the other input.

Shift Circuits

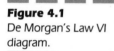

\Boolean Arch\One Bit Shifter.vi

The **One-Bit Shifter VI** shown in Fig. 4.2 uses AND functions to enable its three outputs. The input data bit feeds each of the three-input AND gates, implemented by the LabVIEW **Compound Arithmetic** node set to AND mode. The *Left Shift* and *Right Shift* control lines pass to the corresponding AND gates and their inverted values pass to the other two AND gates. In this way, when the *Left Shift* bit is true, it enables the AND gate that sends the *Left Out* bit, and its inverse disables the other two AND gates and their output bits. If neither shift bit is true, then the output

Figure 4.1
De Morgan's Law VI diagram.

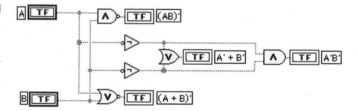

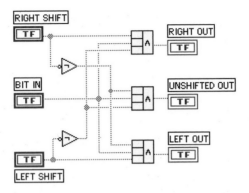

Figure 4.2
One-Bit Shifter VI
diagram.

passes to the *Unshifted Out.* The case where both shift control bits are true (an illegal state) disables all three AND gates.

Bit slice machine architectures combine components like the One-Bit Shifter to create circuits *n* bits wide. An *n*-bit shifter can be built with *n* One-Bit Shifters and *n* three-input OR gates. Figure 4.3 shows a **Four-Bit Shifter VI** built by combining four One-Bit Shifters and three-input OR gates. The OR gates combine up to three outputs from the shifters. Only one of the inputs to the OR gate will be enabled and possibly true. The other two inputs will be false due to the disabling done in the shifter and will not drive the OR gate. This VI handles the four least significant bits of the input number. You could expand upon the logic shown here to handle any number of bits.

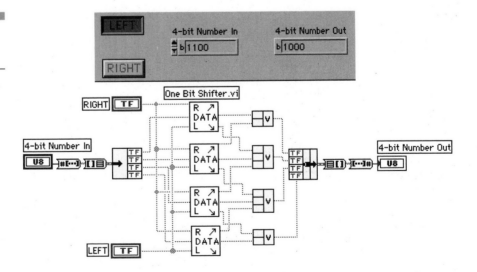

Figure 4.3
Four-Bit Shifter VI
diagram.

Latches and Related Circuits

Every computer system relies on memory circuits to store data and programs. These memory circuits must remember their most recent input values. The **SR latch** circuit provides a memory building block. This circuit has two inputs, S and R. The S input sets the latch, and the R input resets it. The latch has two outputs, Q and $\overline{Q}$, where $\overline{Q}$ is the complement of Q The outputs of the SR latch depend on the state of the inputs as well as the most recent state of the outputs. Defining the characteristics of the SR latch requires both a truth table (also called a characteristic table) and an **excitation table**. The excitation table defines the time-dependent characteristics of the circuits. Tables 4.2 and 4.3 are the truth table and the excitation table, respectively, for the SR latch. The excitation table lists the current state of output Q as $Q(t)$, and the next state as $Q(t+1)$. The first row can be interpreted as saying that if $Q(t)$ equals 0, and we want $Q(t+1)$ to remain 0, then the S input must remain 0, and the R input has no effect.

The SR latch remembers its last state by feeding the previous outputs back to the inputs. LabVIEW does not allow a function's output to be wired to its inputs (yet), so we must use an alternate approach. Shift registers provide a solution for this problem, but require a loop structure. The LabVIEW emulation of this circuit, shown in Fig. 4.4, uses a For Loop with two shift registers and two NOR functions. Two loop iterations pro-

\Boolean
Arch\SR Master
Latch.vi

TABLE 4.2

SR Latch Truth
Table

S	R	Q	$\overline{Q}$	Comment
0	0	0/1	0/1	Q, $\overline{Q}$ keep most recent value
0	1	0	1	
1	0	1	0	
1	1	0	0	Not used

TABLE 4.3

SR Latch Excitation
Table

$Q(t)$	$Q(t+1)$	S	R	Comment
0	0	0	x	State maintained as long as S = 0
0	1	1	0	Q transitions to true when Set true
1	0	0	1	Q transitions to false when Reset true
1	1	x	0	To maintain Q = 1, do not reset

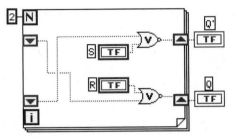

Figure 4.4
SR Master Latch VI
diagram.

vide the needed feedback. The first iteration reads the inputs and NORs them with the last outputs, and the second iteration NORs the inputs with the outputs from the first iteration. After two iterations, the latch reaches a consistent state: more iterations do not change the output state of the function.

\Boolean Arch\D Latch.vi

The truth table for the SR latch (Table 4.2) shows two ambiguous output states where the two inputs are equal. In the case where both are false, the latch retains its previous state. The case where both are true presents a problem. In this case, both outputs go to false, which violates the complementary state relationship. Further, when both S and R return to false, the circuit becomes nondeterministic: The input that remains true the longest determines the output state. In the VI, both inputs may transition simultaneously. This is also known as a race condition and must be avoided. In this case, the outputs remain unchanged at false. The D latch, shown in Fig. 4.5, prevents the ambiguous states from occurring by using only one input, D, and its complement. The circuit replaces the S input with D and feeds $\overline{D}$ to the R input.

A **clocked latch** can be constructed by enabling the inputs with a clock signal and AND gates. This effectively disables the inputs until the clock signal goes true. **Flip-flops** closely resemble clocked latches. A flip-flop uses edge triggering, while a latch uses level triggering. The edge-triggered behavior is difficult to implement in software because the transition from old values to new values occurs atomically. Therefore we ignore the difference between latches and flip-flops in the VIs and in related discussions.

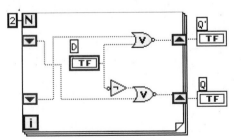

Figure 4.5
D Latch VI diagram.

\Boolean
Arch\JK Flip-
Flop.vi

SR latches combined in a master-slave configuration create a **JK Flip-Flop VI** as shown in Fig. 4.6. The corresponding excitation table appears in Table 4.4. The JK flip-flop also resolves the SR latch's ambiguity. This VI presents an interesting problem. The initial values of the shift registers default to false. This disables the rest of the logic in the VI, since no matter what values J or K have, the shift registers disable them. This VI automatically initializes itself by substituting true values for the shift register values until one of the shift registers takes a true value.

The ALU and CPU

\Boolean
Arch\One Bit
ALU.vi

One of the most important circuits in a computer is the **Arithmetic Logical Unit** (ALU). The ALU accepts two inputs, both of which can be loaded with the contents of any register, and processes them in one of several possible ways. Figure 4.7 shows the VI diagram for a single-bit ALU. The ALU consists of three subVIs: the **Logical Unit VI**, the **Full Adder With Enable VI**, and the **Two-Bit Decoder VI**. The Logical Unit subVI performs the following logical operations: A AND B, A OR B, and logical inverting of the B input. The Full Adder VI implements the arithmetic operation. The Two-Bit Decoder VI interprets the function bits (*f0* and *f1*) and enables or disables the functions of the Logical Unit and Full Adder VIs.

The One-Bit ALU VI takes three data inputs: the *A bit,* the *B bit,* and a *Carry In* bit. The ALU performs only one of four possible operations on the inputs. The *f0* and *f1* bits specify the operation of the ALU. The Two-Bit Decode VI takes *f0* and *f1* and delivers four *enable* lines whose values depend on the inputs. The first three enable lines control which (if any) logical operation the Logical Unit VI performs. The final select line

Figure 4.6
JK Flip Flop VI
diagram.

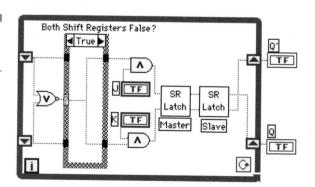

TABLE 4.4

JK Flip-Flop
Excitation Table

Q(t)	Q($t+1$)	J	K	Comment
0	0	0	x	State maintained as long as J = 0
0	1	1	x	Q transitions to true when J is true
1	0	x	1	Q transitions to false when K is true
1	1	x	0	To maintain Q = 1, leave K false

\Boolean
Arch\Two Bit
Decoder.vi

enables the Full Adder VI. Although the Full Adder and the Logical Unit VIs both execute, the absence of an enable signal will cause the output of a logical false value that has no influence on the OR function that feeds the *Output* bit.

The **Two-Bit Decoder VI** appears in Fig. 4.8. The VI takes two bits, x and y, as input, and outputs four bits D0–D3. Each of the output bits could be considered to represent a line on the truth table for two inputs. The first line of the truth table has input values of (0,0). So when the input bits take this value bit, D0 goes true. We implement this logic by inverting both inputs and feeding them to the AND gate, which feeds D0. The possible combinations of x, $\bar{x}$, y, and $\bar{y}$ determine the other output bits. Since the four possible outcomes are mutually exclusive, only one output bit will go true for each possible combination of inputs.

Figure 4.7
One-Bit ALU VI
diagram.

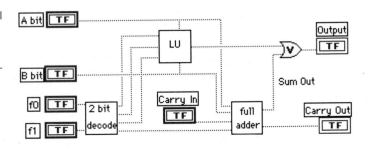

Figure 4.8
Two-Bit Decoder VI
diagram.

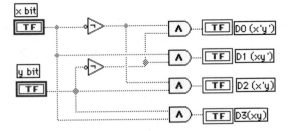

\Boolean
Arch\Logical
Unit.vi

\Boolean
Arch\Full Adder
With Enable.vi

\Boolean
Arch\Four Bit
ALU.vi

\Boolean
Arch\Four Bit
CPU.vi

The **Logical Unit VI** Diagram appears in Fig. 4.9. The logic functions form the three possible operations (AB, A + B, and $\overline{B}$.) Their outputs feed AND gates driven by the three enable inputs. The outputs of the AND gates are ORed and fed to the *Output* bit. Since only one of the three enable lines will be true, only one of the three ANDs can possibly drive the output OR true.

The Full Adder truth table appears in Table 4.5, and the VI diagram appears in Fig. 4.10. Analysis of the truth table and logical manipulation of the relationships allows the arithmetic operation to be implemented with logical components. The *Sum* output bit goes true when one or all of the inputs go true. Two XOR functions provide this behavior. The *Carry Out* bit goes true when there are two or more true inputs.

An n-bit ALU can be constructed by connecting the *Carry Out* bit from the ith bit to the *Carry In* of bit $i + 1$. This circuit is easily implemented in software either by using n instances of the One-Bit ALU VI or by using one instance of the VI in a loop with shift registers passing the *Carry Out* bit to the next bit computation. Figure 4.11 shows the VI diagram for a Four-Bit ALU.

The ALU VI provides subtraction with the A + B operation when A or B have negative values. This VI uses unsigned integers that do not represent negative numbers. However, negative numbers can be represented with a two's-complement encoding scheme and processed like any other number. Two's-complement reserves the most significant bit as a sign bit. Negating a number takes two steps. First, invert each bit in the number, then add 1 to the number. The results from a two's-complement operation must be decoded in the opposite way. First subtract 1 from the number, then invert all bits.

The Four-Bit ALU and Four-Bit Shifter combine to simulate the main processing portion of a Four-Bit CPU. The Four-Bit CPU VI appears in Fig. 4.12.

Figure 4.9
Logical Unit VI
diagram.

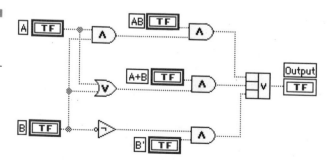

TABLE 4.5

Truth Table for
the Full Adder

X	Y	Carry In	Carry Out	Sum
0	0	0	0	0
0	0	1	0	1
0	1	0	0	1
0	1	1	1	0
1	0	0	0	1
1	0	1	1	0
1	1	0	1	0
1	1	1	1	1

The Four-Bit CPU processes the A and B inputs with the Four-Bit ALU. The *ALU Op* input determines the ALU function. The ALU output passes to the Four-Bit Shifter VI. Combining the ALU and shifter provides some processing shortcuts. For example, the ALU does not provide a multiplication operation, but some multiplication operations can be done. The shifter provides multiplication and division by 2: Left shifts double the input, and right shifts halve the input. A multiply by 2 can also be done with the ALU by adding A and B (where $B = A$). A multiply by 4 combines the ALU's A + B operation with a shift left operation. The average of two numbers can be approximated with the A + B operation combined with a right shift (this generates the *floor* of the average; the Binary Search VI uses this computation.) The CPU VI shows how the basic functionality of a computer is implemented in hardware.

Figure 4.10
Full Adder VI
diagram.

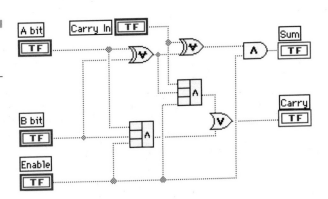

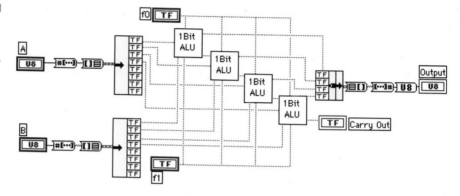

Figure 4.11
Four-Bit ALU VI
diagram.

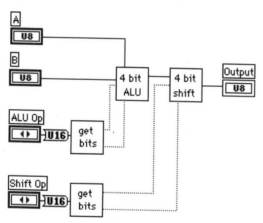

Figure 4.12
Four-Bit CPU VI
diagram.

Summary

The VIs presented here demonstrate that many logic components and circuits can be emulated with LabVIEW code. When coded using the basic logic functions, the VIs closely resemble the circuits' logic schematics. The One-Bit Shifter VI and One-Bit ALU VI show the design of important bit slice architecture components. The Four-Bit Shifter and Four-Bit ALU VIs show how the bit slice components combine to create the *n*-bit–wide implementations. The modern computer provides powerful functionality that comes from the combination of basic logic functions that create the CPU. While the CPU provides some processing shortcuts, such as the floor of average discussed earlier, most of its functionality comes from simple circuits. With a bit more effort, a comprehensive computer architecture simulation is clearly feasible in LabVIEW.

Cryptography

Joseph Damico

Sandia National Laboratories, Livermore, CA

When cryptography is outlawed,
bayl bhgynjf jvyy unir cevinpl.

Cryptography, the art of keeping messages secure, has been practiced for thousands of years throughout the world, yet has remained virtually unknown outside of governments until only recently. The popularity and insecurity of the Internet and controversies over the United States' export policies and proposed key escrow systems have brought cryptographic systems to the attention of the general public. Many modern cryptographic systems rely on computers to execute the algorithms needed to secure messages. **Cryptanalysis**, the art of breaking the code of secure messages, relies even more on computers.

Anyone transmitting private, proprietary, or otherwise important data over the Internet or any other open means of communication should consider some level of encryption. The data's value and the likely threats against it determine the amount of encryption security needed. This section introduces some of the important concepts of cryptography and cryptanalysis, and provides simple VIs to demonstrate the algorithms discussed. The VIs do not provide sufficient security for most applications. They are presented only to demonstrate the algorithms and show their LabVIEW implementations.

Terminology and Background

A typical cryptographic system takes a **plaintext** message M and encrypts with an **algorithm** E, which outputs a **ciphertext** message C. This is stated as

$$C = E(M) \tag{5.1}$$

The encryption algorithm relies on **confusion** and **diffusion** to obscure the original plaintext message yet retain enough information to allow the message to be recovered. Confusion hides the relationship between the plaintext and the ciphertext. The Caesar Cipher, discussed later, uses simple alphabetic substitution to create confusion (that's how the quote at the beginning of the chapter was encrypted).

Most languages contain a certain amount of redundancy: We don't need to see all the letters in a word or all the words in a sentence to understand the meaning. The encrypted quote above follows the familiar bumper sticker form: "If something is outlawed, only someone will have something else." Without any cryptanalysis, we can guess most of the message. This is redundancy. Diffusion reduces the plaintext redundancies by spreading small plaintext changes over a wide area of the ciphertext. Permutation, or transposition, spreads the plaintext throughout the ciphertext.

Once encrypted, the ciphertext C can be safely transmitted over insecure communications channels. The **decryption** algorithm D restores the original plaintext from the ciphertext.

$$M = D(E(M)) \qquad (5.2)$$

The cryptanalyst eavesdropping on the communications channel will see only the seemingly random ciphertext. Recovering the message without knowledge of the encryption algorithm and keys constitutes a difficult task because the ciphertext yields little information about the original plaintext. Attempts to break the ciphertext should cost more than the value of the message it contains, or should take longer than the meaningful lifetime of the message.

Designers of cryptographic systems assume that any adversaries know the algorithms they have used, so they do not expect the algorithm alone to ensure security. The most important security component in a cryptographic system is the key. Even if an adversarial cryptanalyst knows the encryption algorithm, he or she must still guess the key.

A key's security comes from the 2^n possible values in an n-bit key space. If there are k possible keys, an adversary using a brute-force guessing approach must test an average of $k/2$ keys before finding the encryption key. Determining the correct key is not trivial; in fact, some incorrect keys may produce decryptions that seem reasonable. Decryptions of text messages can be tested for correctness by eye or with spell-checking software. Evaluating the decryptions of nontext data requires some knowledge of the message format and content and presents a harder problem in general. In any case, as the number of possible keys k grows larger, testing half of the keys becomes a computationally infeasible problem.

The Caesar Cipher

\cryptography\Caesar Cipher.vi

The ancient Romans used the **Caesar Cipher**, making it one of the oldest known algorithms. This encryption algorithm simply adds an offset to each character, then applies a modulo operation to the sum. This effectively shifts the alphabet to the right by the offset's value. With a modulus of the alphabet's size, the modulo operation wraps characters shifted at the end of the alphabet back to the beginning. The decryption algorithm subtracts the offset from the ciphertext and then applies the same modulo operation. Figure 5.1 shows a LabVIEW implementation of the encryption and decryption code for the Caesar Cipher.

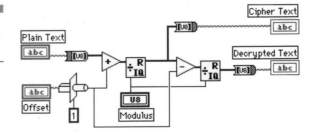

Figure 5.1
Caesar Cipher system
VI diagram.

This algorithm provides confusion with a simple substitution, and that is its weakness. Every instance of the letter *e* will be replaced by the character (*e* + offset) modulo *n* for an *n*-character alphabet. Character frequency analysis of the ciphertext allows the cryptanalyst to guess the offset and break the code. Since *e* is the most commonly used letter in the English language, the code for *e* should appear as one of the most frequent symbols in the ciphertext. While the exact frequencies vary, they apply to almost any ciphertext with some small modifications. Since we can guess several of the encrypted words in the quote above, we don't need to do any character frequency analysis to break the code. Guess the code for the letter *o*, and the rest of the code follows. The Caesar Cipher introduces confusion into the ciphertext, but does not provide enough diffusion to hide the character frequencies.

Variations of the Caesar Cipher use multiple alphabets and offsets. Since there are a finite number of alphabets, the period of each can be deduced and character frequency analysis can be applied to each alphabet to break the code.

One-Time Pad System

The Caesar Cipher algorithm demonstrates how the ciphertext can reveal information about the plaintext to the cryptanalyst. An encryption system provides **perfect secrecy** when the ciphertext reveals no information about the plaintext. Only the **One-Time Pad** (OTP) algorithm offers perfect secrecy; all other encryption algorithms include some plaintext information to the cryptanalyst.

The OTP algorithm, shown in Fig. 5.2, uses a simple XOR function. The key, or pad, consists of a continuous random string of bits. The XOR between the plaintext and pad produces a random ciphertext output. The ciphertext can only be decrypted by XORing it with the original pad. This

\cryptog-
raphy\One Time
Pad.vi

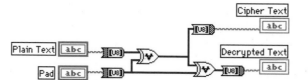

algorithm solves the character frequency weakness of the Caesar Cipher by encrypting each character with a different portion of the random pad. Thus the letter *e* will take many different values in the ciphertext.

Although this simple algorithm provides perfect secrecy, it suffers from several problems that limit its usefulness. Key size presents a major problem. The key must be as large as the plaintext message. As the name implies, the algorithm uses each part of the pad only once. Reuse of the pad provides information that can be used to decrypt previous messages. All recipients of a ciphertext message must have a copy of the pad to decrypt it. This creates a huge key distribution and storage problem that limits the OTP's use to low-bandwidth systems.

Generating the massive keys for the OTP presents a problem, too. The pseudorandom number generators provided by most computer systems are not random enough to use with this algorithm. These generators have long cyclic patterns of numbers (on the order of 2^{90} for the LabVIEW random number function) that the cryptanalyst exploits. Random numbers suitable for the OTP must come from random natural events such as emissions from radioactive decay.

Public Key Cryptography: The RSA Algorithm

The Caesar Cipher and the One-Time Pad are both **symmetric** cryptographic systems where the encryption and decryption algorithms use the same key. **Public key** cryptographic systems use different keys to encrypt and decrypt messages. As the name implies, one of the keys can be published for general use. One of the most popular public key cryptographic systems, the **RSA algorithm**, takes its name from the inventors of the algorithm—Rivest, Shamir, and Adleman.

The RSA algorithm requires two large primes, *p* and *q*. The product *pq* determines a third value *n*. An encryption exponent *e* is chosen such that *e* and *n* are relatively prime (the greatest common divisor [GCD] of *e* and

n is 1). The **GCD VI** on the CD-ROM tests this condition. Small values of *e* reduce the exponentiation computation. The formula

$$d = e^{-1} \bmod (p-1)(q-1) \tag{5.3}$$

computes the decryption exponent *d*. In this formula, the term e^{-1} denotes the modular inverse of *e*. This modular inverse has some value *v* where

$$ve \bmod (p-1)(q-1) = 1 \tag{5.4}$$

\cryptog-
raphy\X Inverse
Mod N.vi

The **X Inverse Mod N VI** computes e^{-1} given *e* and *n*. The values of *d*, *p*, and *q* are kept secret and those for *e* and *n* are published. The private key is *d* and the public key is *e*. Since *e* and *n* are public, but *p* and *q* are not, the secrecy of *d* depends on the difficulty of factoring *n*. (Factoring of large numbers often makes the national news when somebody manages to set a new record for *n*.) To increase the security of the system, use larger values of *p* and *q*.

The RSA examples presented here use the following values:

p = 251
q = 241
n = 60,491
e = 7
d = 17,143

The values of *p* and *q* are not really large primes. They were chosen to keep within the range of 16-bit integers. Real implementations use key lengths from 512 to 2048 bits.

A plaintext message *M* is encrypted with the function

$$C = M^e \bmod n \tag{5.5}$$

and the ciphertext is decrypted with the function

$$M = C^d \bmod n \tag{5.6}$$

\cryptogra-
phy\Fast Modular
Exponentiation.vi

The encryption and decryption functions both rely on modular exponentiation. A fast modular exponentiation algorithm appears in Fig. 5.3. This algorithm computes B^e in approximately $\log_2 e$ iterations. The right shift at the top of the diagram halves the exponent with each iteration. The algorithm squares the shift register variable initialized with *B* with each iteration to correspond to the halved exponent. If $e = 16$, this computes $((((B^2)^2)^2)^2)$. The shift register initialized with 1 holds the partial product of

Figure 5.3
Fast Modular
Exponentiation VI
diagram.

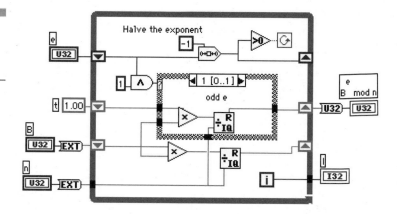

each iteration. On iterations where e is even (e AND $1 = 0$), the value passes through the 0 case unchanged. When e is odd, the value is multiplied times the product of the B squared series. The modulo function has the added benefit of preventing any product from growing too large. Despite this, the possibility of overflow exists when multiplying two large values. Using the extended-precision floating point format within the VI solves this problem.

To encrypt large inputs, the string can be broken into blocks that are then processed individually. The processed blocks are then concatenated. The algorithm fails to work in cases where the text input block value exceeds n. Choosing sufficiently large values of p and q and sizing the text blocks appropriately mitigates this problem.

The RSA algorithm can also be used for authenticating a message. Authentication certifies that a message came from a particular sender. Figure 5.4 shows the **RSA Authentication VI** and Fig. 5.5 shows the **RSA Verification VI**. To authenticate a message with the RSA algorithm, the sender passes the message through a hash function, encrypts the hash function output with the private key, and appends the encrypted hash value onto the original message. The sender does not encrypt the original message, just its hash value. To verify a message's authenticity, the recipient strips the encrypted signature and hashes the message with the same hash function used by the sender. The recipient decrypts the signature with the sender's public key and compares it to the computed hash value. If the

\cryptogra-
phy\RSA Authen-
tication.vi

\cryptogra-
phy\RSA Verifica-
tion.vi

Figure 5.4
RSA Authentication VI
diagram.

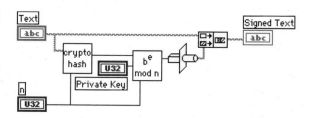

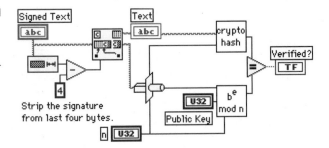

Figure 5.5
RSA Verification VI
diagram.

decrypted hash result matches the message hash, then the recipient knows that the message came from the sender (assuming no one else knows the sender's private key). While the recipient could create a signature with the public key, he or she cannot forge the sender's signature. Only the sender's private key will correctly decrypt the signature. The authentication fails when other users test the forged signatures with the public key.

The RSA algorithm offers the flexibility of a public key system, which significantly reduces key management overhead. However, the algorithm does have some serious drawbacks. The exponentiation operations used in encryption and decryption are very slow even when the fast modular exponentiation algorithm is employed. The time required to encrypt a message has been used to more accurately guess the private key, since a larger value requires more time to compute. This problem is addressed by adding delays to the encryption operation to make most values of e take the same amount of time. This fix only aggravates the slowness of the algorithm. The RSA algorithm does have a place in modern encryption systems: It is used to encrypt session keys for the Data Encryption Standard (DES) or other algorithms in hybrid systems.

Summary

The VIs presented in this chapter demonstrate the range of complexity in cryptographic systems. The most secure algorithm, the One-Time Pad, has a simple algorithm based on the XOR function. The RSA algorithm relies on a much more complex and computationally intensive public key system. Regardless of the algorithm used, the security of a cryptographic system relies on the secrecy of the keys used and the difficulty of guessing or deriving them. The larger the key space, the more guessing is needed to find the right key. The same computationally infeasible tasks that vex computer scientists provide security to the cryptographer.

LabVIEW and Mathematics

Lothar Wenzel

LabVIEW Consultant

Advanced programming techniques in LabVIEW's G language allow a systematic, thorough exploration of many of the current uses of this graphically oriented language. It's even more fascinating, however, to look for new fields of application for LabVIEW. In the ideal case, the solution you come up with works as well in practice as it does in theory.

Network operations are a good example—they are supported by LabVIEW with regard to both the platform and the protocols they use. Because of this, it's really not difficult to use G to program relatively complex network problems. The graphically oriented and data-driven concept leads to fast, easy solutions because of its similarities to network operations.

The next three chapters discuss ideas that should enlighten you further on this aspect of LabVIEW. First, we'll look at the relationship between mathematics and LabVIEW. Next, we'll consider whether or not G is a suitable simulation language or will be in the near future. Finally, we'll turn our attention to new LabVIEW applications in signal processing, a field in which LabVIEW has been well represented since its introduction.

The National Instruments **G Math Toolkit** is a collection of mathematical and theoretical signal routines that go above and beyond what the Advanced Analysis Library can do. In fact, entirely new doors are opening up for LabVIEW using this toolkit with suitable G programs; this also applies to mathematics, simulation calculations, and signal theory.

After you read the following three chapters, you might think that LabVIEW's G fits right in with these fields for several reasons. First, the conversion of algorithms to G is often easier and more efficient than the classical sequentially oriented description. Second, as a rule, the run time performance is very good and platform independence is guaranteed. Finally, in contrast to most other mathematics and simulation programs, interfacing with the real world is no problem. Only time will tell whether these advantages will be enough to catapult LabVIEW into completely new frontiers.

G and Classical Programming Languages

LabVIEW was primarily developed to improve applications involving automated test equipment and data acquisition. Until recently, we didn't actually know whether LabVIEW could also handle more demanding mathematical problems. Although we had several examples that converted more complex mathematical routines into G, the majority of these examples were designed purely for demonstration purposes. However, we can probably call some of these programs the beginnings of a new generation of algorithmic descriptions with a graphically determined background. This raises the question of whether LabVIEW's G has the expressive power to build important functions and procedures.

The answer to these questions would be easy if you were only interested in implementations based on C, FORTRAN, or Pascal. LabVIEW can use the Code Interface Node (CIN) to link user-specific external code, but there are some disadvantages to going about it this way. In particular, there is a platform dependence that requires as many solutions as the number of available computer architectures. You may also lose the asynchronous capabilities of LabVIEW in this case. A third argument involves the data structures—every modification of a data type requires a new program cycle consisting of editing, compiling, and linking. And you have to repeat this cycle for every platform you're interested in, with special adaptations for each one.

All these disadvantages of conventional languages contrast with the very real advantages of LabVIEW's G. In G, platform independence is guaranteed and the asynchronous working part of LabVIEW creates great freedom of movement both for the programmer and for the user.

You might be asking yourself, "If the advantages are so heavily in favor of G, why hasn't this concept won out in the contest with classical languages?" It's because, until now, the matchup between classical languages and completely new approaches (including G) hasn't happened. Why? Because, for centuries, mathematical algorithms have been recorded in text form and almost always sequentially. Each new generation adopted this style, which is understandable because all publications use it. You can imagine that sometimes algorithms had to be forced into sequential text form, but nothing is harder to change than researchers and programmers who are set in their ways.

Wouldn't it be really cool if all the algorithmic knowledge accumulated up until now could be modeled after examples like G? Even if you didn't consider any other advantages, the internal structure of algorithms would be much easier to see!

Obviously, LabVIEW is more than just capable of handling mathematical questions; it can also be a handy tool in those investigations. It might even be the *best* approach available right now, but a conclusive answer would require rewriting a lot of the existing algorithmic literature.

G as Formula Language

LabVIEW is capable of the demanding job of algorithm description. In some ways LabVIEW, or more generally, a well-defined graphically oriented and data-driven programming language, is probably the best method of converting a given algorithm. The following example should help demonstrate this idea.

Figure 6.1 represents the C program for the famous **Runge-Kutta** algorithm. This method solves ordinary differential equations and is one of the most popular routines in applied mathematics. The corresponding G version of this algorithm is represented in Fig. 6.2. In purely structural terms, the G version is clearer and easier to understand than the C version. In addition, the graphical notation eases modification of the code.

For many mathematical applications using LabVIEW, you need a formula input mechanism. Although LabVIEW has its own formula node, it is *compiled,* which means that it's very fast but you can't input new formulas while the program is running. You have to know ahead of time which formulas you intend to use in the program. This limitation isn't all that severe if you design a parser that you can access at run time.

Figure 6.1
The famous Runge-Kutta method in C notation.

```
void rk4(float y[], float dydx[], int n, float x, float h,
    float yout[], void (*derivs) (float [], float []))

{
    int i;
    float xh,hh,h6,*dym,*dyt,*yt;

    dym=vector(1,n);
    dyt=vector(1,n);
    yt=vector(1,n);
    hh=h*0.5;
    h6=h/6.0;
    xh=x+hh;
    for (i=1;i<=n;i++) yt[i]=y[i]+hh*dydx[i];
    (*derivs)(xh,yt,dyt);
    for (i=1;i<=n;i++) yt[i]=y[i]+hh*dyt[i];
    (*derivs)(xh,yt,dym);
    for (i=1;i<=n;i++) {
        yt[i]=y[i]+h*dym[i];
        dym[i] += dyt[i];
    }
    (*derivs)(x+h,yt,dyt);
    for (i=1;i<=n;i++)
        yout[i]=y[i]+h6*(dydx[i]+dyt[i]+2.0*dym[i]);
    free_vector(yt,1,n);
    free_vector(dyt,1,n);
    free_vector(dym,1,n);
}
```

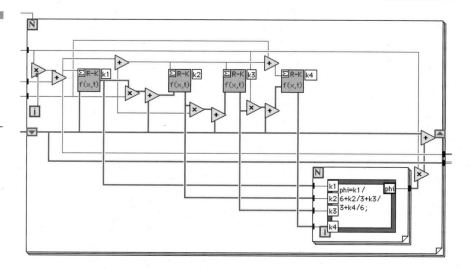

Figure 6.2
The Runge-Kutta method in G notation. The subVI carries out the calculation of the underlying function f.

A *parser* is a program that converts text strings into formulas that the underlying program understands. It's a classic computer science exercise, often involving recursion (where a function calls itself). You might think that designing such a thing is an impossible task because of the repetition involved, if you're basing it on a data flow language like G. Formulas are split into subformulas, which in turn are split into sub-sub-formulas, and so forth. At first glance, LabVIEW isn't capable of handling this, but if you look again you can find detours to help you get around the problem. It's not easy, but it is possible if you limit the scope of the parser's capability.

The definition of a formula starts out being rather vague. It becomes concrete only after you establish the rules—rules concerning the number of variables and their nomenclature, the allowed functions, and the data structures you want to use. The G Math Toolkit parser is simple in both design and operation. It works exclusively with real-valued numbers, and the variable names are two characters at most, with the second character being a number. From an engineer's standpoint, this isn't a major limitation. However, you'll have to expand the present parser if you plan to study more demanding mathematical questions, particularly if you're getting into simulations. In that situation, you'll need parsers that can handle complex numbers, vectors, and matrices, and that have more flexibility in naming variables. In addition, you'll need the ability to declare complicated new functions. Such parsers are entirely possible in G, which makes LabVIEW's future secure in this area as well.

A Brief Description of the G Math Toolkit

To assist LabVIEW users in the expression of mathematical relationships, the G Math Toolkit was created. It consists of a collection of interwoven libraries, the parser being the most important (Fig. 6.3). Each library represents a particular field of operation.

This richness of this combination will be explained later. Table 6.1 lists the fields of operation that are covered by the individual libraries.

The connections between all these parts are numerous and, as already mentioned, constitute the real strength of the G Math Toolkit. The 1D Explorer library uses program parts of Zero, Optimize, Function, Visualize, and Parser as service VIs. You, as the user, have complete freedom to build up your own solutions of any complexity.

Overall, the total package consists of about 100 core VIs, completed by a few dozen subVIs. All these VIs can be used directly, and all core VIs are documented in detail. Let's take a look inside the toolkit, beginning with the parser.

The Internal Structure of the Parser

There are an infinite number of ways of implementing a general parser. The parser of the G Math Toolkit realizes formulas with the aid of **tree structures** and interprets these trees on the basis of the **three-register**

Figure 6.3
The basic structure of the G Math Toolkit. The parser takes the central role, but only the interplay of all the libraries allows the solution of demanding and complex problems.

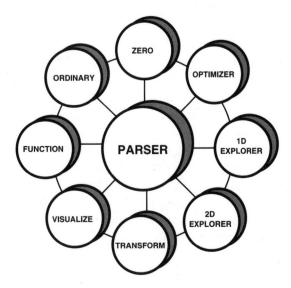

TABLE 6.1

Fields of Operation
Covered by the
Libraries in the
G Math Toolkit

Library Name	Description
ZERO	Zero-point determination of 1-D and n-D real-valued functions that are described by the parser
OPTIMIZE	Optimization of 1-D and n-D real-valued functions that are described by the parser, supplemented by fitting algorithms and by routines of linear programming
1D EXPLORER	Investigation of 1-D real-valued functions, function graphs, extremes, zero points, curve lengths, and more
2D EXPLORER	Investigation of 2-D real-valued functions, plots, extremes, zero points, partial derivatives, and more
TRANSFORM	Collection of important transformations in signal theory that, however, are not part of the Advanced Analysis Library
VISUALIZE	Tools for the 2-D and 3-D representation of functions and data
FUNCTION	Collection of frequently used functions that, however, are not part of the Advanced Analysis Library
PARSER	Formula interpreter that is used in all parts of the package
ODE	Routines that can be used to solve ordinary differential equations both in numerical and in symbolic form

machine known from information technology. A tree is a basic structure both of theoretical and of applied mathematics. We're interested mainly in **binary** trees, which are highly suitable for parser operation (Fig. 6.4). Binary trees can cope with both unary and binary operators in any combination (Fig. 6.5).

Figure 6.4
The binary tree
shown represents
the very simple for-
mula $a + b$.

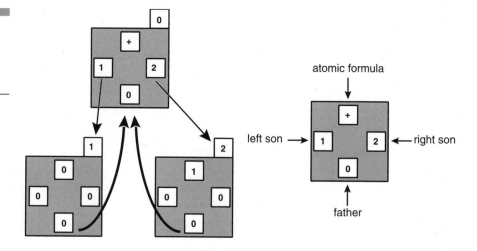

Figure 6.5
Two typical binary
tree structures. The
example at *left* stands
for binary operators
such as +, −, *, or /;
the example at *right*
stands for the unary
operators such as sin,
exp, or cosh. The
entire tree can have
any desired structure;
narrow parts can
subsequently build
up many branches,
subbranches, and
so forth.

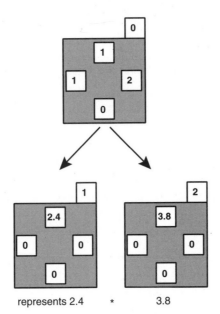

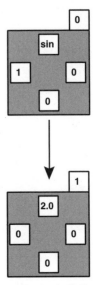

represents 2.4   *   3.8

represents sin (2.0)

In essence, the **analyzing** portion of the parser transforms formulas into tree structures. This usually proceeds smoothly, but with a limitation: entering a formula isn't as simple as a click with a mouse. You could make any number of erroneous inputs, in particular when entering really complicated formulas. As a general rule, remember that a parser has to invest a lot of time in error checking. Error checking means both detecting and localizing the faulty input with appropriate indications for the user. The parser of the G Math Toolkit supplies the error code −23001 if something has gone wrong. In addition, an error cluster (Fig. 6.6) is included, which supplies you with more detailed information when errors occur.

Figure 6.6
All parser routines
use LabVIEW stan-
dard error clusters.
The *error in* reflects
the error situation
at the beginning of
the analysis, while
the *error out* docu-
ments the new situa-
tion after the analysis.

Figure 6.7
Both the direct (top)
and the indirect (bot-
tom) modes of oper-
ation of the parser
are represented dia-
grammatically. In vir-
tually all applications,
the indirect mode
is the means of
choice. The analysis
of the formula is sep-
arated in time from
its interpretation.

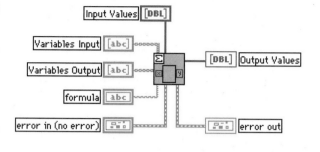

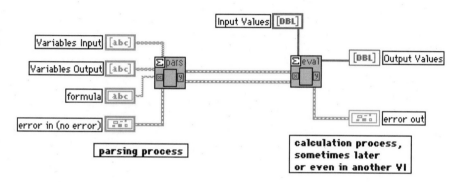

The parser actually has two principal modes of operation, **direct** and **indirect**. In many applications, you have to handle formulas directly. This means you have to calculate a string representing a formula directly. An example of this is a VI that is to act like the formula node of the Lab-VIEW system. Internally, this is also a two-stage process, although it will be invisible to you.

After analyzing or interpreting the string, the second step performed by the parser is always the **calculation**. For a direct operation, calculation immediately follows interpretation. However, indirect handling of a formula is used more frequently. A good example of this is the solution of ordinary differential equations. This normally requires managing a series of equations, initial conditions, and variables. In this case, interpreting the formulas many times would be highly inefficient. It's much better to separate the interpretation phase from the actual calculation. The calculation phase then makes repeated use of the results from the interpretation step. The G Math Toolkit has a special data structure for this purpose. Figure 6.7 demonstrates both strategies and the connection between the two phases of the indirect method.

The Explorers and Examples

There are six libraries of examples within the total scope of the G Math Toolkit: Graphics, Math, Mechanics, Optimization, Signal Processing, and Miscellaneous. These libraries consist of examples of different degrees of difficulty, and some of these demonstrations are so complete that you could call them independent applications. The explorers represent both useful applications and programming details that are important in using the G Math Toolkit. The following paragraphs outline the functionality of some of the explorers.

1D EXPLORER EXAMPLE VI   This example calculates the function graph of a 1-D real-valued function. The user has a choice between determining extreme values, zero points, integrals, derivatives, and curve lengths.

2D EXPLORER EXAMPLE VI   Similar to the 1D Explorer Example, this example graphs 2-D functions and displays extremes of the functions (Fig. 6.8).

Figure 6.8
The front panel of the 2D Explorer Example.vi. This VI supplies both the graphs and the extreme values of a function defined by the user.

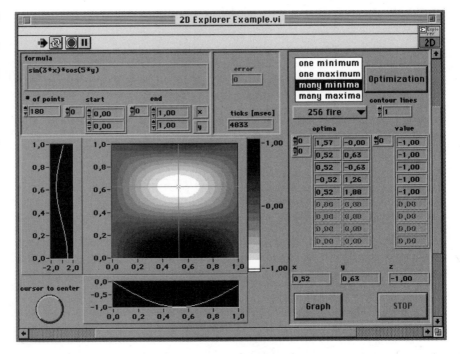

EQUATION EXPLORER EXAMPLE VI This VI solves systems of nonlinear equations. The solutions of these systems are found by means of randomly determined starting points inside an *n*-dimensional rectangle defined by the user.

ODE EXPLORER EXAMPLE VI This VI solves systems of ordinary differential equations. The systems can be of any order. The user can choose between the standard methods of Euler, Runge-Kutta, and Cash-Karp.

PROCESS CONTROL EXPLORER EXAMPLE VI This example represents a real-world problem. A water tank having an inlet and an outlet is modeled. Both the rate of inflow and the rate of outflow can be adjusted by the user of the program. The VI checks whether the water tank runs dry, approaches a stable cycle, or finally overflows. The rates of inflow and outflow can be specified by formulas. This example will be discussed later in this chapter.

TRANSFORM EXPLORER EXAMPLE VI This VI demonstrates the calculation of the Short Time Fourier Transform (STFT). The STFT is set up in this case on the basis of symbolically specified functions.

TRANSPORT OPTIMIZATION EXPLORER EXAMPLE VI This real-world problem concerns optimization, which is very important in practice. A number of producers of a specific product must supply numerous dealers. The transportation of a product unit from a given producer to a given dealer generates fixed costs. The VI determines an optimal strategy whose total costs are at a minimum in global terms. In addition, the results of the optimization are displayed graphically.

The Handling of Mathematical Problems in LabVIEW

In this section we'll look at some practical examples of handling math problems in the LabVIEW paradigm. Although it is possible to master mathematical problems directly without using the G Math Toolkit, the toolkit plays a big part in simplifying programming in many applications.

Determination of Characteristic Measuring Parameters

In the practice of measurement, you often have to match your data to prescribed models; in some cases, you can find the right fit by using known formulations like polynomials or trig functions.

Usually, given pairs of measured values (x_i, y_i), you interpret y_i as the actual measured value at the instant x_i, with the index i running from 1 to the final value of n. Also, you can assume that the model equation $y = f(a, x)$ is given. The parameter a might consist of several individual components. Your goal is to find an a such that the sum

$$\sum_{i=1}^{n} |y_i - f(a, x_i)|^2$$

turns out to be as small as possible. This is the classic **least-squares** approach.

In practice, we often solve this problem by using the **Levenberg-Marquardt method** (Press et al. 1993), which also works with nonlinear functions. LabVIEW's Advanced Analysis library offers the Levenberg-Marquardt method, but you have to fix the functional model $f(a, x)$ while you're programming.

You'll get more degrees of freedom if you use the G Math Toolkit. The benefits in this case are the free input of the model equation in the form of symbols on the front panel and the ability to use all the functions known by the parser. The distinction between model parameters and independent variables is performed by appropriate components of a cluster.

Figure 6.9 shows how to handle a fitting problem. To make things easier to understand, the initial data wasn't generated by a measurement process. Rather, it came from another G Math Toolkit feature: the ability to generate arbitrary function values for a prescribed equation. In this case, you can use random terms in the definition, thus giving rise to a true fitting problem. If the originally specified function and the model equation have an identical or at least a very similar structure, you can easily check whether the expected parameters and the actual ones really correspond. In the diagram you see the use of two VIs from the toolkit—one to evaluate the formula and the other to do the fit.

Gyroscopic Motion in 3-D Space

Now let's briefly look at G Math's capabilities in solving differential equations. The toolkit gives you access to methods according to Euler, Runge-

LabVIEW and Mathematics

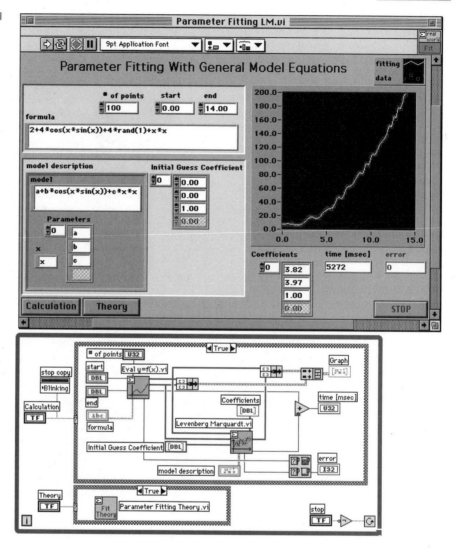

Figure 6.9
The G Math Toolkit allows you to manipulate formulas when you're fitting measured values while running the program. The model equations, the variable quantity, and the parameters that occur are fixed (*bottom left* in the cluster). For easier understanding, the initial data in the example was also generated using a formula (*top of panel*). Additional random terms ensure that you get a true fitting problem. The diagram is simplicity itself.

Kutta, and Cash-Karp, as well as to numeric and symbolic operating routines for systems of linear differential equations and differential equations of the nth order. As an example, let's look at describing the motion of a gyroscope. You can do this by fixing the gyroscope's center of gravity in three-dimensional space (Gander and Hrebicek 1993). There are many parameters that determine the behavior of this system. Figure 6.10 shows the panel of an example VI that displays the equations of motion solved by the G Math Toolkit.

Figure 6.10
The user interface for treating the gyroscope problem. You can see the actual differential equations in the middle part of the upper figure. The three components completely describe the gyroscope's position in space and time.

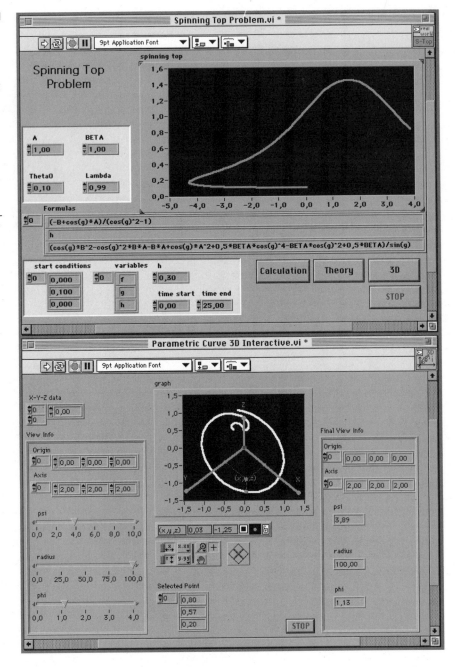

One of the substantial advantages of LabVIEW's G Math Toolkit is the ability to admit measured values as parameters of differential equation models *and* to feed back the results of these calculations to the process by means of digital-to-analog conversion or other interfaces. Thus, if you're investigating differential equations, you could very well get specific parameters directly from process measurements, and the results could also have a feedback effect on the process through digital-to-analog conversion or other actuators. These features far surpass the performance of other mathematics and simulation packages.

A Numerical Experiment: Newton-Raphson Method

For many reasons, LabVIEW is well suited for carrying out numerical investigations. The three most important arguments are:

■ You can describe many algorithms in numerical analysis quite well by using a data flow machine in conjunction with graphical orientation.

■ The user interface allows you to react quickly to new situations, so you can easily visualize each auxiliary variable. This leaves room for you to experiment and study new phenomena.

■ As a rule, you can use simple wiring or branching of existing structures on the programming side, which helps you achieve the preceding argument.

The Newton-Raphson method is a good example of a numerical investigation. You can use this method to determine zeros of a given function $f(x)$ by using the derivative of this function. For practical reasons, the Newton-Raphson method succeeds because it has good convergence properties, and you can use this method for both 1-D or n-D real-valued functions as well as 1-D or n-D complex-valued functions.

The fundamental idea of the method is based on the approximation formula (only the 1-D case is shown here):

$$f(x_0 + h) = f(x_0) + hf'(x_0) \tag{6.1}$$

from which it follows, after transformation, that

$$h = -f(x_0)/f'(x_0) \tag{6.2}$$

assuming that $f(x_0 + h) = 0$. In other words, if you consider x_0 as a good approximation for a zero point of f, and it holds that $f(x_0 + h) = 0$, you can estimate the unknown h in accordance with Eq. 6.2. An iteration algorithm for determining a zero of f follows from this.

A. Start with a guess for x0.

B. If x_n is an approximation of the zero point, let

$$x_{n+1} = x_n - f(x_n)/f'(x_n) \tag{6.3}$$

C. If the approximation x_{n+1} is sufficiently good, or if the number of iterations is large enough, then stop. Otherwise, proceed to B.

Let's look at a special case. Given $f(x) = x^3 - 1$, permitting not only real-valued x, but also complex numbers, the formula in Eq. 6.3 will then look like this:

$$x_{n+1} = x_n - (x^3_{n-1})/3x^2_n \tag{6.3a}$$

Now we can experiment with this formula. You begin the iteration process using the starting value x_0, which you can select with complete freedom. Remember that x_0 is a complex number, so you can visualize properties of these values in the complex plane. One of these properties is whether a prescribed starting value converges toward the zero point $x = 1$ while iterating. You can't take this for granted—after all, there are two other zero points, exp $(2\pi i/3)$ and exp $(4\pi i/3)$, and even there convergence isn't guaranteed. The question also remains as to which complex numbers x_0 converge toward 1 in steps A through C of the iteration process.

The reality of this situation turns out to be very exciting. Based on symmetry, one third of the complex plane (initial values being intended) converges toward 1, one third converges toward exp $(2\pi i/3)$, and one third converges toward exp $(4\pi i/3)$. If you ignore rotations and displacements, the corresponding convergence zones should be identical. You would expect a simple threefold division of the complex plane into pie pieces, with 1, exp $(2\pi i/3)$, and exp $(4\pi i/3)$ somehow situated in the center of these parts.

This really happens, but you'll see a strange breakdown. Figure 6.11 shows the results obtained using LabVIEW to investigate a square of the complex plane starting at $(-2, -2i)$ and ending at $(+2, +2i)$. You can see stable islands (for which the convergence proceeds undisturbed toward 1) among bizarre structures that have completely different convergence properties, creating a fractal structure with truly fascinating details.

Figure 6.11
Fractals made by LabVIEW. The white part of the graph is the region of convergence.

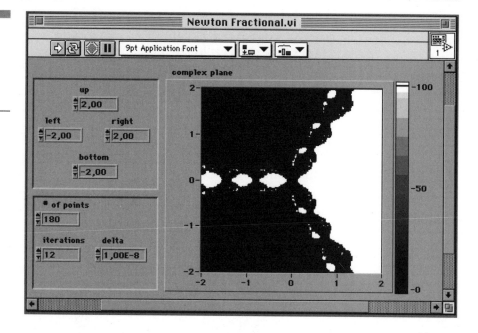

The experimental possibilities are endless. Once you obtain part of an image, you can recalculate on a magnified scale, or you can make variations in the program. In the original version, you're only investigating whether the starting values are close enough to the target value of 1 after a certain number of iterations. If they are, you'll mark the corresponding starting value with white, otherwise with black. You can also investigate how well you reach the target value of 1 after a fixed number of iterations, and you can mark this quantity with color. You'll end up with colorful topographic maps, which are attractive in their own right. You can usually do the programming modifications for this purpose in about a minute.

You can accomplish steps A through C, and the subsequent visualization, easily with LabVIEW. Note that you won't be able to use the Formula Node to implement the formula in Eq. 6.3a, since you can't treat complex numbers with this tool. You would need a formula node that operates with complex numbers—a good idea for a future version of LabVIEW. Right now, you still have to convert Eq. 6.3a directly.

Iterative Function Systems

The previous program shows that you can produce fascinating images from relatively simple mathematical relationships. You can actually create artificial worlds this way on a conveyor belt, as it were. What comes next, however, exceeds this by far.

Let's look at an arbitrary image. To make this as uncomplicated as possible, the image you consider should consist of black and white points only. You'll be able to see structures inside the image, assuming, of course, that the image really does represent something.

The key here is the concept of self-similarity. If you look at a piece of the image under a magnifying glass, you'll see something that looks very much like the starting image. It might be rotated slightly, or even deformed, but basically it will be the same as the original. In practical terms, you need to detect so-called **affine transformations** T_i $(i = 1, ..., n)$ of the image B, which possess additional properties. Affine transformations are very easy to describe in mathematical terms. An affine transformation in a plane has the general form of

$$x_{new} = a * x + b * y + e \qquad \text{(6.4a)}$$

$$y_{new} = c * x + d * y + f \qquad \text{(6.4 b)}$$

Here, (x,y) is the starting point, while (x_{new}, y_{new}) is the transformed point in the plane. The constants a, b, c, d, e, and f determine the exact character of the affine transformation. The pair (e,f) is responsible for the displacement of points, while the other parameters a, b, c, and d cause compressions, elongations, and rotations.

In the *specific competing* affine transformation T, you can interpret self-similarity in such a way that in the case of the image, $T(B)$ coincides nicely with a part of B. If you take this a step further, it might be possible for you to detect a range T_i $(i = 1, ..., n)$ of competing affine transformations that recreate the total image in miniature. If you match all this in such a way that the relationship

$$B = T_1(B) + T_2(B) + \cdots + T_n(B) \qquad \text{(6.5)}$$

is satisfied at least approximately, you get an output image that in some respects is completely coded by the transformations $T_1, ..., T_n$. This coding is extremely efficient, since each transformation is completely described by the six values a to f. Now, what about decoding? As it turns out, there is a brilliant solution: chance reconstructs the output image.

Before we look at an example, let's review the solution algorithm for the fractal description of structures:

A. Determine a range of competing affine transformations $T_1, ..., T_n$ with the property described in Eq. 6.5.

B. Determine probabilities $p_1, \ldots, p_n$, which are oriented toward the magnitude of $T_1(B), \ldots, T_n(B)$ referred to B. It holds that $p_1 + \cdots + p_n = 1$.

C. Fix the starting point $(x,y) = (0,0)$.

D. Decide on precisely one of the transformations $T_i\,(i = 1, \ldots, n)$ using the probability $p_i\,(i = 1, \ldots, n)$. Let $i = j$ have been selected.

E. Calculate $(x_{new}, y_{new}) = T_j(x,y)$.

F. Plot the point (x_{new}, y_{new}).

G. Set $(x,y) = (x_{new}, y_{new})$ and proceed to D.

You can shorten the process as required. It's next to impossible to go wrong regarding the probabilities that arise. If you choose unfavorable values, the process merely lasts longer before the image emerges. However, the points you plot at the beginning are mostly outliers—they actually shouldn't even occur in the graphs at all. You can avoid these exceptions easily: simply start plotting from the point with the number 1000.

It is possible for you to grant one transformation absolute authority (selected with the probability of 1) while the other transformations have no say at all. Since the transformation you selected acts in a competing fashion, the preceding algorithm terminates quickly. In other words, you quickly reach a fixed point after which you can't go any further. These images turn out to be rather plain. As soon as a second transformation with a positive probability comes into play, you won't approach any more stable end points. The other transformation shows up occasionally, and as a result, the current point is immediately repositioned.

Enough theory; let's take a look at a practical application. Our aim is to go through a complete cycle of coding and decoding using the existing structures of Fig. 6.12. A few auxiliary constructions have already been started in the image; these can be seen in two places. First, at the upper right you see the overall image in a form that is slightly smaller and rotated by several degrees. You can easily determine the corresponding competing affine transformation. Second, with the exception of the lower part just mentioned, you can generate the spiral shape from the overall image information. You can determine the corresponding parameters a–f by fixing three original points and three image points and noting corresponding systems of equations.

These simple transformations allow you to code the spiral object on the basis of 12 individual values (two a–f data records). In today's world, it's theoretically possible to code any meaningful image like this. You'll end up with a few hundred competing affine transformations that can completely generate the image's content. What's so great about that? Well, imagine that

The user interface and the diagram of a data compression algorithm based on affine transforms. The mathematics employed can be taken directly from the diagram.

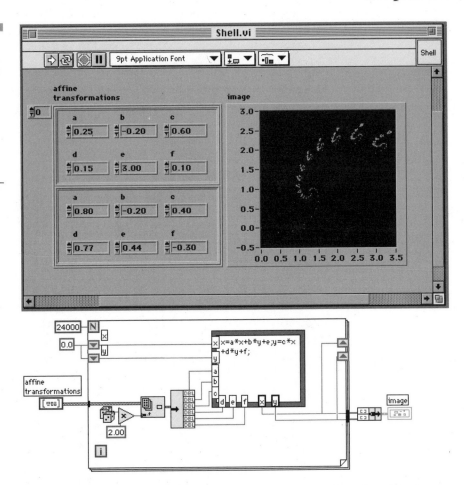

a 90-minute film is available as sequences of images. For simplicity's sake, pretend that it's a black-and-white film with a resolution of 4000×4000 individual points per image. Assume that a supercomputer has coded the film's individual images in the sense discussed previously. We want each image to have 100 transformations, meaning that we'll need to store perhaps 2 Kbytes. By contrast, the total content of an image is 16,000,000 bits or about 2 Mbytes. This is a 1000-to-1 compression of the original.

Shortest Paths in the Graph

Looking at a generalized **directed graph**—a structure of *nodes* and *edges*—you'll notice that several pairs of nodes are connected by edges, while others are not. The edges themselves are directional, and are also weighted with nonnegative numbers. In this case, you interpret the weightings as lengths, costs, or the like (Fig. 6.13). Let two different nodes A and B of the graph be fixed. What is the shortest (or most cost-effective) path from A to B? You can find the length of the path by adding the weightings of the individual edges, but there are also other conceivable definitions for the path length.

First, let's look at the current algorithmic solution to the problem of the shortest path in graphs: the **Bellman principle**. The starting point is a property of the shortest path that was first used by the mathematician Bellman. Specifically, each path from A to C, the aim being for C to lie on the shortest path from A to B, is itself a shortest path from A to C. You can easily see the correctness of this statement. If it didn't hold, it would be possible to construct a new path from A to B. This would mean you would have to adopt the second segment from C to B without making changes, while the original path from A to C would be replaced by the hypothetically shortest from A to C. You end up with a path from A to B that is shorter than the original segment that you've already recognized as being a minimum. You can only resolve this contradiction by requiring that the path from A to C is a minimum.

You can derive an effective marking algorithm from this simple relationship. Nodes are occupied by specific numbers. Initially, you allocate the node A the number 0, while all other nodes are labeled ∞. The length of a shortest path from A to each node is presented as a dimension at that tar-

Figure 6.13
Directed graphs consist of nodes and edges. Some pairs of nodes are connected by edges. Weights for the edges are provided by nonnegative numbers. You can interpret the sum of these weightings of a path as its length. The challenge is to figure out the shortest path between two given nodes.

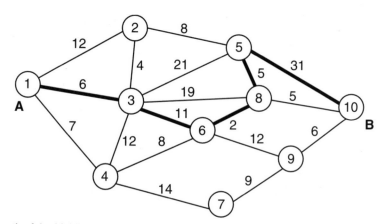

Length of the highlighted path = 6+11+2+5+31 = 55

$\underline{8}$ weighting of an edge

② node 2

get point only after everything has been done. However, you'll recognize the shortest path from A to B immediately. Specifically, you obtain the node lying directly in front of B on the said minimum path by adding all nodes connected directly to B, the previously mentioned dimension, and the edge length of the precursor of B to B itself. At least one sum is exactly as large as the length of the shortest path from A to B. The node that satisfies this equation is the point lying directly in front of A on the shortest path from A to B. You can continue this theme recursively, resulting in knowledge of the exact course of the entire shortest path from A to B.

Let's get back to the marking algorithm, which, as it were, is like putting a cart before the horse we just described. You make multiple passes for this purpose: in each pass you subject all the markings to a common (i.e., synchronous) assessment. To be precise, you calculate the sums

$$\{d_{ij} + M_i \mid (i,j) \text{ the edge of the graph}\} \tag{6.6}$$

for each node j. Here, d_{ij} is the length of the edge from the node i to j, and M_i is the old weighting of the node i. You select the minimum of all these numbers and compare it with the value M_j. If the minimum is smaller than M_j, it becomes the new marking of the node. This all proceeds entirely synchronously for all nodes. At the conclusion of a pass, all the marking numbers M_j are simultaneously updated. If there aren't any changes to the M_j values within a pass, the algorithm is terminated. You can prove that the required number of passes is less than or equal to the number of nodes.

A simple and elegant LabVIEW solution to the shortest paths problem using the Bellman principle is shown in Fig. 6.14. You can find this VI in the LabVIEW examples in LabVIEW\examples\analysis\mathxmpl.llb\ Shortest Paths Example.

All that really matters to the LabVIEW programmer is that a data flow machine is available. Because of this, the actual problem moves into the foreground more than ever before. As you can see, programming the problem of the shortest path is easy using G. Two conclusions you'll probably reach are:

- Theoretical graph problems can be handled by LabVIEW.
- Recursion in an algorithm does not automatically spell curtains for LabVIEW.

The second statement has, by the way, already been confirmed in connection with the design of the parser and is discussed in detail in Chapter 3, "Algorithms."

Figure 6.14
Figure 6.14
LabVIEW diagram for the Bellman princi- ple, which is the ker- nel of the solution to the shortest path problem.

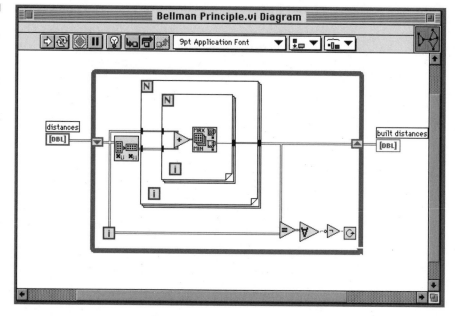

Optimization of a Production Process

You can find some of the most striking and important applications of the theory of convex figures in **linear optimization**. This involves many variable quantities that have to satisfy linear inequalities *and* maximize a certain objective function. You can denote the variables by $x_1, x_2, \ldots, x_n$. In purely mathematical form, it looks like this:

System of linear inequalities:

$$\left.\begin{cases} a_{11}x_1 + a_{12}x_2 + \cdots + a_{1n}x_n \geq b_1 \\ \vdots \qquad\qquad\qquad\qquad \vdots \\ a_{m1}x_1 + a_{m2}x_2 + \cdots + a_{mn}x_n \geq b_m \end{cases}\right\} \tag{6.7}$$

Objective function:

$$c_1x_1 + c_2x_2 + \cdots + c_nx_n = \text{max!} \tag{6.8}$$

All the a and c components are linearly coupled to the x values, and we know all the a_{ji}, b_j, and c_i ($i = 1, \ldots, n$; $j = 1, \ldots, m$) values in advance. Our aim is to find a vector $(x_1, \ldots, x_n)$ that satisfies all the inequalities and max- imizes the objective function.

Systems of the types shown in Eqs. 6.7 and 6.8 are solved worldwide every day—for example, problems that address the transportation of goods from producer to vendor. We've known an effective solution algorithm for tasks in linear optimization for over 40 years, but recently problems of immense size (≥10,000 unknowns) have led to interesting new developments.

Be that as it may, all the methods of solution are based on properties of convex figures. To be precise, an equation of the form

$$a_{j1}x_1 + a_{j2}x_2 + \cdots + a_{jn}x_n = b_j \qquad (6.9)$$

describes nothing but a hyperplane in n-dimensional space. If you replace the equality sign in Eq. 6.9 by an inequality, something happens in n-dimensional space that you can easily interpret. Specifically, all the points that lie on one side or the other of the hyperplane (depending on the inequality sign) are brought out. If several inequalities of the type shown in Eq. 6.9 are satisfied at the same time, you can translate that into the language of geometry. It's simply a question of causing an appropriate number of half-spaces to intersect with one another. All the half-spaces are infinitely large convex figures. Because of this, the intersection of a limited number of such half-planes is also convex. Three situations can happen in this case: The intersection can produce a finite polyhedron in n-dimensional space; it can be unlimited; or it can contain nothing at all.

It is mostly x vectors that satisfy the system of inequalities of Eq. 6.7 that you can denote as permissible. The third case is awkward in this respect: If there are no permissible points present, there is nothing to optimize. In other words, the inequalities contradict one another. Consequently, we're really only interested in the first two cases. This is where the objective function comes into play. You interpret the requirement of Eq. 6.8 geometrically. Specifically, for a concrete value of the variable c,

$$c_1x_1 + c_2x_2 + \cdots + c_nx_n = c \qquad (6.10)$$

again describes a hyperplane in n-dimensional space. Of course, c is unknown during the optimization process. On the other hand, we've found a way to solve the problem. You have to bring the family of hyperplanes from very far above (because of the search for the maximum) to the intersection of the half spaces (Eq. 6.9) in such a way that you reach a corner point of the polyhedron. The values of $x_1, x_2, \ldots, x_n$ that you're looking for turn out to be the coordinates of the corner points.

The search for the optimum takes place largely on the surface of the convex polyhedron. Beginning at a permissible starting point (i.e., the system of inequalities is satisfied), the first step is to move along a specific hyperplane, which is a structure of dimension $(n-1)$. In the next step, you fix an $(n-2)$-dimensional hyperplane. Continue this procedure for each hyperplane down to dimensions 3, 2, and 1. These are just normal spaces, planes, and straight lines, respectively. Finally, you involve corner points of the n-dimensional polyhedron. The **simplex method** then ensures a corner migration. In this process, you approach the optimum step by step. Because the number of corners of a customary n-dimensional polyhedron is finite, the result is generally good. Special algorithms have been developed, by the way, for exceptional cases.

The following example is a typical representative of the class of problems known as **linear optimization**, but you're likely to encounter much harder touchstones in practice.

Problem:

A factory produces two products P and Q. A profit of $40 is returned per item for P, but the figure for Q is $120. For reasons of storage, the total number of items may not exceed 100. Furthermore, material costing $10 and $20, respectively, is required to produce a product P or Q. The maximum permissible overall material cost is $1100. The wage costs, however, amount to $10 and $40, respectively, per individual product. The wage costs must together remain below $1600. Given these conditions, what does an optimum production strategy look like?[1]

To obtain a solution, let x_1 denote the number of samples of P produced, and x_2 the same for Q. The following restrictions result from the problem:

$$x_1 + x_2 \leq 100 \quad \text{(storage costs)}$$

$$10x_1 + 20x_2 \leq 1100 \quad \text{(material costs)}$$

$$10x_1 + 40x_2 \leq 1600 \quad \text{(wage costs)}$$

$$x_1 \geq 0; \, x_2 \geq 0 \quad \text{(less than 0 is not permitted)}$$

The objective function is:

$$40x_1 + 120x_2 = \text{max!}$$

There are a couple of things to remember:

1. The solution must actually consist of natural numbers x_1 and x_2. There are special methods that also guarantee that the solutions are

---

[1] Just about now, I consider it a blessing that I'm an engineer and not a businessman. *Ed.*

integral. However, a "bent solution" can certainly be useful as an approximation.

2. The inequality sign changes in the relationships. The form desired by the simplex method can, however, always be provided simply by multiplying by −1.

The solution in the example is, by the way, $x_1 = 60$ and $x_2 = 25$, which you can determine directly by using the **Linear Programming Simplex Method VI** in the G Math Toolkit Optimization library (Fig. 6.15).

The Water Tank Problem

The G Math Toolkit can build up very complex solutions by joining elementary services. We can demonstrate this by solving a physical problem that leads to an ordinary differential equation.

A water tank (see the right lower part of Fig. 6.16) can, as a function of time, be filled with liquid via an inlet or be emptied via an outlet. The incoming flow is determined by the volumetric flow $f_i(t)$, while the outgoing flow is determined by the cross section $a(t)$ of a valve. Additional important parameters are the cross-sectional area A of the tank and the initial level h_0 of the water at the instant $t = 0$.

As you can see in Fig. 6.16, the functions $f_i(t)$ and $a(t)$, which depend on time, can be entered directly by the user. Of course, in accordance with

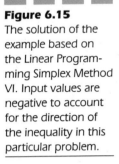

Figure 6.15
The solution of the example based on the Linear Programming Simplex Method VI. Input values are negative to account for the direction of the inequality in this particular problem.

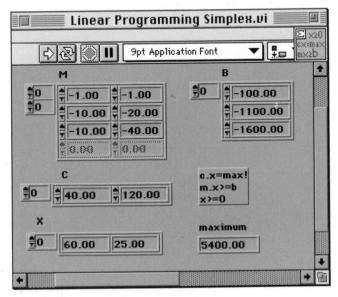

these stipulations the question arises as to how the level profile of the water tank will change with respect to time. The water tank problem concerns the solution of an ordinary differential equation with the initial conditions at the instant $t = 0$.

The physics behind this application are fairly easy and are represented at bottom right in Fig. 6.16. This, by the way, is another advantage of the G Math Toolkit that shouldn't be underestimated. Documentation and explanations can take place both on the front panel and in the diagram.

Figure 6.17 shows one of the numerous conceivable solutions of this problem using the G Math Toolkit. You determine the actual solution with the aid of the Runge-Kutta method, which is depicted in the diagram in the upper Case structure at the right margin. The lower Case structure implements an animation of the solution obtained, while the actual level of the water can be read both on the tank itself and as a highlighted point on a graph.

The **Process Control Explorer Example VI** discussed here is a part of the example section of the G Math Toolkit. You'll also find many other VIs there that will help you understand the toolkit. Most of these examples are well documented, with the mathematical and physical background supplied.

Figure 6.16
Solving the water tank problem. The basic theory is also shown on the front panel. The incoming and outgoing rates of flow can be entered with the aid of formulas. After the calculation, the variation in the level of the water in the tank can be animated. This VI is located in the Explorer example library.

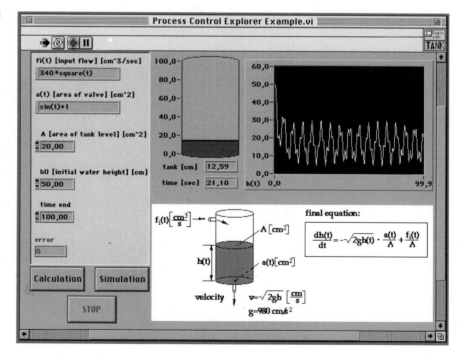

Figure 6.17
Diagram for a solu-
tion to the water
tank problem using
the LabVIEW
G Math Toolkit.

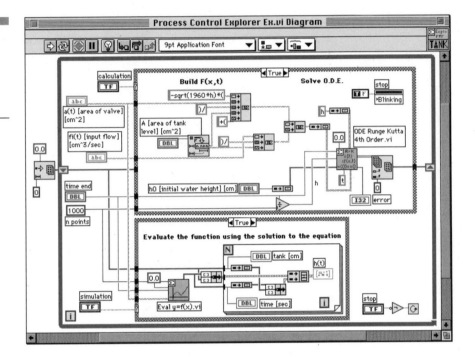

One-Way Codes

Ever since there have been messages, there has also been a need to protect
them against unauthorized access. Basically, the problem has not changed
in the last two to three thousand years. A sender attempts to supply a
receiver, mostly far removed, with a message via a so-called channel.
Throughout most of history, the channel could be formed, for instance,
by a runner or a rider. Obviously, secure transportation of the message
wasn't guaranteed because the entire procedure had weak points. A lot
depended on the human qualities of the bearer of the message. The information could be passed on by the bearer to a third party without the
sender or the addressee knowing anything about it.

Sensible short code keys use a mathematical property that everyone
learns in school: the difference between calculating a function and its
inversion. Hardly anyone will have a problem calculating the square of a
number, but what if you're looking for the square root? Even a pocket calculator needs a few extra milliseconds for the second task than for the first.

You can use some number theory tricks to increase the difference dra-
matically. Imagine a very large prime number p of, shall we say, 50 to 100
places. You distinguish prime numbers by the fact that they can be

divided only by 1 and by themselves. You also have a second natural number that is somewhere between 2 and $p-1$. Finally, $a^x \bmod (p)$ denotes the remainder the number a^x leaves when divided by p. For specific values of a, you can prove that where the x values are run through from 1 to $p-1$, the same thing happens with the variables $a^x \bmod (p)$. In other words, if y is some number between 1 and $p-1$, there is only one x that satisfies the equation

$$a^x \bmod (p) = y \qquad (6.11)$$

You end up with a function that assigns a y to each x and that is uniquely reversible. It's relatively easy to calculate the a values that serve as a basis.

The point is that it's possible to calculate a y for a prescribed x—if not easily, then at least with acceptable results. The inverse is a different story entirely; it turns out to be very complicated. The term *one-way function* is a result of this discrepancy between the two directions.

Some additional remarks are in order on realizing the one-way functions by computing. Because of the enormously large number of places used in the variables a, p, x, and y, there is no way to avoid good old-fashioned arithmetic. At best, you can use self-written special routines; some tools such as Mathematica from Wolfram Research even have arithmetic of arbitrary accuracy as a standard feature.

If you want to use LabVIEW, a problem arises. The integer formats stop in LabVIEW at U32 or I32; that is, the order of magnitude of 2^{32} sets the limit beyond which no numbers exist at all in principle. Although you could push the limit further with skillful use of real-valued number formats, you still couldn't advance into regions of 100, 200, or more places. The situation becomes even more dire if you envision real-valued numbers of any size and accuracy.

\math
Superlong Arith

A workable LabVIEW solution is based on strings rather than numeric data types. That is, every number is noted down as a chain of characters. You perform this conversion both at the start of the calculation and right before outputting the result. The **Superlong Arithmetic** library on the CD-ROM implements additions, subtractions, divisions with remainder, multiplications and relational operators, and specific special functions with integers of any length. Figure 6.18 shows a concrete example of a multiplication using the superlong arithmetic library.

It's easy to convert the previously mentioned functions or relational operators into LabVIEW notation. Essentially, you convert the chain of characters into arrays of numbers, then carry out additions just like you

Figure 6.18
An example of a mul-
tiplication operation
with integers of
(almost) any length.
The VI is based on
the treatment of
strings.

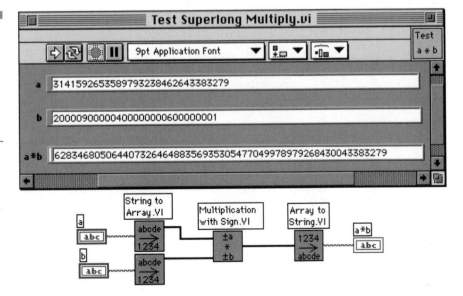

would with pencil and paper. You can also use a similar procedure to treat real-valued numbers with any number of places before and after the decimal. A further word on the fascinating cross contacts between mathematics and signal theory: You can multiply very large numbers very efficiently if you keep Fourier transformations in mind!

How can one-way functions be used as a coding instrument? Well, messages aren't transmitted in accordance with the previously mentioned scheme. Instead, you use them as access control. Anyone who wants access must find the solution to $a^x \bmod (p) = y$, which is something that can't be found purely by guessing or even by using super-quick computers for systematic testing. The generation of an arbitrary number of keys, in addition, won't give you any trouble.

Open cryptocodes are closely related in approach to one-way functions. These codes are quite suitable for coded message transmission. They are widely applied in practice (for example, banking). In contrast to the one-way functions described above, a very well-known family of the open cryptocodes proceeds not from one, but from two prime numbers of about 100 places. If these two prime numbers are multiplied, the prior history of the product is no longer visible in it. Even if you know that you're looking at the product of two prime numbers, it's impossible to make out the individual factors. That's precisely why open cryptocodes are so enormously powerful.

◼ ◼ The Next Steps

The new operational areas opened up by the G Math Toolkit are valuable additions to the LabVIEW package. In many practical applications, it's now possible to fuse measured value processes and demanding, user-defined evaluation. In addition, LabVIEW is being used more and more in simulation calculations and as a supporting tool in training in signal theory, mathematics, and general engineering. This will be taken into account in the future when a specially designed student version is introduced. Some other desirable improvements for future versions of the G Math package might be a complex parser (formula interpreter) and symbolic components.

◼ ◼ Bibliography

Walter Gander and Jiri Hrebicek, *Solving Problems in Scientific Computing using Maple and Matlab*, Springer-Verlag, New York, 1993, chap. 12.

William H. Press, Saul A. Teukolsky, William T. Vetterling, and Brian P. Flannery, *Numerical Recipes in C*, Cambridge, University Press, Cambridge, UK, 1993, chap. 15.5.

Readers are also encouraged to consult the references listed at the back of the *G Math Toolkit Reference Manual*, available from National Instruments.

LabVIEW as a Simulation Tool

Lothar Wenzel
LabVIEW Consultant

In addition to everyday tasks such as word processing and the calculation of tables or graphs, modern computers also offer a multitude of further possibilities. This is mainly due to their enormously high processing power and to their employment of the user interface, which translates alphanumeric elements to graphic ones. The power of present-day computers is particularly evident in science and technology applications. We've known the mathematical preconditions for many years. What has been lacking until recently is the computing power, but this has become less of a problem. The world of simulation is an area where great advancement has been made, and with the right tools, LabVIEW makes an outstanding simulation environment. The G Math Toolkit and the built-in analysis libraries in LabVIEW make simulation jobs relatively easy.

Simulation and Reality

The importance of simulation calculations is growing. You might choose simulation calculations over real experiments for many reasons:

- Price advantages when compared to real experiments
- Possibility of variant calculations
- Ability to simulate dangerous or virtually impossible experiments
- Exact repeatability
- Ability to test nonexistent apparatus and developments

The advantages are significant, but you can also run into all sorts of problems in the world of simulations. In most cases, the exact model equations are so complicated that you have to make an appropriate approximation. Your skill as a developer determines whether or not this simplification alters reality.

Simulation calculations require a different kind of software support than most other projects because the degree of abstraction is fairly high. Usually this requires demanding mathematics and signal processing routines whose internal details aren't visible to the developer.

The question is whether LabVIEW's G language can support simulation projects efficiently.

Is G a Suitable Simulation Language?

Many specially developed simulation languages exist that are widely used in science and technology. Ideally, such a language should have the following properties:

1. Suitability to the problem; that is, it should be easy to translate the tasks into the programming language.
2. Good data visualization possibilities.
3. Simple treatment of variant calculations and parameter domains.
4. Range of data structures that are significant for simulation calculations.
5. Well-constructed mathematics and signal theory.
6. Possibility of linkage to the real world.

If you take a closer look at these requirements, you might decide that although LabVIEW has some good points, it doesn't meet the criteria of a simulation language. You need to use supplementary toolkits to really succeed. This can be true for other software packages as well.

The most obvious weaknesses are in points 1, 2, and 5, but you can eliminate these shortcomings by using various toolkits in signal theory and G Math, or by using the Picture Control Toolkit for point 2. You can also eliminate point 1 from consideration, since LabVIEW's virtual instruments can simplify mapping of complicated problems when used with the toolkits.

The rest of this chapter shows various simulation calculations based on LabVIEW's G language. Our goal is to start working with the standard LabVIEW package with its Advanced Analysis library, and then to go on to additional toolkits.

Scientific Simulations

Simulations for dynamic systems are becoming increasingly important due to the cumulative economic, safety, and environmental demands being placed on companies as they strive to remain competitive in world markets. As a result, simulations for dynamic systems have undergone significant changes since the 1970s, when the availability of inexpensive digital technology began a radical change in instrumentation technology. Pressures associated with increased competition, rapidly changing economic conditions, more stringent environmental regulating, and the need for more flexible yet more complex processes have given engineers and scientists an expanded role in the design and operation of almost all industrial sectors.

Lattice Gas Theory

The **lattice gas computer** is a topical research subject that is very promising. Lattice gas methods are discrete techniques for efficiently solving partial differential equations. In years past, researchers found that in a series of pending calculations, a numerical solution was impossible because of the extremely complex structure. The computing architectures currently available don't seem to be capable in principle of breaking out of the dilemma. Massively parallel systems indicate a way out, but if used consistently this avenue would also require abandoning traditional hardware elements.

Lattice gas computers have roots in theoretical computer science. They have close connections with *Turing machines*, with the so-called *cellular automatons*, and, in particular, with *parallel processing*. LabVIEW can treat all these topics in an obvious way; we can say in general that G's nature is highly suitable for these projects.

CELLULAR AUTOMATONS   Cellular automatons originally cropped up as purely theoretical models in the literature for three important reasons. First, cellular automatons are an excellent approach to questions of self-reproduction. From a historical perspective (von Neumann and Burks 1966), that was the reason for introducing and investigating this theoretical class of computer architecture. Second, cellular automatons were used to "stake out" the very limits of computers. It turned out that, in terms of power, cellular automatons have the same quality as conventional computers, a power that corresponds to that of a Turing machine. This contributed greatly to the stability of theoretical computer science. Finally, future cellular automatons could prove to be particularly suitable for concrete calculations in conjunction with physical modeling.

The third point looks very promising, particularly in light of recent successes in miniaturizing computer components. Specifically, what you'll notice in this field are breakthroughs in *microtechnology, nanotechnology,* or *quantum dots.* The simple structure of a cellular automaton searches efficiently for the linkage with these modules.

Cellular automatons operate **discretely**; that is, they occur in only a few different states. Individual cells are assembled to form homogeneous structures. The simplest examples of cellular automatons (Fig. 7.1) are one- and two-dimensional lattices, but many other basic structures are also permissible. Each cell has a local neighborhood that consists of only a very few individual elements of the same shape. A cellular automaton operates in a clocked fashion, but the clock doesn't necessarily play a dominant role the way it does in a conventional computer. At the starting time, each cell is provided with a specific state. With each clock pulse, these states change in accordance with a fixed set of rules that you prescribe. All the cells of the automaton obey the same set of rules, and all the cells have a new state at the end of the clock pulse. The dynamics of this process over many clock pulses constitute the essence of a concrete cellular automaton.

Figure 7.1

The simplest cellular automatons. Many further types are conceivable.

One-dimensional cellular automaton with two neighbors

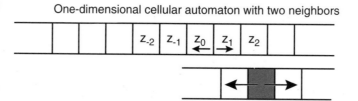

Two-dimensional cellular automaton with four neighbors

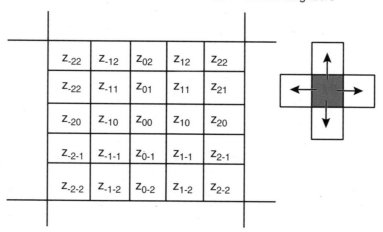

A very simple cellular automaton can act as follows. The basis is a square array where the cells in each case have two states (dead or alive). The neighborhood is defined as all eight directly adjoining cells. The aim in the next clock pulse is for a cell to live if an even number of neighbors are alive at the same time. You can use this scenario to simulate life processes or social relationships. What might surprise you is the astonishingly high suitability for calculating complex physical sequences. This modern direction is being pursued intensely and is taking shape under the name **lattice gas theory**.

Another thing that might surprise you is the handling of numerical material in digital computers, mostly involving bandwidths of 32, 64, or still more bits, in a quasi-continuous fashion. In addition, you don't treat the bit positions equally; instead, you favor the significant bits in calculations. Approaches based on lattice gas theory use bit numbers of the order of magnitude of 5 and are therefore digitally oriented. Note in this connection that results of physical simulation calculations usually don't require a higher accuracy than these few bits. In other words, cellular automatons perform what is necessary and sufficient. On the other hand, conventional digital computers are virtually forced to work with an overload and continually have to struggle with rounding problems.

BELOUSOV-ZHABOTINSKY MODELS   Even before the term *lattice gas model* was coined, reaction and diffusion systems were being treated by means of cellular automatons. The **Belousov-Zhabotinsky** reaction and diffusion system played a pivotal role in such investigations (Langton 1988). The mathematics behind this are difficult, since the most interesting models are nonlinear, and that makes a closed solution impossible.

In the following example, three different cell properties are given: motionless, active, and passive. According to a Greenberg and Hastings model (Langton 1988), you can describe a reaction and diffusion system on this basis using discrete time steps. If a_{ij}^t is the state (i.e., one of the properties of motionless, active, or passive) of the cell in column i and row j at the instant t, the relationship

$$a_{ij}^{t+1} = R(a_{ij}^t) + D(a_{i-1j}^t, a_{i+1j}^t, a_{ij-1}^t, a_{ij+1}^t) \qquad (7.1)$$

holds. The letter R stands for a reaction component, and D stands for the diffusion term. R relates to the same cell one clock pulse back, while D relates to properties of the four neighboring cells in the clock pulse before the instantaneous observing time. Although this formula isn't very complicated, you can nevertheless use it to carry out realistic simulations. The important thing to remember is that the functions R and D have to be suitably defined.

The functions R and D shown in Fig. 7.2 are a good basis. At the same time, the result of a concrete simulation procedure with the aid of a solution in G code is shown. Such results are very dependent on their initial occupancy at the instant $t = 0$. You can see the structure of the cellular automaton on closer inspection of the diagram.

HEAT CONDUCTION EQUATION WITH CELLULAR AUTOMATONS The link between physics and simulation calculations in the form

Figure 7.2
The Greenberg-Hastings model leaves plenty of room for experiments. A very simple approach is shown, but it can lead to complicated structures.

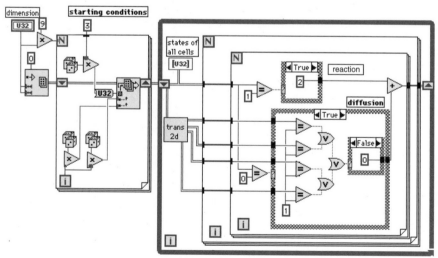

of lattice gas and **cellular automatons** is already over 70 years old, although the terminology is fairly new. In particular, this concerns a known physical problem, the **heat conduction equation**. While searching for a computing scheme to solve this problem, researchers encountered a structure that would be called a spreadsheet in modern terminology. Imagine that a flat plate is heated at the edges at a temperature-dependent location. After a certain amount of time, a stable temperature profile will form on the plate, and this is what you need to calculate.

If you look at the plate as a structure consisting of many individual square cells, you can interpret the temperature compensation process as continuous communication between neighboring cells. At the start, each cell bears a specific item of temperature information that is available in discrete form: for example, in stages of tenths of a degree. With each following clock pulse, each cell interrogates all its neighbors and generates a new temperature value of its own from these data. This value can be a rounded average of the neighboring temperatures. This heuristic looks eminently sensible, since you can view any compensation process as a continuous exchange of information with local surroundings. In fact, this transformation of a physical formulation of a problem into a cellular automaton can be completely successful.

The solutions of heat conduction equations and the differential equations related to them have mathematical properties behind their strategy that contribute to their success—specifically, certain properties of averages. For instance, a solution at a point in space is precisely the average of the solutions in an area surrounding the original point.

The programmer has another decision to make. Both the fourfold neighborhood (the directions of the compass) and the more extensive eightfold neighborhood (the four diagonally positioned neighbors are added) are sensible variants. The procedural mode is then based on a lattice network whose nodes are occupied by the temperatures specified at the beginning. In each computing step, the temperature at an internal node point of the lattice is replaced by the arithmetic average of the neighboring values. Given a sufficiently long computing time, the system arrives at a stable state; that is, the plate is in the heated-through state. The temperature in the interior of the plate is then a function only of the prescribed and temporally constant temperature stimulus at the edges. It's also possible to determine the precise temporal sequence of the heating process within the simulation framework, but this would require the availability of specific physical characteristics, for example the thermal conductivity of the plate material.

You can find the solution described in the Example Section of the Advanced Analysis Library manual and in the **Heat Equation Example VI** in the LabVIEW example library mathxmpl.llb.

Artificial Ants (Artificial Life)

Let's demonstrate some of LabVIEW programming's other characteristics with the following example. Our goal is to simulate a process that is interesting from a theoretical computer science point of view.

Imagine an ant on an infinitely large chessboard, with all the squares starting out being white. The ant is initially sitting on a specific square, but it continuously changes its location according to fixed rules, and colors certain squares black or white. The precise rules are shown in Fig. 7.3.

The set of rules for the movements of the ant is extremely simple, but the results are surprising. After the ant wanders around for a relatively long time without any apparent goal, very regular movements become apparent. In other words, order appears out of chaos. At present, we know very little of the background of this change, but numerous computer theorists believe that we are on to a new basic principle of nature.

Figure 7.3

The rules for the locomotion of the ant and for the coloring of the squares are very simple. Nevertheless, over time very irregular structures are produced at first, followed later by very homogeneous variations.

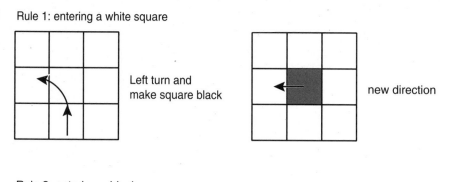

Rule 1: entering a white square

Left turn and make square black

new direction

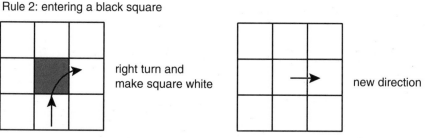

Rule 2: entering a black square

right turn and make square white

new direction

LabVIEW has no problem implementing such simulations. Figure 7.4 shows both the user interface and the programming of the ant simulation. Our own experiments support the proposition in each case that order is suddenly generated from apparent disorder. We can also demonstrate this effect if the original chessboard pattern is arbitrarily occupied by white and black squares.

Figure 7.4
The ant simulation in G.

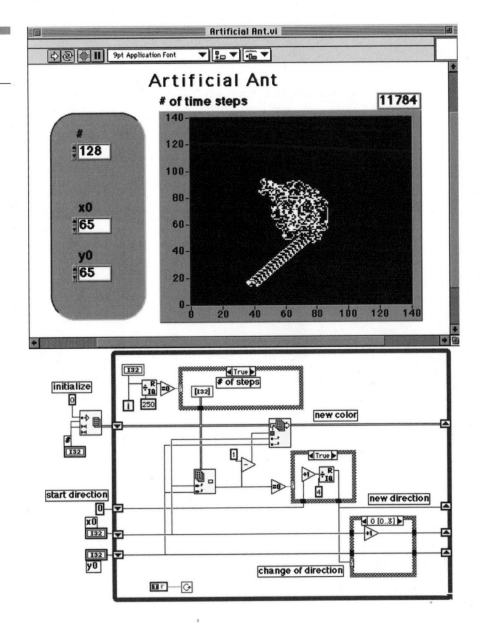

Instabilities

Any numerical method starts and ends in the primeval forest of numbers. In other words, conducting numerical methods means transforming input values into output values in accordance with fixed rules. If the transformation responds sensitively to changes in the inputs, the outputs can become relatively worthless. Remember that the numerical material at the start of the calculation often comes from measurements or from other calculations and thus is only approximate in nature. Sometimes you can save the numerical transactions by using other methods, but this doesn't always work.

This problem becomes very clear in an application that doesn't look very promising. The Advanced Analysis library of LabVIEW has a method for determining zeros of real and complex polynomials. But what about the two following examples?

$$p(x) = (x - 1)(x - 2)\cdots(x - 20) = x^{20} - 210x^{19} + \cdots$$

$$q(x) = p(x) - 2^{-23}x^{19}$$

(7.2)

The two polynomials differ only minimally, and yet the distribution of the zeros is completely different (the second polynomial has nonreal zeros at $16.73073 + 2.81262i$ and $16.73073 - 2.81262i$, while $p(x)$ has the zeros $1, 2, \ldots, 20$). Stated more generally, each demanding method has surprises hidden somewhere. The two examples should be tested directly with Lab-VIEW. But first, a virtual instrument has to be written that takes over the task of multiplying out in the expansion of $p(x)$. If you have the G Math Toolkit available, there is no problem, because, conveniently, you can calculate the binomial coefficients occurring in the expansion of $p(x)$ directly with the aid of the package.

Simulations in Practice

The examples set forth so far have had a theoretical background. The next simulation, by contrast, is more practical.

Simulation of Tomographic Photographs

During the last few decades, a lot has been done in the field of processing measured data. We can demonstrate an interesting tendency. Originally, individual measured values or series of measured values occupied center stage, but the desire for graphic representations of quantitative relationships soon arrived. There is, after all, a big difference between lengthy lists of numbers and pictures.

Of course, graphic representation assumes that you'll follow conventions on the interpretation of the data material. These conventions are sometimes arbitrary, but they're not all that important. The temperature field of a workpiece surface can be understood easily by the layperson when shown in the form of colored areas. The choice between black-and-white or colored images is of secondary importance. Finally, the assignment of numerical value and gray level (or color) is usually artificial.

The two-dimensional representation of measured data requires powerful computers as essential components. Fields such as image processing wouldn't have come into being at all without computers. Now, two-dimensional representations like the one previously mentioned seem to be everywhere. Every X-ray photograph falls into this category; thermal photography is another example.

Sometimes the origin of a picture is a mystery. You can traverse the surface of a test specimen using an ultrasonic scanner. At well-defined points on this surface, you send an ultrasonic pulse perpendicularly into the specimen. Then you use the response pulse characteristics as a measure of the flaws in the test specimen. In the end you get a measured value for each point on the surface, and with the appropriate interpretation this is just a black-and-white picture. The expert can then judge the quality of the object in a single glance.

Our world is three-dimensional. For this reason, you might want to look into the *interior* of objects. However, the brutal approach using a hammer and other tools to look inside is very seldom appropriate (think of medicine in this regard!). The third dimension is becoming more and more important, which brings us to the concept of **tomography**. The phrases you encounter most often are *computer tomography, nuclear magnetic resonance tomography, X-ray tomography,* and *ultrasonic tomography.* Although the operating principles cover a wide range, they have a lot in common.

As an example, imagine a solid cuboid made of metal and having some irregularities in the interior. A single X-ray photograph can supply only a projection of the three-dimensional reality onto a surface. However, there is another fascinating possibility. It really is possible to look into the interior of the cuboid if you use a little trick.

You need to mount both the cuboid and the X-ray film on rotatable plates (Fig. 7.5). The plates have to rotate simultaneously and uniformly. In addition, the rotating plate that holds the X-ray film must be slightly inclined with respect to the plate that has the cuboid. After a complete revolution of the two plates, you can see an image on the film that corresponds directly to a section through the cuboid in the plane of the plates. You get a complete reconstruction of the solid cuboid by combining the individual sections if the cuboid moves upward and downward. What causes this?

Given a specific setting of the two plates, a projection forms instantaneously on the film that is proportional to the size of the flawed region in the cuboid. The rotation sums up these projections in such a way that the interior is precisely reconstructed.

The film located on the slightly inclined plate is just an elegant method of obtaining a linear scan. You're mainly interested in the projection of a wafer-thin slice of the original material when X-raying. In the age of computers and digital image processing, a CCD line-scan camera can directly replace the second plate without changing the essence of tomography.

Let's consider a test specimen that contains in its interior three inhomogeneities in the form of spherical flaws. Since we're only interested in sections of the test specimen, the flaws take on the form of circles of different radii. In our example, the circles don't overlap, although this will

Figure 7.5
Arrangement of test pieces and X-ray equipment for a tomography photograph. Currently, imaging systems (image sensors and CCD cameras) are used more than an X-ray film.

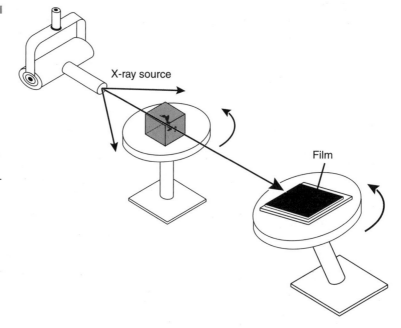

X-ray source

Film

often be the case in real applications. Take a look at the **Simulation of Tomography VI** from the LabVIEW analysis examples, which displays various graphic windows during operation (Fig. 7.6). The section through the specimen at the upper left shows the three circular inhomogeneities.

In the Simulation of Tomography VI the X-ray equipment revolves around the test specimen. By contrast, the source of radiation was stationary in our initial concept. However, the two approaches are identical because only the relative movements are important in tomographic photographs. The revolving source can simply be better represented in the simulation. In many medical applications of tomography it's actually the stationary item (the patient) that's the subject of investigation.

When the Simulation of Tomography program is running, you can see a small revolving symbol in the *real situation* graph that represents the X-ray source. The picture you see under this shows the shot currently being taken. At this instant, the X-ray source has a certain position at the edge of the test specimen (in the current plane of section). The radiation source causes a reaction on the uniformly co-rotating film, which is shown in the *situation at time t* graph. The *analog reconstruction* graph adds up these individual shots. Normalization of the colors in the Intensity Graph occurs at the same time.

In a successful reconstruction, the *analog reconstruction* graph must largely correspond to the *real situation* graph. You can improve the quality of the reconstruction by taking as many individual shots as possible during one revolution of the two plates (or of the X-ray source in this example). Shots are taken continuously in tomographic photography with the two plates described above. In contrast, the simulation requires the acquisition (or generation) of discrete images. Nevertheless, the results are the same.

Simulations with the Aid of the G Math Toolkit

The simulation examples we've looked at so far mostly manage without using the G Math Toolkit. In other words, LabVIEW's G is already powerful enough to conduct very demanding simulation calculations. Of course, the situation only improves if additional tools are used. In this sense, the G Math Toolkit is a valuable supplement to the existing range of functions. The same also applies to further toolkits.

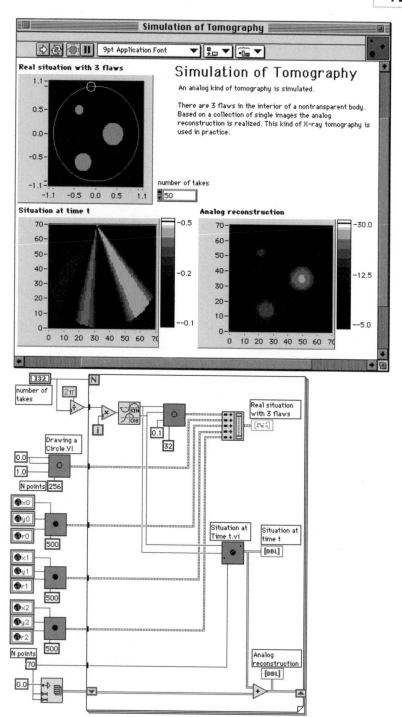

Figure 7.6
The simulation of X-ray tomography is illustrated both at the user end and from a programming point of view. The true structure of the flaws is reconstructed very well.

In particular, the G Math Toolkit offers three features that strongly favor simulation projects. First, there is the **parser**, which permits the free input of formulas given the presentation of specific model equations. Second, there are tools that permit the solution of differential equations—a lot of simulation problems are based on differential equations. Finally, the possibility of visualizing the results proves to be valuable when combined with a free configuration of the user interface. The following examples demonstrate all three components.

Wave Equation

One of the most important partial differential equations in practice is the **wave equation**, which describes sound propagation processes in homogeneous media as well as the propagation of electromagnetic waves in homogeneous dielectric materials. In addition, you can use the wave equation to model physical quantities such as gas density, gas pressure, velocity potential, and the field strength components of electric or magnetic fields. In the simplest case of the one-dimensional homogeneous wave equation, there is a clear formula with a closed solution.

You might wonder what would be a suitable calculating tool for studying such solutions. You want to allow the use of spatially distributed sources for the resultant field in the calculation. In acoustic applications, these can be sound sources installed at different positions. In such cases, the analytical solution you specify in principle can no longer be visualized directly.

A solution based on the G Math Toolkit is illustrated in Fig. 7.7. You can freely enter the number of external sources, their spatial arrangement, their direct-time characteristic, and the derivation's direct-time characteristic. You accomplish this with the aid of formulas. You can investigate the temporal and spatial behavior of the resultant field precisely by viewing the solution of the wave equation as shown in Fig. 7.8. One possible application is the design of an artificial source with special properties that is a superposition of spatially distributed and simply structured sources. Thus, sinusoidal sources can simulate every artificial source of interest, given a suitable arrangement.

Laplace Equation and Soap Films

The tendency to steer toward an optimum is one of the most basic principles of nature. A light beam always runs in stratified glass plates such

Figure 7.7
More demanding simulation calculations can also be performed with the G Math Toolkit. This example shows the structure of external sources.

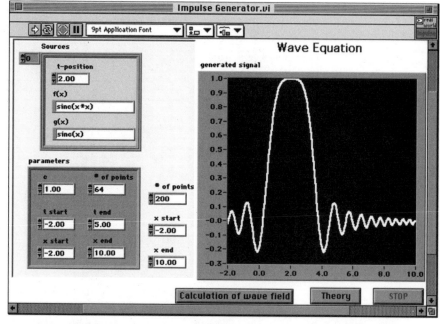

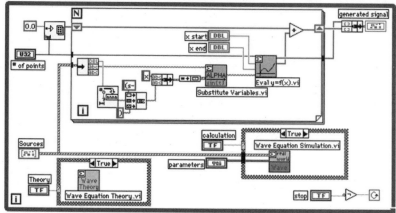

that the propagation time is as short as possible. A ball located in the middle of an inclined surface will roll downhill. Something similar applies when you perform the venerable soap bubble experiment. You take a small, closed, and at the same time spatially curved wire frame and dip it briefly into a soap solution. A thin soap film forms inside the wire. It's a surface that has a tension value that can't be lowered.

The solution to the soap film problem is very easy if your starting point is a circular wire frame that is bent only in the direction of depth;

Figure 7.8
Solution to the wave
equation with
sources defined in
Fig. 7.7.

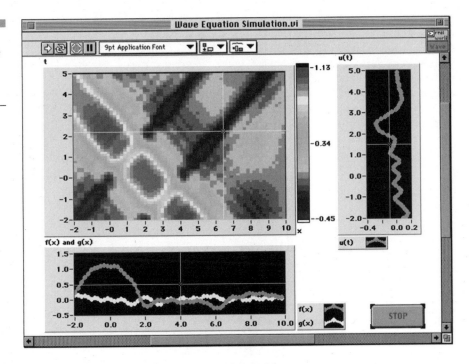

that is, that still appears as a circle in top view. In this case, you can specify the solution in a closed fashion and you can implement it with the aid of Fig. 7.9. You can enter the level of the bulge in the VI by using a formula that is evaluated by the parser. This information is sufficient for calculating the soap film in the interior of the wire frame.

The **Laplace PDE on a Circle VI**, from the G Math examples, displays the variation of the soap film as a color map. You can also obtain an output of contour lines or even three-dimensional representations by using the G Math Toolkit.

From a physical point of view, this problem is equivalent to calculating the thermal characteristic of a thin circular disc to which a defined quantity of heat is applied to the boundary. Therefore, it's also possible for you to interpret the results as a temperature characteristic, if you're interested in the heated-plate problem.

The Control and Simulation Toolkit

A new add-on for LabVIEW, the **Control and Simulation Toolkit**, was released by National Instruments just as this book went to press. The

Figure 7.9

The Laplace PDE on a Circle VI is an example in the G Math Toolkit and can handle both the soap film problem and the heat distribution of flat plates. The behavior at the boundary is fixed with the aid of a formula.

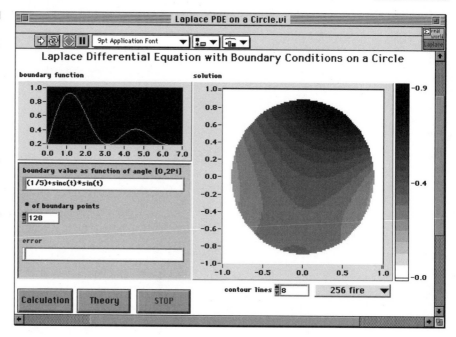

package includes features for high-level simulation, modeling, and control, using blocks and symbols familiar to control engineers. It offers capabilities similar to Matlab's Simulink, but with higher performance and the ease of integration with real I/O hardware that we take for granted in LabVIEW.

You can directly enter transfer functions in Laplacian notation, such as $H(s)$, or use z transform notation for discrete systems. That makes it a snap to enter existing system equations. You can also build up models using discrete or continuous time function blocks, such as integrators and differentiators, all within an ordinary LabVIEW diagram. Higher-level blocks, such as signal sources, PID controllers, and filters, simplify many tasks.

One trick the developers included in the package is a way to model feedback. As you probably know, it's illegal to wire a *cycle* in LabVIEW, where an output of a VI is wired directly to an input. System topologies with feedback are commonly drawn with exactly this kind structure, so it initially appears that LabVIEW fails to implement this notion. But there's an easy solution: Shift registers or local variables can transfer VI outputs to inputs on subsequent iterations of a loop structure. The resulting diagrams (particularly with the local variable solution) are highly intuitive and efficient. As a bonus, such diagrams can easily be modified to work with real I/O, such as a DAQ board.

Example VIs cover a wide range of topics, such as an inverted pendulum, cascaded water tanks, chemical reactors, thermostatic or PID-based heating, RLC network simulation, Bode plot generation, and satellite attitude control. Overall, it's a very flexible package and shows how far you can go with the G language.

Bibliography

C. G. Langton, *Artificial Life*, Addison-Wesley, Reading, MA, 1997.

John von Neumann and Arthur W. Burks, *Theory of Self-Reproducing Automata*, University of Illinois Press, Urbana, IL, 1966.

8

Digital Signal Processing

Lothar Wenzel
LabVIEW Consultant

One of the numerous, extremely well laid out pages of LabVIEW relates to signal processing. The LabVIEW Full Development System includes a wide variety of signal theory routines in the Analysis library. In addition, as an open programming environment, LabVIEW is very capable of simulating relatively complex situations. This chapter includes examples that address some of these difficult problems. Most of the themes mentioned here are currently very important and seem to indicate new directions of development within signal theory, which is certainly not a small field.

The LabVIEW DSP Library

The acquisition of measured data is closely connected with digital signal processing. Many of National Instruments' hardware components have integrated signal processing circuits; for example, low-pass filters for filtering out higher-frequency interference signals. In addition, LabVIEW's Full Development System offers numerous signal theory routines within the Advanced Analysis library (AAL).

The assignment of specific parts of the AAL to mathematics or to signal theory isn't exactly easy. The transitions are simply too fluid, and, in a sense, signal theory without the use of mathematical aids is inconceivable. However, in some circumstances you can use the breakdown in Table 8.1 as an aid to orientation.

Each of these libraries consists of numerous VIs. For improved efficiency, the LabVIEW developers used Code Interface Nodes (CINs) almost exclusively at the lowermost level of the analysis library. The LabVIEW concept is strong enough, however, to implement all the previously named libraries entirely in G.

National Instruments also offers numerous toolkits devoted to special problems in signal theory. Specifically, these are:

- Signal Processing Suite
- Third-Octave Analysis Toolkit
- Digital Filter Design Toolkit
- Joint Time-Frequency Analysis (JTFA) Toolkit
- Wavelet and Filter Bank Design Toolkit

The availability of toolkits enables you to extend the basic LabVIEW package in a targeted fashion for use with special problems. You can also use the toolkits as stand-alone programs without LabVIEW. But the VIs

TABLE 8.1

Organization of the
Advanced Analysis
Library

Mathematical Libraries of the AAL	Signal Theory Libraries of the AAL
Curve fitting	Signal generation
Probability and statistics	Digital signal processing
Linear algebra	Measurement
Array operations	Filters
Additional numerical methods	Windows

that National Instruments offers might be more valuable, because you have more degrees of freedom in implementing your own projects.

The LabVIEW Full Development System performs the basic load of work in signal theory right out of the box. You can tackle many advanced problems by using one of the toolkits mentioned, so the need for new routines in signal processing is actually rare. This statement is true in principle, but there are grounds that justify higher ambitions in this field. In particular, look at experimental investigations both in practice and in training. Again, the advantage of G's clear notation is obvious. Usually, signal theory applications profit to a much greater extent from the data flow concept than other applications do.

More Demanding DSP Tasks

A few solutions to difficult digital signal processing tasks based on G are presented in the following sections. Information about the algorithmic background of each problem is discussed as well.

Fractional Fourier Transform

There is probably not a more important operator in signal theory and mathematics than the **Fourier transform**. In signal theory, the Fourier transform is the link between the time domain signal and a physically interpretable frequency spectrum. The Fourier transform is encountered many times in mathematics: It is present starting with Fourier series (the pendant to the Taylor series for periodic functions), via the theory of distributions, and as theoretical computer science (computer models, compression algorithms, and so forth), to name just a few applications.

From a historical perspective, the Fourier transform has even blocked our view of further-reaching generalizations because it's been so dominant. Although we've been aware of two-dimensional and multi-dimensional Fourier transforms for quite a while, as well as the **Walsh-Hadamard transforms** based on the **Haar functions** (Rao 1985), it is, nonetheless, only recently that we've grasped the full scope of signal theory transformations. **Wavelet transforms** (Fig. 8.1) are clearly a tool suitable for rendering this overview possible. However simple the definition of wavelets may appear today, many decades passed by before it was discovered. The unconventional abandonment of dimension in the transformation operation is probably responsible for this (Fig. 8.2).

In practical applications, you're forced to set a time-discrete and digitized world against the continuous, analog real world. Because these two standpoints produce results that are virtually identical, two preconditions are necessary. On one hand, you have to provide a firm foundation (e.g., the sampling theorem) for the effects of discretization and digitization, which were initially poorly understood; on the other hand, the computer has to be available and sufficiently powerful. Both preconditions were fulfilled by the middle of the 1960s.

Figure 8.1

Unlike the Fourier spectra (*bottom*), wavelets do not transform time signals (*top*) into one-dimensional signals. Rather, wavelets (*center*) produce a mixture of temporal and spectral components.

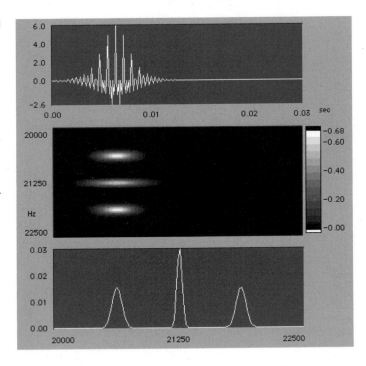

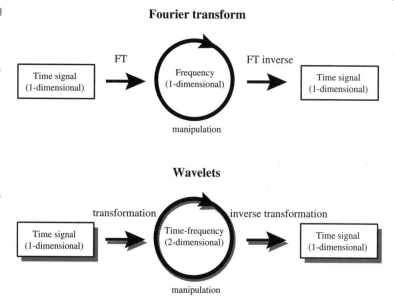

Figure 8.2
Wavelets transform time signals into domains that can't be interpreted immediately in physical terms. Nevertheless, wavelets appear to be more important for signal theory than the classical approaches.

At the same time, a flood of publications arrived on quick and efficient conversions of discrete variants of the Fourier transform. The first high point was a famous article by Cooley and Tukey in 1965 on the **Fast Fourier transform (FFT)**, which is among the most quoted works of signal theory. Cooley and Tukey used the **butterfly** strategy, which is basically a slick modification of the "divide and conquer" principle. Inherent in the butterfly strategy is that the signal lengths must be powers of 2. In the final analysis, this requirement proved to be drastic and unpopular, but the FFT approach's efficiency in terms of computing and storage is considerable compared to earlier discrete Fourier transform approaches.

Immediately everyone wanted to extend the very effective idea of the FFT to arbitrary signal lengths. Two different approaches to a solution arose at the start of the 1970s. One came from Rader and is based on properties of prime numbers, while the other, developed by Bluestein, later found a larger breadth of application. However, Rader's strategy was initially more successful.

Prime Numbers and Fourier Transforms

Rader starts with a signal length that is a prime number p. This is the sharpest conceivable contrast to the number of a power of 2, which is highly composite. The key to success proves to be a circular convolution of signals with a length of $p - 1$. This trick displaces a Fourier transformation of a signal of length p onto a convolution of two signals of length $p - 1$ that can be covered essentially by three individual Fourier transforms. The latter number can generally be effectively decomposed into individual factors, permitting the use of a procedure in accordance with the Cooley-Tukey algorithm.

However, practical use assumes background knowledge of number theory—complications arise in implementing this idea in a program. A theme is taken up recursively, because decomposing the number $p - 1$ into factors can, in turn, lead to relatively large prime numbers.

Rader's idea is a constituent of the G Math Toolkit as a VI called the **Prime FFT VI**. Figure 8.3 shows the essential points of the Prime FFT VI in diagram form. Figure 8.3(*a*) implements the previously mentioned circular convolution, which can be ascribed in the final analysis to three individual Fourier transforms. You can see these three FFTs clearly as icons. Figure 8.3(*b*) is a special routine that is used by the Prime FFT VI. This is a question in number theory whose answer is an essential component of the virtual instrument Prime FFT. It's a question of whether a given number is a prime number at all; if it is, you must determine a generator of the multiplicative group of the p residual class. Here, g is a generator if the powers g^i with $i = 0, 1, ..., p - 2$ yield precisely all the numbers from 1 to $p - 1$.

Figure 8.3

(a) The implementation of a cyclic convolution with the aid of three Fourier transforms. This structure is an essential component in converting the prime FFT. (b) Block diagram for determining a generator of the cyclic multiplicative group modulo p and is thus an example of the G coding of a problem in number theory.

A.

B.

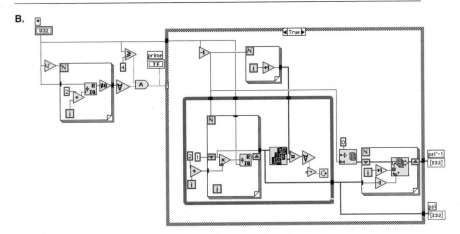

This LabVIEW solution is also an example of converting a problem in number theory to G. LabVIEW's powerful debugging tools become useful in applications like this.

Chirp-z Algorithm

The most successful access to the problems of Fast Fourier transformation for general signal lengths is presently designated the **chirp-z algorithm** and is directly associated with the fractional Fourier transform. The term *chirp* indicates a quadratic dependence in the time domain (the twittering of birds is an example). In fact, the apparent detour used in the chirp-z method is the key to a very transparent method of implementing the Fourier transformation.

The original definition of the Fourier transform FT

$$FT(x)(j) = \sum_{k=0}^{n-1} \exp\left[-2\pi i j k \cdot \alpha\right] x_k \tag{8.1}$$

is written down with the aid of the relationship

$$2jk = j^2 + k^2 - (k - j)^2 \tag{8.2}$$

in the form

$$FT(x)(j) = \exp\left[-\pi i j^2 \alpha\right] \sum_{k=0}^{n-1} y_k z_{j-k} \tag{8.3}$$

in which use is also made of

$$y_k = x_k \exp\left[-\pi i k^2 \alpha\right] \quad \text{and} \quad z_k = \exp\left[\pi i k^2 \alpha\right] \tag{8.4}$$

Here, x is the original discrete signal and j and k, respectively, run from 0 to $n-1$ for a signal length n. The factor α can be arbitrary; hence the name *fractional*. In the conventional Fourier transformation, it is precisely $\alpha = 1/n$. Equation 8.3 recalls a conventional circular convolution. This is also the case if the y component and z component, respectively, are supplemented as appropriate up to the first power of 2 beyond n. In the next step, you implement the circular convolution in the usual way by means of the FFT of signals having a length that is a power of 2. At the very end, you must further reduce the result to the appropriate length of n.

This method is very easy to convert to a program, and you can use it many ways. In particular, you can master the discrete formulation of the

Laplace transform by means of a generalized approach. (The variable α can even be an arbitrary complex number.)

The **Fractional FFT VI** of the G Math Toolkit provides the conversion of the FFFT in G code. Figure 8.4 shows the diagram of this VI, which shows that the use of the chirp-z algorithm is relatively easy.

Sparse Signals

When Fourier transforms are used in practice, you often see that only a relatively short initial piece of a lengthy signal is filled with values other than 0. A typical situation is that all the frequency components of an already-transformed signal are blanked out outside a certain band, after which the inverse transformation has to be carried out (band-pass or signal compression). Of course, you'd want to treat these limited signals with a highly efficient method developed for that purpose. This happens easily with the aid of the fractional Fourier transform.

Let a signal of length n be prescribed for this purpose, with only a segment of the length m of this signal filled starting on the point of j_0. In this case, according to Eq. 8.1,

$$\text{FT}(x)(j_0 + j) = \sum_{k=0}^{m-1} \exp\left[-2\pi ik(j_0 + j) \cdot \frac{1}{n}\right] x_k \tag{8.5}$$

You can interpret the right side of this identity as a fractional Fourier transform with $\alpha = 1/n$ and a signal of length m, and you can calculate it very quickly according to the procedure described earlier. Direct rivals are

Figure 8.4
The programming of the fractional Fourier transform isn't a big problem in LabVIEW. You can see at *bottom right* a cyclic convolution with the aid of three ordinary Fourier transforms. The rest of the VI produces appropriate input values for this convolution.

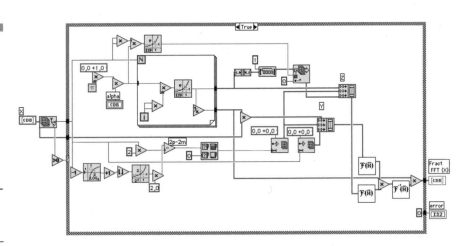

a complete FFT with subsequent reduction, or a direct use of Eq. 8.1 without the use of the FFT (the so-called **discrete Fourier transform** [DFT]). The latter is sensible only if m is small compared to n.

On closer examination, you can see that the fractional FFT approach is suitable whenever n becomes large while m remains relatively small. Remember that in practical applications Fourier transforms of signals having some 10,000 interpolation points are certainly useful. For instance, an audio signal of CD quality with a sampling rate of 44.1 kHz and a duration of 10 seconds consists of 441,000 individual values. Two-dimensional images can even exceed this magnitude. Clearly, the computational problem can be immense.

Subspectra

One task that closely relates to the problem of sparse signals is trying to determine only a narrowly demarcated spectral range of a Fourier transform. The classic FFT method doesn't work for this because it operates globally. In other words, the entire output signal and all the intermediate values determined must constantly be further processed. The solution algorithm must be designed to save time. In this case, recasting the FFT by using many tricks proves to be a good way of mastering this problem.

Let the signal x itself be of length n, and assume that you want the first m values of the Fourier transform of the signal x. You can assume for the purpose of simplification that n is a multiple of m $(n = d \cdot m)$. It then holds that

$$\mathrm{FT}(x)(j) = \sum_{k=0}^{d-1} \exp\left[-2\pi i j k \cdot \frac{1}{n}\right] \sum_{l=0}^{m-1} \exp\left[-2\pi i l j \cdot \frac{1}{m}\right] x_{k+l \cdot d} \qquad \textbf{(8.6)}$$

If you look closely, Eq. 8.6 proves to be a multiple calculation of FFTs of length m, followed by multiplications and summations.

Both the treatment of the subspectra and the FFT of sparse signals are integral constituents of the G Math Toolkit, and you can adopt them directly into your own applications. Figure 8.5 shows a block diagram that demonstrates the fact that implementation of special FFT routines is easy in G.

Both problems leave plenty of room for you to set further tasks. For example, your interest might center on several separate but short segments in the spectrum, or you can structure the output signal according to this scheme. The method presented can help in these cases and others like them.

Figure 8.5
The Fourier transform of sparse signals can be reduced to the fractional Fourier transform of a specially conditioned signal. You can see the icon for the fractional Fourier transform in the loop structure at *right*.

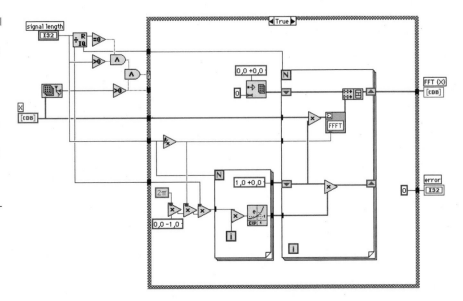

Period Determination in Signals

When you're investigating periodic signals, you usually assume that the sampling operation executes in harmony with a fundamental frequency inherent to the signal. Strictly speaking, however, it rarely happens. This becomes clear when you use a function generator to generate a simple sinusoidal oscillation and offer it to a spectrum analyzer. What you'll see in this case (Fig. 8.6) looks only a little like the sharp peak that you actually expect in a fundamental frequency of the sinusoidal oscillation. This phenomenon is known as **spectral leakage**.

Spectral leakage is a problem in many situations, possibly the simplest being the determination of the true fundamental frequency of a sinusoidal oscillation using a discrete Fourier transform. Further problems arise directly if you add harmonics and noise.

It's possible to read off a rough estimate of the true fundamental frequency from the fuzzy spectrum in accordance with Fig. 8.6, with a deviation that is no more than one of the signal units (*frequency bins*) employed. You can determine the fundamental frequency exactly with the aid of these enclosing brackets [$f, f + 1$]:

$$f + \frac{n}{\pi} \arctan \left\{ \frac{\sin \dfrac{\pi}{m}}{\cos \dfrac{\pi}{m} + W} \right\} \qquad (8.7)$$

Figure 8.6
Fourier spectra of sinusoidal oscillations don't always exhibit a sharp peak. Fuzziness in the spectrum—*spectral leakage*—occurs if the sampling rate is not tuned to the fundamental frequency.

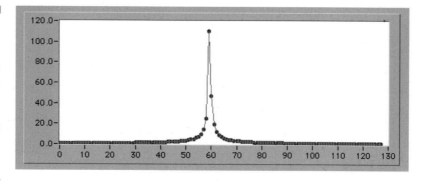

in which

$$W = \frac{|FT(x)(f)|}{|FT(x)(f+1)|}$$

This formula is exact for pure sinusoidal oscillations; it's sufficiently close to the correct value even given the occurrence of harmonics or of relatively weak interference. A related solution, for **total harmonic distortion** (THD) analysis, appears in the LabVIEW analysis examples.

Another way to solve the same problem is by using the fractional FFT. In the first step, you determine the enclosing brackets [$f, f + 1$] in turn by using an FFT. Then you perform further refinements artificially in the interval [$f, f + 1$] by determining spectral values for f, $f + \Delta$, $f + 2\Delta$, ... by means of fractional FFT if you have a permanently selected Δ. In this case, an α is selected according to Eq. 8.1 as Δ/n, and $\Delta = \sqrt{m}$ is frequently the suitable value. Of course, then you use the original signal x as the point of departure. The peak that corresponds most closely to the value you're looking for is sought in this artificially refined spectrum.

You can also make a comparison with the **Buneman Frequency Estimator VI** of the G Math Toolkit. Essentially, this VI is a LabVIEW implementation of Eq. 8.7.

Walsh-Hadamard Transform

The family of Fourier transformations is based on complex exponential functions, or on collections of functions that are appropriately tuned to each other. You might want to introduce other basic systems that are even simpler than those of the Fourier transform and at the same time preserve important properties of the Fourier transform. First and foremost among these is the **convolution** law (transformation of the convolution is equivalent to the product of the transformations). The **Walsh-Hadamard transform** (Gumas 1997) turns out to be the best in this regard and is implemented by stairstep functions.

The Walsh-Hadamard transform, a constituent of the G Math Toolkit, has an advantage and a disadvantage. On the positive side, it's fast and easy to calculate—only additions and subtractions are required. On the negative side, the transformation doesn't allow a direct physical interpretation. Nevertheless, you can define spectra and related terms that you can use very sensibly. For instance, the Walsh-Hadamard transform can detect global as well as local properties of signals. A major application of this transform is in cellular telephone communications, where it provides a means for multiplexing many signals within a given bandwidth. Other applications include edge detection and character recognition. In the case of one-dimensional signals, you can use this transform to watch the (artificial, not physical) spectral behavior of the signal. If a change is detected, you can then calculate the more time-consuming Fourier transform.

Joint Time-Frequency Analysis (JTFA)

Investigations of signals or systems are commonly carried out in the time domain or, alternatively, in the frequency domain. Although the two forms contain essentially the same information, they do change the viewer's perspective in such a way that each approach has its own independent justification. Mixed methods that consider the aspects of time and frequency simultaneously have recently been more successful—hence the name **joint time-frequency analysis** (JTFA) (Quian and Chen 1996). Completely new insights have been discovered in many practical applications that couldn't have been obtained either through a pure time analysis or through a pure frequency analysis.

The pure time domain signal often isn't very informative. For instance, speech does not lend itself well to computer-based time domain analysis or generation. Another example is noisy images or audio sequences whose quality you want to improve. Again, it's very difficult to undertake such measures directly on the time domain signal.

Transformations that change the prescribed time signal into another signal may be more suitable for these difficult contexts. The Fourier transform, which converts temporal information into frequency information, is by far the most important representative of this class. The great advantage of Fourier transformation, apart from the mathematical simplicity and elegance, is the physical relevance. Frequency components have a unique relationship with energy components. Clearly, things like spoken words or noisy signals are reflected directly in frequency spectra.

You shouldn't underestimate the importance of the Fourier transform either from a theoretical or a practical point of view. However, it isn't a cure-all. One of the most important limitations of Fourier transformation that you must consider is that it is *stationary*. This means that spectral properties of the signal can't depend on the time of viewing. If you're considering a chirp signal, and the spectrum is calculated, the output signal is obviously not stationary. Figure 8.7 suggests that low frequencies dominate at the start, but higher ones dominate later. This is a snapshot of the **Transform Explorer Example VI** found in the G Math Toolkit.

To better analyze these complex signals, you'll need a suitable combination of temporal and frequency components. A lot has happened recently due to the rapid advances in computer engineering, resulting in completely new types of ideas for applications. In particular, two main directions have taken shape for dealing with these problems: the **linear** and **quadratic** approaches. Quadratic approaches are also called **bilinear transforms**. These methods encompass the field of joint time-frequency analysis.

Figure 8.7
A snapshot during operation of the Transform Explorer Example VI, part of the G Math Toolkit. A formula is used at *top left* to generate the signal. Represented in the *right* part of the figure are the time signal, the power spectrum, and the Short Time Fourier Transform. The example calculates the Short Time Fourier Transform of a chirp signal.

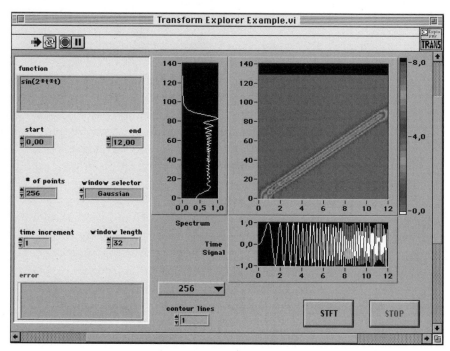

Short Time Fourier transforms and **wavelets** are the most important representatives of linear transformation. The bilinear transformation class is wider, with one of the most important representatives being the **Wigner-Ville distribution**. Let's look at the mode of operation of these transformations with the aid of G programs.

Short Time Fourier Transform (STFT)

Among the linear transformations, the Short Time Fourier transform (STFT) is the simplest representative. Conventional Fourier transformation characterizes signals with the aid of sinusoidal or complex-valued exponential functions. You wouldn't expect any differentiation on the temporal plane. The STFT, by contrast, proceeds from basic functions that are concentrated in time *and* frequency. Gaussian functions are an important representative; they are even optimum with regard to simultaneous concentration of time and frequency.

The STFT of a given signal $s(t)$ is determined in accordance with the formula

$$\text{STFT}(t,\omega) = \int s(\tau)\gamma^*(\tau - t)e^{-i\omega\tau}\,d\tau \tag{8.8}$$

Here, you still have to determine the window function γ, and the quality of your choice determines the quality of the resulting STFT. This window function is usually gaussian in nature.

In contrast with conventional Fourier transform, which transforms a time signal into a frequency signal, in the STFT a time signal is converted into a function of both time and frequency. This gives you many advantages in direct evaluation, but it also complicates the treatment of this transformation. Therefore, the inversion of an STFT is much more demanding than the inversion of an ordinary Fourier transform. In the second case, you know that the inversion coincides with the Fourier transform itself.

The concrete calculation of Eq. 8.8 is relatively simple. For a fixed t, the right side is nothing more than the definition of a Fourier transform, and the function you are transforming is concentrated in time because of the window property of γ. Consequently, you can look at the mode of operation of an STFT as if a window were moving in time over the signal and executing local Fourier transforms.

In most applications, you use the square of the STFT, which has an absolute (positive) value. The term **STFT spectrogram** was coined for this purpose. The **STFT Spectrogram VI** is an implementation of the STFT and is included in the G Math Toolkit. You can see the associated diagram of the core routine in Fig. 8.8.

Wavelet Transform

The second important representative of linear transformations is formed by **wavelets**. In contrast with the Fourier transform, which operates with sinusoidal functions of staggered frequencies (or with complex-valued exponential functions), wavelets use base functions that are both scaled and time-shifted. The nonscaled and nonshifted basic function is called the *mother wavelet*. One of the best-known mother wavelets is the **Daubechies4 function**, which we generated in Fig. 8.9 with the aid of a VI in the G Math Toolkit.

Interestingly enough, the basic idea is rather old, but the extremely rapid development of wavelets began only in the last ten years. In its continuous version, you can write the wavelet transformation in the general form

$$\mathrm{CWT}(a,b) = \frac{1}{\sqrt{|a|}} \int s(t)\Psi^*\left(\frac{t-b}{a}\right) dt \qquad a \neq 0 \tag{8.9}$$

where Ψ is the mother wavelet. The term $(t - b)/a$ represents the scaling and shifting of the mother wavelet. A significant difference from the STFT is that the wavelet transform assigns additional requirements for Ψ,

Figure 8.8
The core routine for calculating the Short Time Fourier Transform is relatively easy in G. The outer loop controls the temporal component of the two-dimensional STFT; the spectral component is calculated in the interior.

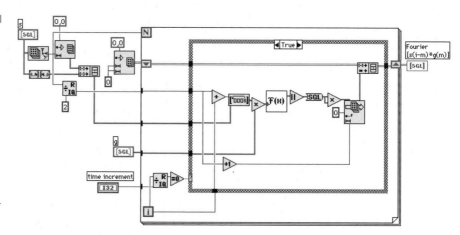

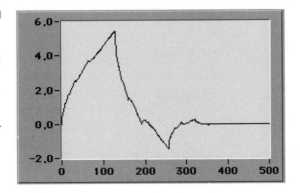

Figure 8.9
The most famous mother wavelet is the Daubechies4 function, which in detail exhibits very bizarre structures.

while the definition of STFT manages without additional conditions. The requirement placed on Ψ takes the form

$$C_\psi = \frac{1}{2\pi} \int \frac{|\psi(\omega)|^2}{|\omega|} \, d\omega < \infty \qquad (8.10)$$

where $\psi(\omega)$ is the Fourier transform of Ψ. If this condition is fulfilled, the inverse transformation is achieved:

$$s(t) = \frac{1}{C_\psi} \iint \frac{1}{a^2} \, \mathrm{CWT}(a,b)\psi\left(\frac{t-b}{a}\right) da \, db \qquad (8.11)$$

Note that given real-valued signals and real-valued mother wavelets Ψ, the wavelet transform itself is real-valued. This is an advantage by comparison with STFT, which usually leads to complex-valued results.

Wigner-Ville Distributions

Despite its relatively simple definition, the **Wigner-Ville distribution** is a very powerful tool in signal analyses. The original applications were in the field of quantum physics; presently, signal processing is a more popular field of use. The definition of the Wigner-Ville distribution (WVD) might remind you of the autocorrelation of a given signal $s(t)$:

$$\mathrm{WVD}(t,\omega) = \int s\left(t + \frac{\tau}{2}\right)s^*\left(t - \frac{\tau}{2}\right) \exp\left(-i\omega\tau\right) d\tau \qquad (8.12)$$

The Wigner-Ville distribution supplies a real-valued transformation result and is a constituent of the G Math Toolkit and the JTFA Toolkit.

Treatment of Nonequidistantly Sampled Data

Another problem you might encounter with the Fourier transform is that it requires that the sampling intervals be equal for all data points. This is not always the case for real-world data. The classic example is daily stock market rates, which aren't available on holidays or weekends. This situation also arises in technology and science.

Interpolation strategies constitute a current remedy. Measured values that don't really exist are produced artificially at equidistant points through interpolation. Often there isn't a good starting point for executing this interpolation—you have no background information on the physical model or equation representing these measured values. It's possible in such cases to work with splines. This can certainly function well in individual cases. Unfortunately, in most cases the results generated by these interpolated measured values after a Fourier transform will have very little to do with the actual process.

A promising approach that largely avoids these disadvantages is offered by the **Lomb periodogram**. This algorithm can handle the raw data directly—the sampling structure plays only a subordinate role. For the Lomb periodogram, you calculate the spectrum as follows.

Let the data x_k be given at the instants t_k, that is, $X = (x_0, x_1, ..., x_{n-1})$ with sampling times $\{t_0, t_1, ..., t_{n-1}\}$. Furthermore, the mean and standard deviation of the data are defined by the familiar expressions:

$$\bar{x} = \frac{1}{n} \sum_{k=0}^{n-1} x_k \quad \text{and} \quad \sigma^2 = \frac{1}{n-1} \sum_{k=0}^{n-1} (x_k - \bar{x})^2$$

The Lomb normalized periodogram is then defined as follows:

$$P(\omega) = \frac{1}{2\sigma^2} \left\{ \frac{\left[\sum_{k=0}^{n-1} (x_k - \bar{x}) \cos \omega(t_k - \tau) \right]^2}{\sum_{k=0}^{n-1} \cos^2 \omega(t_k - \tau)} \right.$$

$$\left. + \frac{\left[\sum_{k=0}^{n-1} (x_k - \bar{x}) \sin \omega(t_k - \tau) \right]^2}{\sum_{k=0}^{n-1} \sin^2 \omega(t_k - \tau)} \right\} \quad \textbf{(8.13a)}$$

with

$$\tau = \frac{1}{2\omega} \arctan \left(\frac{\sum_{k=0}^{n-1} \sin 2\omega t_k}{\sum_{k=0}^{n-1} \cos 2\omega t_k} \right) \tag{8.13b}$$

This formula is not very simple in structure, but implementation in G doesn't pose a problem (Fig. 8.10). For comparison, the Fourier spectrum and the Lomb periodogram are displayed on the front panel for a time signal that is sampled nonequidistantly and is constructed as the superposition of four different sinusoidal functions. You'll notice immediately that the Fourier spectrum can't reveal the structure of the signal—the spectrum seems to be constructed more in accordance with the stochastic principle. By contrast, the Lomb periodogram clearly detects the four sinusoidal functions. This demonstration is available as the **Generalized Fourier Spectrum VI** from the G Math Toolkit examples.

The ability to freely manipulate and visualize input signals turns out to be very helpful in programming and testing the Lomb Periodogram VI. This option alone significantly shortens the development time, and it

Figure 8.10
Power spectra of nonequidistantly sampled data can be estimated very precisely with the aid of the Lomb periodogram. This example VI produces such signals and calculates both the classic power spectrum and that according to Lomb. The data of the power spectrum are of no value in this case. The Lomb spectrum detects very accurately that the signal is a mixture of four different sinusoidal oscillations.

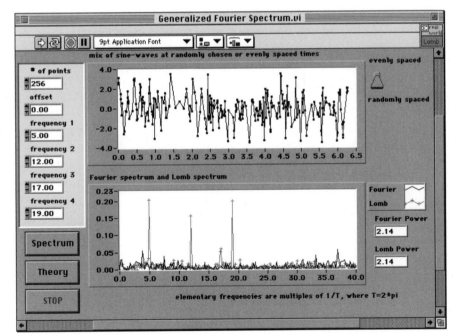

provides deeper insight into the mode of operation of a new algorithm. The key is training, which can't be mentioned enough.

A General Function Generator

Let's look again at the description of the parser of the G Math Toolkit. You can use the ability to input formulas from the front panel directly in constructing a general function generator. However, the word *direct* isn't quite accurate, because ideally a function generator is intended to generate quite different patterns one after another in time. In the world of test and measurement, such an instrument is called an **arbitrary function generator**, or *arb* for short.

Let's look at a concrete example. Let a test pattern be generated that is to have the following characteristic:

$$f_1(x) = 2 \sin (\pi x) \quad 0 \leq x < 1$$

$$f_2(x) = 0.5 \quad 1 \leq x < 2$$

$$f_3(x) = \text{sqrt}(x) \quad 2 \leq x \leq 4$$

in which the signal is to start 4 s after a trigger. In addition, you have to prescribe a sampling rate. That is, it must be clear how many individual values you want to calculate every 4 s. In the example, this number is 1000, which means that 250, 250, and 500 values go, respectively, to the individual constituents f_1, f_2, and f_3.

In addition to the representation of such artificially produced signals and a possible use in the case of calculations, transformations, or simulations, we'll be interested in outputting the test pattern via the D/A converter on a plug-in board. The parser produces real-valued numbers between 0 and 2 in the example. You shouldn't have any problem scaling that to an appropriate voltage for the D/A converter.

The fly in the ointment is that although in its original form the parser can deal with the individual components f_1, f_2, and f_3, it isn't capable of combining these three functions. You can, however, remove this obstacle with a bit of programming. Let's learn more about handling the parser and its various modes of operation.

Let the previously given notation be the basis of a general signal definition; in this case, the designations f_1, f_2, and f_3 can even be eliminated.

All you have to do is make some minor adaptations to match the parser conventions. Finally, in this example the input to the parser looks like this:

$$2 * \sin (pi(1) * x)$$

$$0.5$$

$$\text{sqrt}(x)$$

\math\
G Math Function Generator.vi

You always use x as the time variable. Given these preconditions, the general signal generator is implemented on the basis of the parser of the G Math Toolkit, as shown in Fig. 8.11. Values of x are calculated, beginning with the value for *Start* and continuing through each interval ending

Figure 8.11
The block diagram shows an implementation of an arbitrary function generator. Analysis of the array of user-defined functions is handled by the Eval $y = f(x)$ VI from the G Math Toolkit.

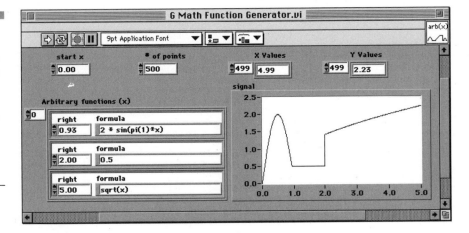

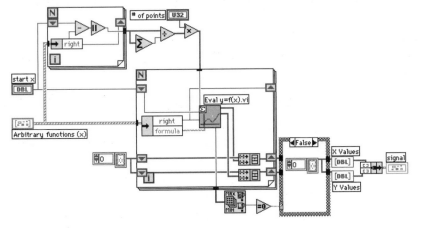

with the value defined by *right*. You can see from the diagram that the mathematical work is incorporated into the parser VI, **Eval** $y = f(x)$.

DSP and Education

In contrast with other software products designed with mathematics and signal theory in mind, the education sector currently has a minimal role for LabVIEW. This should change very quickly for two reasons. The first is that the programming language G is easily learned, particularly if you're already familiar with the data flow concept. The other reason is the ease of experimentation, which is generously supported by LabVIEW's user and programmer interface. Two examples support these arguments.

The Gibbs Phenomenon

Let's select a problem that has long been a subject of controversy: the Fourier series of signals that are periodic in the interval [0,2π].

At the end of the last century, Michelson and Gibbs (Oppenheim and Willsky 1983) recognized that, for many functions, the Fourier series converges in a specific sense toward the original function. Although this convergence exists when viewed in integral terms (more precisely, in the quadratic integral norm), it's often not uniform for all points of the range of definition. In other words, while the Fourier series is a good representation of the signal when viewed from a distance, there may be significant errors visible when you take a closer look. This effect is easiest to see with discontinuous functions. The **step function** is a simple representative of this class that assumes the values 0 and 1 only.

You can visualize this effect, currently known as the **Gibbs phenomenon**, directly with the G Math Toolkit example, the **FFT Symbolic VI** (Fig. 8.12). Here you can freely select both the functions to be investigated and the number of parameters for the interpolation values, as well as the order of the approximation (number of the series members). You can see the systematically occurring overshoots in the vicinity of discontinuities in the given function. Increasing the order of approximation doesn't provide a remedy; all that happens is that the range of greatest deviation becomes narrower with increasing order.

You'll note that, in general, LabVIEW's possibilities in education and simulation have been largely underestimated. The advantages of Lab-

Figure 8.12
The Gibbs phenom-
enon describes
unavoidable over-
shoots in the case of
Fourier series expan-
sions in the vicinity of
discontinuities of
given functions. If the
order of the approxi-
mation is increased,
the overshooting
range does become
narrower, but the
maximum absolute
value of the deviation
remains largely
unchanged.

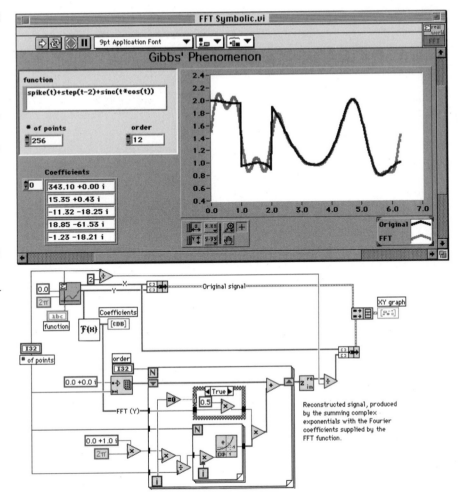

VIEW compared to products such as Matlab or Mathematica are found, in particular, in the fields of visualization and direct linkage to the real world in the form of measured values or data outputs. In addition, many algorithms in signal theory or applied mathematics can be represented very efficiently and clearly in a graphics-oriented data flow language such as G. Another advantage of LabVIEW is the ease with which you can modify a program, which is something that shouldn't be underestimated in education or in simulation calculations. In the demonstration of the Gibbs phenomenon it's not a problem to represent additional information on the absolute or square difference between a given function and an approximation. In more complex tasks, this experiment-friendliness receives much stronger support.

Construction of Optimum FIR Filters

The design of optimum filters is one of the most important and most demanding tasks in theoretical signal theory and its application. The aim of the **finite impulse response** (FIR) filter design is to simulate a prescribed frequency response $G(\omega)$ by the relatively simple model

$$G(\omega) = \sum_{n=0}^{M} a[n] \cos(n\omega) \tag{8.14}$$

The problem is to determine the coefficients $a[n]$. FIR filters operate without feedback and are therefore based only on the data to be filtered. The more complex **infinite impulse response** (IIR) approach, by contrast, uses data that have already been computed, that is, filtered.

Figure 8.13
Comparison between the results of the FIR design using the Parks-McClellan algorithm and with the aid of the routines, contained in the G Math Toolkit, for linear optimization.

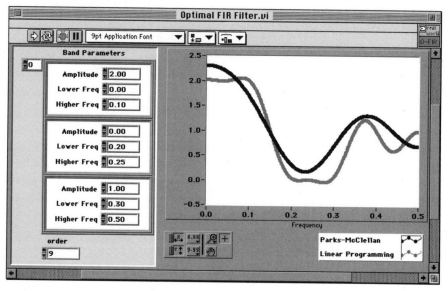

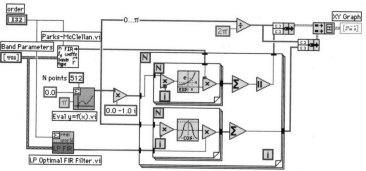

The frequency response you want to achieve is usually prescribed as a sequence of prescribed amplitude response characteristics of disjoint frequency intervals. In other words, you have to configure the filter such that the functionality of a superposition of weighted bandpass filters is realized. For this purpose, the Full Development System of LabVIEW offers the **Parks-McClellan algorithm**, which is based on skillful exchange operations (Remez Exchange). However, different sorts of optimization strategies are offered from the point of view of design.

Since the G Math Toolkit contains tools for optimization, you can formulate this filter design problem like a well-known problem in linear optimization. In this case, you formulate the absolute deviation between the desired frequency response and that obtained in the form of linear inequalities (Parks and McClellan 1972) and attempt at the same time to minimize this deviation.

Figure 8.13 demonstrates the solution of an FIR design with reference to a concrete problem. Specifically, the frequency response you want to achieve is compared with the optimum response within the framework of the specification. Remember that when a finite number of coefficients are available, it's only possible to approximate the theoretically prescribed frequency response.

Bibliography

Charles C. Gumas, "A Century Old, the Fast Hadamard Transform Proves Useful in Digital Communications," *Personal Engineering and Instrumentation News,* November 1997.

Alan V. Oppenheim and Alan S. Willsky, *Signals and Systems,* Prentice-Hall, New York, 1983, chap. 4.

T. W. Parks and J. H. McClellan, "A Program for the Design of Linear Phase Finite Impulse Response Filters," *IEEE Trans. Audio Electroacoustics,* vol. AU-20, no. 3, pp. 195–199, August 1972.

Shie Quian and Dapang Chen, *Joint Time-Frequency Analysis,* Prentice-Hall, New York, 1996.

K. Ramamohan Rao, "Discrete Transforms and Their Applications," in *Benchmark Papers in Electrical Engineering and Computer Science,* van Nostrand, New York, 1985.

ActiveX and Application Control

Brad Hedstrom

Advanced Measurements, Inc.

LabVIEW 4 and 5 for Windows includes support for **ActiveX**, a Windows mechanism that allows applications to manipulate each other using a specific type of messaging. In keeping with the pace of change in the software industry, ActiveX was formerly called **OLE Automation**, which in turn was formerly called **Object Linking and Embedding**. In this chapter, we will use the term ActiveX, but don't be surprised if you see the other terms used synonymously. To get started, read National Instruments Application Note 081, *Using OLE Automation in LabVIEW.*[1] It provides a good overall introduction to ActiveX.

LabVIEW 5 adds a feature called the **VI Server**. This allows LabVIEW to expose many of its capabilities (through *methods* and *properties*) to other applications. These other applications could be other LabVIEW applications running on the local machine or on a remote machine, or they could be developed in other environments (VisualBasic, Visual C++, Excel, etc.). The VI Server is platform independent, using TCP/IP, in contrast to ActiveX, which is currently restricted to 32-bit Windows 95 and NT. While this chapter concentrates on ActiveX, the VI Server is not exclusive to ActiveX and thus the final section applies to LabVIEW running on all platforms. The programming model used for the VI Server is very similar to that of ActiveX, and thus you may gain some insight into using the VI Server even if you're not using ActiveX.

We will first look at an example of an ActiveX Automation client that is supported by LabVIEW 4 and 5. We will then look at a simple example using the VI Server with a LabVIEW client.

LabVIEW as an ActiveX Client

LabVIEW 4.0 and later provides VIs that allow LabVIEW to communicate with ActiveX servers via their exposed objects. This allows LabVIEW to "take control" of the automation server application and cause it to perform particular tasks. LabVIEW 5.0 provides enhanced functionality, and adds server capability as well, so all examples in this chapter will be based on LabVIEW 5 functions. This section will show specifically how LabVIEW can act as an ActiveX client where Microsoft Access is the Automation server.

In this example we will use LabVIEW to acquire, present, store, and print data. LabVIEW will be the only application with which the user

---

[1]Available from the http://www.natinst.com or the Instrupedia CD-ROM.

interacts. The collected data is to be stored in a Microsoft Access database, and a nicely formatted report is to be printed at the end of each task. We would like the operator to be able to press a *print* button on the front panel, preview the report, and then send it to the printer if satisfied. The operator should not have to switch applications to perform these tasks. (Remember, from their perspective, operators should only see one application.) How can this be accomplished? With ActiveX.

The best way to describe the use of ActiveX is with a real-world example. Let's say that the application is an ATE system that performs a suite of tests. After the tests have been run, the operator needs to be able to review and optionally print individual test results. After the operator has reviewed the data, a summary report is automatically printed. Let's review the requirements to see if they will help us determine a methodology.

- LabVIEW will be the main application. The user will only start one program to perform the task, and that program will be built using LabVIEW.

- The application will collect data from some sources (DAQ, GPIB, whatever), present it to the user, and store it in an Access database.

- At the end of the test the user will review the collected data by examining reports on-screen.

- The user will be able to print any of the displayed reports on demand.

- A summary report will be printed automatically when the user has finished the test.

One of the advantages of using a database application is its reporting capabilities. Access is very good at generating high-quality, complex reports (something that LabVIEW on its own is not). So we should use Access for all of the report generation (both on-screen and printed). How is this accomplished? Let's tackle the requirements one at a time.

I love examples. To keep this discussion as practical as possible, it will be based on the development of a relatively simple ATE system that incorporates the five requirements listed previously. We'll keep it simple so we don't get bogged down in the details of the project requirements.

Our ATE system will be used for production testing of a piece of telecommunications equipment. Data is collected via serial, GPIB, and plug-in DAQ. There are three tests that are run on each unit under test (UUT): phase noise over the frequency band, gain at the center frequency, and minimum rejection in the stop band. The first test will gather several samples where each sample is a frequency and phase noise measurement.

The second test will supply single samples (center frequency and gain), as will the third (frequency and rejection). All results will be stored in the database for statistical process control (SPC) use. For acceptance testing, all tests will be compared against specifications and each test will pass or fail.

If a unit passes, it is delivered to the shipping department, and the next unit is tested. If a unit fails, a report or reports will be printed for each failed test, and the unit will be delivered to the repair station. At the end of a product run or a production shift, a summary report of all tested units will be printed.

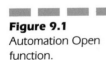

\ActiveX
Access ATE.mdb

Included on the CD-ROM is a sample Microsoft Access database for this ATE system already containing test data (**Access ATE.mdb**). There is also a LabVIEW application that simulates the test scenario. The application has been written so that LabVIEW does not actually store any data in the database. Therefore, the **SQL Toolkit** (available from National Instruments) is not required to run the example.

LabVIEW Controls Microsoft Access

Since we want LabVIEW to be the main application, we need a way for LabVIEW to control Microsoft Access. Luckily for us, Access 8 (included with Microsoft Office 97) can act as an ActiveX server. By turning our LabVIEW application into an ActiveX client, we can effectively control Access and make it do exactly what we want from LabVIEW. The operator will never (knowingly) interact with Access.

In order for Access to act as an ActiveX server it must be running in the background. Thus LabVIEW needs to be able to launch Access. This is a good place to start.

All ActiveX tasks in LabVIEW start with a call to the **Automation Open** function (Fig. 9.1), which does two things. First, it starts the server application if it's not already running. Second, it returns an *automation refnum* that will be used by subsequent OLE VIs. But where does the automation refnum input come from? Everything in OLE is an **object**. Objects can have properties, respond to events, and perform methods. The object name is used to refer to any particular object. Object names are built hierarchically: library.class. Each server application will have its own

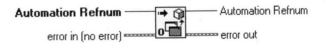

Figure 9.1
Automation Open
function.

group of objects. So the Automation Open function needs to know to which automation server we wish to connect. This is accomplished by popping up on the **Automation Refnum** terminal or control and selecting an *ActiveX Class* as shown in Fig. 9.2. Any previously opened classes will be displayed (as Access is here); new ones are added by selecting Browse, which prompts the user to find a new type of library (Fig. 9.3). If the object is not listed in the objects list, additional types of libraries can be opened by selecting Browse from the Select Object dialog.

The easiest way to find out what objects are available is to use an **object browser**. There is one in Access itself called, of all things, Object Browser (see Fig. 9.4). The object browser lists all of the objects for a class and may also be linked to on-line help that provides usage information for the objects.

Figure 9.2
Setting the Automation Refnum input terminal on the Automation Open function.

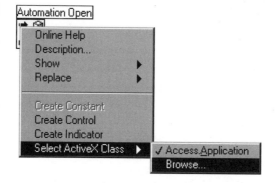

Figure 9.3
Selection of an object from a type library.

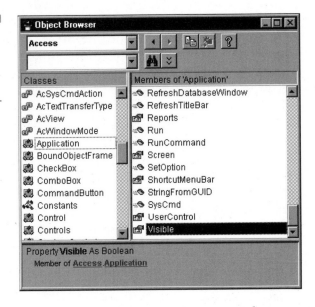

Figure 9.4
Microsoft's Object
Browser, available
from Microsoft
Access.

For our requirements we don't want the operator to even know that Access is running; hence when we launch Access via Automation Open we don't want it to be visible. This can be controlled by setting an Access **property** called access.application.visible, which you select from the Object Browser. The Object Browser can also provide the help screen shown in Fig. 9.5. Properties can be read (get) and written (set) by the **Property Node** function, which is quite similar to the VISA Attribute

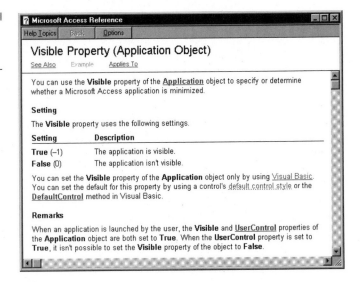

Figure 9.5
An OLE Help
(Reference) page.

function. The Property Node requires the automation refnum (from Automation Open), the property name, and the property value. The automation refnum provides the access.application part of the object name, so we just need to add the visible property. This is easily selected by popping up on the Property Node and selecting the desired property as shown in Fig. 9.6.

One gotcha. If Access was started by another agent (other program or user), LabVIEW will not have permission to set access.application.visible and the Property Node will return an error. I put a second Boolean into the final version of the VI, called the **Open Access VI**, which will conditionally set the visibility property. The Access Handler VI (described later) has additional error handling in case LabVIEW is denied access to the visibility Boolean.

The Open Access VI starts Microsoft Access, hides it, and returns an automation refnum we can use in other parts of our application. When the user has finished with the application, then LabVIEW needs to exit Access as well. This is accomplished with the **Close Automation Refnum** function shown in Fig. 9.7. If the call to OLE Create Automation Refnum caused Access to be launched, then you can call the **OLE Release Refnum function** (with the same automation refnum) to force Access to exit. If Access was already running when OLE Create Automation Refnum was called, then calling OLE Release Refnum will not affect Access at all.

LabVIEW Collects; Access Stores

LabVIEW is an excellent integration tool because it can communicate with nearly any type of hardware that can be connected to a computer. However, it cannot do everything. Access (for example) is an excellent data

\ActiveX\
OLEAccess\Open
Access.vi

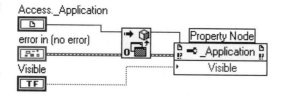

Figure 9.6
Setting the
access.application
.visible property.

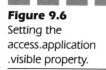

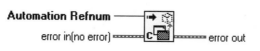

Figure 9.7
Close Automation
Refnum function.

storage, data retrieval, and reporting tool. A complete ATE system can be constructed using LabVIEW for the data collection and user interface and Access for data storage and reporting. We have seen how LabVIEW can launch and display Access, which is the first step in building the ATE system. Next we need some mechanism to store the data collected by Lab-VIEW into Access. There are three methods.

One is to use the **SQL Toolkit for LabVIEW** from National Instruments. The toolkit allows LabVIEW to communicate with any database that supports Microsoft's Open Database Connectivity (ODBC) application programmer's interface (API) via Structured Query Language (SQL) commands. This is the method I prefer, because SQL is very well documented and the same application can be used with many different databases.

In the programming model of SQL, the SQL Toolkit is similar to that of the ActiveX library. In the case of SQL, a connection is made to a database, one or more transactions are completed, and the connection is closed. Figure 9.8 shows an ATE example. First a connection to the database called Widget Tests is established, then the test results (serial number, phase noise, and Q factor) are inserted, and finally the connection is closed. This is a very simplified example; the schema for a real ATE database would be much more complex. It does show how relatively easy it is to store data collected by LabVIEW into a commercial database. Look in **ATE OLE Examples** on the CD-ROM to see how the data was stored into the database file. This LLB requires the SQL Toolkit.

The second method is to use ActiveX. Part of the Microsoft Access ActiveX model is the **Data Access Object** (DAO). Data can be exchanged with Access by generating a DAO automation refnum and executing the appropriate methods. This is a fairly involved process and beyond the introductory nature of this section. Also, using DAO will result in database-specific VIs (different databases will have different objects), whereas the

**\ActiveX\
ATE OLE
Examples**

Figure 9.8
Diagram from
the Simple SQL
Example VI.

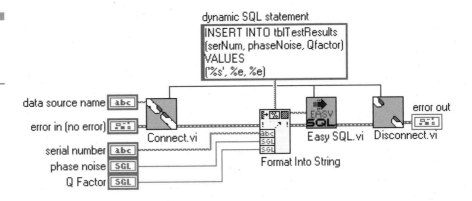

SQL solution will work with any ODBC-compliant database. There is also more overhead with OLE as compared to SQL, so ActiveX-based transaction times will likely be longer. Therefore I'll stick with SQL.

The third method is to use **Dynamic Data Exchange** (DDE). However, DDE is being replaced by ActiveX, so I don't recommend building new applications based on it.

Viewing and Printing Reports

After the test data has been collected with LabVIEW and stored via SQL, the operator needs to be able to review the data and optionally print reports. Since Access will be our reporting engine, it would be nice to be able to use Access to create the on-screen reports as well. This can be accomplished if we let the user transparently "bounce" back and forth between LabVIEW and Access. We can do just that via ActiveX.

We have already seen how to launch, control the visibility of, and exit Access using ActiveX. There are a few more steps required to allow the user to view the Access reports on-screen (assume that LabVIEW has already launched Access and has generated a valid automation refnum).

First we need to tell Access which database (file) has the data to be reported. The object browser reveals a **method** called OpenCurrent-Database (see Fig. 9.9). Properties are similar to variables (they can be written to and read from), whereas methods are more like subroutines in that they perform an action. The OpenCurrentDatabase method can be called by using the **Invoke Node** LabVIEW function (see Fig. 9.10). Again

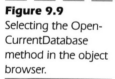

Figure 9.9
Selecting the Open-CurrentDatabase method in the object browser.

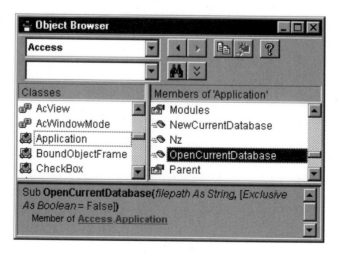

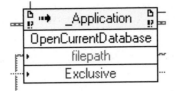

the method is selected by popping up on the node and selecting the desired object. The on-line help can also be accessed from the pop-up menu as shown in Fig. 9.11.

Once the appropriate database has been opened, the desired report can be called and either displayed on-screen or sent to the printer. This can be accomplished by invoking another Access method: DoCmd.OpenReport (see Fig. 9.12). This method requires a report name where the report must reside in the currently open database. It also allows setting the destination (view) of the report (on-screen or sent to the default printer) and permits specifying a *named filter* or a *where* condition. The latter two items select which records will be displayed when the report opens and provide the real power behind this method.

Figure 9.11
OpenCurrentData-
base help page as
displayed in Microsoft
Access.

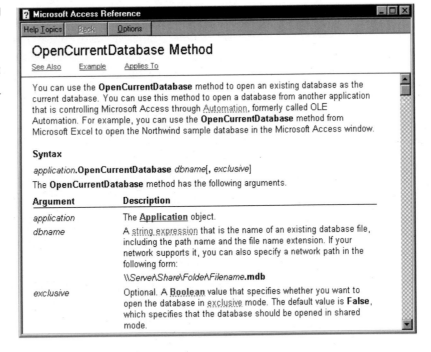

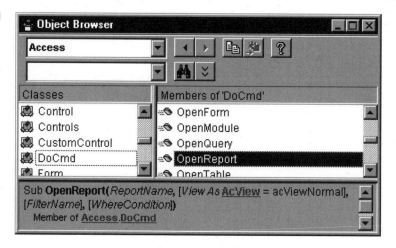

In this case, the OpenReport method is not a member of the Application class but rather of the DoCmd class. This class exposes various methods in the DoCmd class, which allows Access actions to be performed just as they would if they had been selected from a menu. The general format executing the DoCmd method is [application.]DoCmd.method [arg1, arg2, …]. The application refnum being passed in is for the class Access.Application. However, we need to execute the method Access.DoCmd.OpenReport. Therefore a new ActiveX refnum is required, but where does it come from? There is a property called Access.Application.DoCmd that returns a refnum to Access.DoCmd. First a refnum for Access.DoCmd is acquired using the Property Node. Then the Invoke Node can be called using the DoCmd refnum and selecting the OpenReport method. The diagram shown in Fig. 9.13 belongs to the **Access Open Report VI**. Confusing? Yes, but it does work.

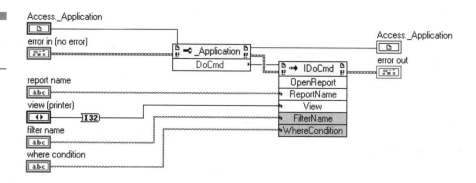

Putting It All Together:
The Access OLE Handler VI

\ActiveX
OLEAccess\Access
OLE Handler.vi

For our ATE application (and many others), only a fraction of the ActiveX objects that Access exposes are necessary. Since I'm lazy I'll only implement the ones that I need. To make controlling Access as easy as possible, I've hidden most of the nasty ActiveX details in an easy-to-use VI called the **Access OLE Handler**, shown in Fig. 9.14. This handy little VI provides all of the functionality that our application requires of Access. The handler VI encapsulates the following operations, selected by the *Operation* enum control:

Open Access—starts Access if it's not already running and creates an application refnum. This operation must be performed once before the VI can perform the other operations. The *Set Visibility* control can be used only if Access is being started by LabVIEW. If *Set Visibility* is true, then the *Visible* Boolean is used to determine if Access will be visible.

Open Database—closes any open database and opens the database specified in *Database Path*.

Open Report—opens the *Report Parameters.Name* in the currently open database and sends the database to the device specified by *View*. A *Named Filter* and/or *Where Condition* can also be specified when the report is run.

Set Status—returns information on any currently open objects and whether Access is visible.

Close Object—closes the *Current Object*.

Close Access—causes Access to quit depending on the value of *Close Options*. Closes the currently open database and frees the application refnum.

Open the **Access OLE Handler Example VI** to see how the handler is used. Finally, open the **View and Print Reports (SQL) VI** if you have the SQL Toolkit or open **ATE OLE Examples\View and Print Reports** if you do not. This top-level VI shows how the user can seamlessly open

\ActiveX
OLEAccess\Access
OLE Handler
Example.vi

Figure 9.14
Connector pane for
the Access OLE
Handler VI. This one
does it all.

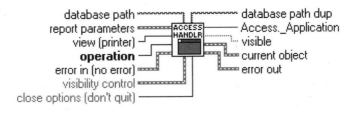

and view Access reports based on data that was collected with LabVIEW and achieves all of the requirements listed at the beginning of this section.

The VI Server

A new feature of LabVIEW 5 is the ability to invoke methods or set properties of other VIs running locally or remotely. This can be accomplished via ActiveX or TCP/IP. The VI Server exposes a set of objects accessible by clients using either ActiveX or TCP/IP (see Fig. 9.15). In general, if the client application is *not* a LabVIEW application, then the ActiveX mechanism should be used. If the client application is a LabVIEW application, then there is no advantage to using ActiveX and the Application Control functions should be used (Fig. 9.16). For examples where LabVIEW is an ActiveX server and other applications access the VI Server via ActiveX, see the examples in the examples\comm directory that ships with LabVIEW.

Next, I'm going to show an example of how LabVIEW can use the Application Control functions to automate a rather tedious operation: generating documentation for a VI hierarchy.

Figure 9.15
VI Server access methods. You manipulate VIs via ActiveX (usually from applications besides LabVIEW) or via TCP/IP.

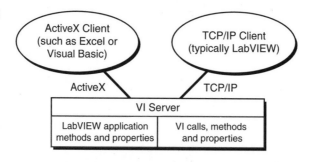

Figure 9.16
The Application Control function pallet.

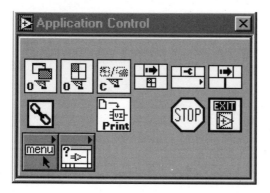

To perform an Application Control operation, you begin by calling the **Open VI Reference** function, which establishes a link with the desired VI. Its output is a *VI reference*, which is another kind of refnum specific to Application Control. To do something useful with Application Control, you wire the VI reference to one of three "attribute" nodes, which are available on the Application Control function pallet. First is the **Invoke Node**, which invokes a method associated with a VI, such as run, abort, print, or Make Current Values Default (a feature we've long been waiting for!). Second is a **Property Node**, which allows you to view and/or modify such items as a VI's name, information, or execution options. Third is the **Call By Reference Node**, which allows you to remotely call a VI with parameters as if it were wired directly into your diagram.

There are a number of VI methods available through the Invoke Node (Fig. 9.17), some of which control printing. Many of these methods are operations that are also available in the LabVIEW menus. Application Control makes these functions available programmatically—VIs can cause other VIs to perform functions that used to be available only through the VI's menu. For example, to print a VI's front panel, you would normally open the VI's front panel and select the Print function from the File menu. The same thing can now be done by invoking the Print VI to Printer method as shown in Fig. 9.18. This is a powerful new feature; explore the other methods and see what else you can do.

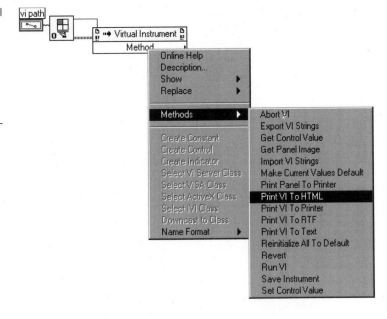

Figure 9.17
Pop-up menu showing the VI Server Methods available from the Invoke Node. This works on all platforms.

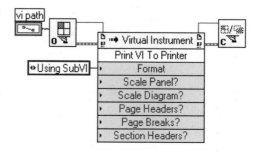

Figure 9.18
Invoking the Print
Documentation
Method from the
Invoke Node.

\ActiveX
Print Documen-
tation\Document
Directory.vi

One immediate application is documentation generation. LabVIEW has some pretty powerful built-in documentation features (via the File>>Print Documentation menu). With LabVIEW 5 you can now programmatically print VI documentation as well. This means that creation of a manual or programmer's reference for a hierarchy of 200 VIs can now be done by running 1 VI! I have created a simple example that will print documentation for a VI library (llb) or a directory to the printer, to a rich text format (RTF) file, or to an HTML file. The **Document Directory VI** is on the CD-ROM for your convenience.

Conclusion

In this chapter I've presented a quick introduction to ActiveX and Application Control by showing some of the common functions and examples of their use. However, I have barely scratched the surface. This is especially true for Application Control—I'm sure that we are going to see some very innovative uses of LabVIEW 5 and remote access, especially with the Internet and intranets.

CHAPTER **10**

Networking
with TCP/IP

Brad Hedstrom

Advanced Measurements, Inc.

Transmission Control Protocol/Internet Protocol (TCP/IP) is an open network protocol standard that allows different computers and operating systems to communicate. Although until a few years ago TCP/IP was relatively unknown outside of the Unix world (government and educational institutions), since the foundation of the Internet and the World Wide Web it is now nearly a household word. All viable operating systems support it, including all operating systems upon which LabVIEW runs. Thus TCP/IP is the only networking protocol that will allow LabVIEW running on different platforms to communicate. It allows communication over the Internet and intranets.

The LabVIEW Model of TCP

The TCP/IP implementation in LabVIEW is quite clean and fairly easy to understand. There are five main VIs required in using TCP/IP in LabVIEW. These VIs can be broken down into two groups: those that deal with managing the connection and those that deal with moving data. For reference, see the *LabVIEW Communications VI Reference Manual* or the LabVIEW on-line help system.

Connection VIs

Three VIs manage the TCP/IP connection: **TCP Listen, TCP Open Connection,** and **TCP Close Connection**. (There are two additional connection VIs, but we'll leave them for later.) These allow the development of **servers** and **clients**. For this discussion, we use the client/server model where the server "listens" for requests for data and supplies this data when requested. Conversely, client VIs request or "open" connections to servers and receive data. The connection can then be closed by either end (or both ends) when it is no longer required. Thus each server VI will have one or more corresponding client VIs. It's also feasible for the client or server to be implemented in a language other than LabVIEW, so long as both ends agree on the content of the messages.

REGARDING PORTS When you establish a connection, a **port** number is required in addition to the Internet address. Port numbers can range from 0 to 65535. Different port numbers at a given Internet address usually identify different services and make it easier to manage multiple connections. For most applications, you manually assign port numbers to clients and servers so that they are guaranteed to connect properly. When you want to specify a local port (for communication between VIs and/or other applications on your own computer), you can use port 0, which causes TCP to choose an unused port.

There are some issues you may run into with port numbers. For example, *fire walls* (network security devices) tend to not allow connections to any port less than 1000 because all of these ports are reserved for specific purposes (FTP, HTTP, Telnet, Finger, etc.). On Unix systems, again for security reasons, after a listener closes the port on which it listens, the port becomes unavailable for listening for a certain time (several minutes) during which you cannot open another listener on it. This makes it harder for a hacker to access a Unix system, but may cause problems for legitimate users as well.

Transmission VIs

Given an established connection, the **TCP Read** and **TCP Write VIs** transfer data between the client and the server. Data can flow bidirectionally between the client and the server.

TCP Read and TCP Write are quite similar to their VISA counterparts except that they use a **connection reference** number instead of a VISA session. As with VISA, the only data type supported for transmission is a string. At first glance this may seem limiting; however, it is really the most efficient way of modeling the data channel. Any type of data may be transmitted using the TCP connection; the TCP/IP protocol doesn't really care what the data is. It is simply a matter of designing the client/server pair such that the sender can convert the data type to a string and the receiver can reconstruct the received string into its actual data type. The **Flatten To String** and **Unflatten From String** functions make this a fairly trivial matter. (Optionally, if the data type is uniform, simple typecasting can also be used). The only requirement is that the receiver must know ahead of time the actual data type being received so the string may be correctly unflattened. This is the same approach used in dealing with bytestream files.

As with VISA, the receiver must know how many bytes have been transmitted so the appropriate number can be read. (There are no magic end-of-message flags in TCP/IP.) This is usually accomplished by adding an I32 integer header to the packet of data. The receiver first reads this I32, which tells it how many bytes of data follow. Alternatively, you could define a fixed-length data message, but that would be rather inflexible.

Example Application: High-Speed DAQ Data Server

This example application is based on a DAQ client/server system developed by Advanced Measurements, Inc. The system is based on two or more computers that need to share small amounts of data in a timely manner. TCP/IP was chosen because it was the only mechanism that could meet the fairly strict time constraints of one of the systems (a 33-ms loop time). The other two options explored were network file sharing, which suffered from Windows' 55-ms timer resolution, and Dynamic Data Exchange (DDE), which has quite drastic Windows overhead and also suffers from the 55-ms timer resolution. Initial testing on 66-MHz 486s using TCP/IP resulted in an 18-ms sustained acquisition rate (that is, performing the DAQ operations and getting the data to the clients). Thus, the server and clients were designed to be as small and as fast as possible.

Provided on the CD-ROM is the basic server and its corresponding client. They are meant to be instructional and to provide a starting point for other TCP/IP client/server systems. The server is composed of three VIs: the main VI and two subVIs. One of the subVIs takes care of converting the actual data type to a string and the other is the server *kernel* that manages both connection and transmission.

\TCP\Fast Example\Data Server.vi

Most of the functionality can be understood by looking at the main **Data Server VI** (Fig. 10.1). The While Loop generates the data (by whatever means), converts it to a string, and signals that new data is available using the new LabVIEW 5 **Notifier** function.[1] The **Single Client Server VI** (Fig. 10.2) has a While Loop that runs in parallel with the one in the Data Server VI, which waits on the Notifier and sends the data, using TCP Write, to the client when new data is available. The Single Client Server VI also manages the connection process by continuously listening on the specified port and accepting a connection request from a client.

The Single Client Server VI is reentrant so that multiple clients may be supported simultaneously. Later we will see an example architecture that can handle multiple connections on the same port. We selected the reentrant solution strictly for performance reasons: It has less overhead.

---

[1]Thanks to Stepan Riha of the NI LabVIEW development team for pointing out the Notifier function—a cool new way of synchronizing that's much better than the old way of using global variables and occurrences.

Figure 10.1
Simple TCP/IP data server diagram.

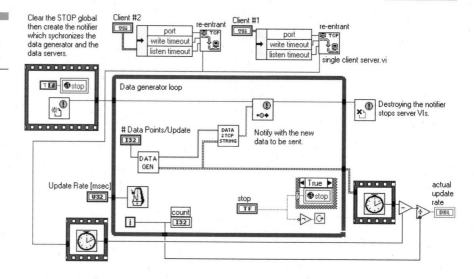

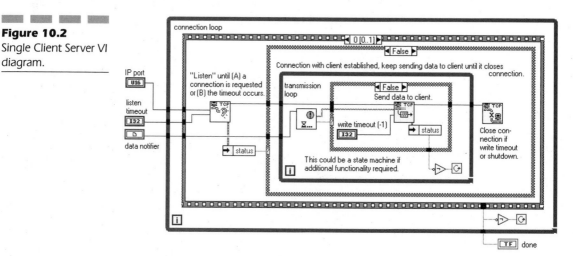

The **Data Client VI** (Fig. 10.3) is really very simple and uses only one subVI, which reconstructs the actual data type from the received data string. The client must know the structure of the data being received so that it can be properly reconstructed (*unflattened*). The data from this VI is then passed on to the application-specific parts of the client. The client requests a connection to the specified machine and port number when it is started and closes the connection when completed. In time-critical operations, timeouts can be used to ensure that the system adheres to the timing specifications; in this example the default timeouts are used.

\TCP\Fast
Example\Data
Client.vi

Figure 10.2
Single Client Server VI diagram.

Figure 10.3
Simple Data Client VI
diagram.

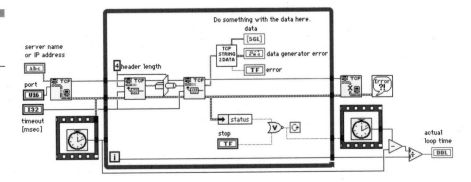

Example Application: Bidirectional Communication and Multiple Clients

The previous example provides unidirectional data flow from the server to the client. But what about applications where the client needs to request particular information (or more generally, services) from the server? Then two-way communication is required. Also, the previous example requires an instance of the Single Client Server subVI for each client as well as a separate port. This is fine for a predefined small number of clients, but what about the more general case where it is not known beforehand how many clients may need to connect? Here a somewhat different approach is required.

Bidirectional communication can be handled in much the same way as it is for instrument control: A particular protocol is used to request and receive information. For example, to get the voltage from a multimeter via GPIB, a command like VOLTS? would be sent to the instrument (which acts as the server). The instrument takes the measurement (performs a service) and then responds with something like VOLTS = 12.342 VDC. The same idea can be used for building a TCP/IP-based bidirectional client/server architecture.

The server has three tasks: (1) listen for and accept connection requests from clients; (2) wait for a client to make a request; and (3) respond to the request. Likewise the client has three tasks: (1) initiate a connection with the server; (2) make requests of the server; and (3) receive the responses from the server. Furthermore, we want to be able to handle an indeterminate number of clients at any time. Thus, our server must be able to accept and manage multiple connections on the same port. This can be accomplished with surprising ease.

**\TCP
Bi-Dir Example\
Request Server
Example.vi**

The three tasks can be performed with two parallel While Loops. One loop handles connection requests from clients and the other loop services the connected clients (see Fig. 10.4). Managing new connections is easily handled with two TCP functions called **TCP Create Listener** and **TCP Wait On Listener**. TCP Create Listener creates a process that listens for connection requests on a particular port; only one listener can be on any single port. TCP Wait On Listener waits until the listener specified by *listener ID* indicates that a new connection request has been made by a client. When a client makes a connection request (via Open Connection), TCP Wait on Listener returns the *connection ID* for that client. By putting TCP Wait On Listener in a loop, we've created a process that continually waits for connection requests on a particular port, thus satisfying the requirement that all clients connect to the same port.

Once the connection request has been made, the *Operations* string array (discussed below) is sent to the client and the *connection ID* is placed in the Connection Queue. The Connection Queue is the mechanism by which the connections are "handed off" from the connection loop (top) to the request loop (bottom). The request loop maintains an array of active connections using the shift register. Any new connections are read from the Connection Queue and appended to the array. The array is then passed into the Poll for Request subVI, which, just as the name suggests, checks each connection ID to see if any requests have been sent by the respective client. This is accomplished simply by calling TCP Read with a short timeout for each client. If the read times out, the client has made no request; otherwise the request is read and passed out of the Poll for

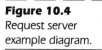

Figure 10.4
Request server
example diagram.

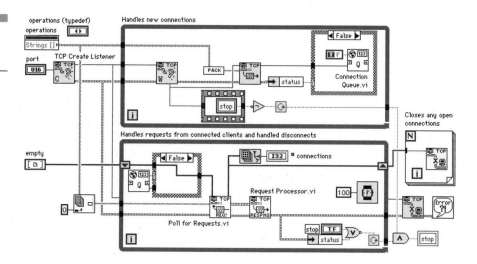

Requests subVI as an element of the *Requests* array. If an error is encountered when reading from a client or the disconnect command is received, that client's connection ID is dropped from the *connection IDs* array and is disconnected. The Request Processor subVI then services each request in the *Requests* array. There are three steps in processing a request: (1) determine which service has been requested; (2) perform the service; and (3) send the results.

In order to make the client and server as generic (and reusable) as possible, I've used command strings to select which service is to be performed (much like an instrument). There is an enumerated type definition called *Operations* that lists all of the services the server can perform (plus two mandatory services: disconnect and error). One method is to use the same typedef for both the client and the server. The problem is that each time the typedef is changed, both the client and server applications need to be rebuilt. I wanted an "old" client to be able to function even after new services were added to the server. That means no *Operations* typedef is allowed on the client. Instead I chose to send the list of services (an array of strings) to the client as soon as it requested a connection (the TCP Write function in the top loop). So, when the client wants to make a request, it just sends the appropriate string from the *Operations* array back to the server. The server then matches the request with the array of operations to see which service had been requested. That's one of the functions of the Request Processor subVI. After it has determined the request, it performs the desired action and then sends back both the request and the result (similar to the above VOLTS = 12.342VDC analogy). As you will see, echoing the request back to the client simplifies its design as well.

There is one special operation that is handled by the Poll for Requests subVI. Element 0 of the *Operations* string array is the disconnect operation. Thus it is indexed out of the array and supplied as an input to the Poll for Requests subVI. If a client sends a request for disconnect, it is disconnected in Poll for Requests and dropped from the *connection ID* array.

The **Request Client VI** (Fig. 10.5) is just as simple as the server. When started, it requests a connection via TCP Open. On the first iteration of the While Loop case 0 is executed, which reads the list of server operations, stores the list in the shift register, and writes the list to the Strings attribute of the *Operation* menu. When the *Submit* button is pressed, the selected operation is sent to the server. If the operation was not disconnect, the subVI Receive Response is called, which reads the echoed response and the resulting data. Using the new and improved LabVIEW 5

\TCP
\Bi-Dir Example
Request Client
Example.vi

Figure 10.5
Request Client
diagram.

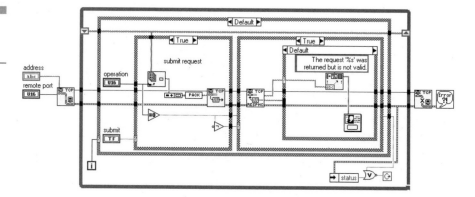

case structure, which supports string selectors, the string responses received from the server cause the appropriate frame to execute. Each time a service (or operation) is added, a new case is required in the case structure. However, the client will still run if additional operations have been added to the server but not to the client; the client will just report an error. Also note that several cases can be combined into one frame as shown in the example of the color responses.[2]

Other Examples

Make sure to look at the TCP/IP examples that come with LabVIEW. Of particular interest are examples\comm\tcpex.llb\Date Server.vi and examples\comm\tcpex.llb\Date Client.vi, which provide a simple example of one-way TCP/IP communication. The two top-level VIs in examples\comm\victltcp.llb, Remote VI Server.vi and Remote Temp Monitor Example.vi, show you how to call and run VIs across the network.

TCP can be used anytime data needs to be shared between two LabVIEW processes running on the same machine or on multiple machines where a client/server architecture applies. Usually this is when real-time data needs to be shared among processes. The solution can be very simple, as in the Date Client/Server example, or a very complex remote control application like the examples\comm\victltcp.llb\Remote Temp Monitor Example.vi or the bidirectional example in this chapter, which is general enough to be used in a variety of applications.

---

[2]Thanks again to Stepan for pointing out this feature.

User Datagram Protocol (UDP)

The **User Datagram Protocol** (UDP) is an alternative to TCP/IP for transmitting data across networks. UDP is not a connection-based protocol like TCP. This means that a connection does not need to be established with a destination before data is sent or received. Instead, the destination for the data is specified when each datagram is sent. The system does not report transmission errors. Typically, UDP is used in applications where reliability is not critical. For example, an application might transmit informative data to a destination frequently enough that a few lost segments of data are not problematic.

The main drawback with UDP is that it does not guarantee data delivery. Each datagram is routed separately, so datagrams may arrive out of order, be delivered more than once, or not be delivered at all. In contrast, TCP guarantees proper ordering. Of course, that adds a bit of overhead.

If you are writing both the client and server, and your system can use TCP/IP, then TCP is probably the best protocol to use because it is a reliable, connection-based protocol. UDP sometimes offers higher performance, but it does not ensure reliable transmission of data.

Using UDP

Using UDP in LabVIEW is quite similar to using TCP/IP. You use the **UDP Open VI** to create a connection. A port must be associated with a connection when it is created so that incoming data can be sent to the appropriate application. The number of simultaneously open UDP connections depends on the system. UDP Open returns a *Network Connection* refnum, similar to the TCP VIs, and it's used in all subsequent operations pertaining to that connection. You use the **UDP Write VI** to send data to a destination and the **UDP Read VI** to read it. Calling the **UDP Close VI** frees system resources when you're done.

The Internet Toolkit

I will close with a few words about the **Internet Toolkit**, which is available from National Instruments. The Internet is built on TCP/IP, so it's appropriate for this chapter. The Internet Toolkit is a set of libraries that allow LabVIEW to support common Internet functions like e-mail and file transfer using the ubiquitous File Transfer Protocol (FTP). It also makes LabVIEW into an HTTP server, which puts LabVIEW applications on the World Wide Web or an intranet with easy access via ordinary Web browsers. LabVIEW can serve static pages, pages with LabVIEW front panels that are regularly updated (like the Weather Station on the National Instruments Web site, www.natinst.com), and even fully dynamic pages using Common Gateway Interface (CGI). This allows LabVIEW VIs to be *controlled* by Web browsers. The possible applications are nearly endless.

Conclusion

In this chapter I've tried to give you an introduction to LabVIEW-LabVIEW communication using TCP/IP. Hopefully, this will help remove some of the mystery from interprocess communication over a network. It really is easy (what isn't with LabVIEW?) and can solve sometimes difficult resource sharing or timing issues in distributed applications. Although TCP/IP guarantees delivery, it does not guarantee *timely* delivery. Thus, for time-critical applications, substantial testing should be performed before developing a TCP/IP-based architecture. For high data volumes or time-sensitive applications it may be advantageous to create a separate network or subnet for the LabVIEW machines.

11

Data Acquisition from Space via the Internet

Ed Baroth, Ph.D., and George Wells
Measurement Technology Center (MTC), Jet Propulsion Laboratory,
California Institute of Technology

Now that you've had a chance to read about the nuts and bolts of networking in LabVIEW, let's take a look at a serious application of those tools. We had the good fortune to be part of the team providing ground support for an experiment on the space shuttle Endeavour (STS-77, May 16–29, 1996). If you were lucky enough to see data from that experiment "live" on the Web (and half a million people did), then you saw the future of data acquisition. The data was sent from Endeavour to the Payload Operations Control Center (POCC, part of Mission Control) at NASA's Johnson Space Center in Houston, then to the Jet Propulsion Laboratory's Measurement Technology Center. From JPL it was sent to National Instruments in Austin, Texas, then out on the Web. Most times it was on the Web 10 seconds after we saw it in Houston (Fig. 11.1).

The Internet has revolutionized data acquisition. In the (very recent) past, data acquisition was a local event. A computer was connected to sensors providing direct data acquisition. Networking was usually rare. A *sneaker net* was often used to take data from the lab to the office for analysis. Data acquisition, analysis, display, and monitoring are now global

Figure 11.1
Path of data from space. (*Courtesy of National Instruments.*)

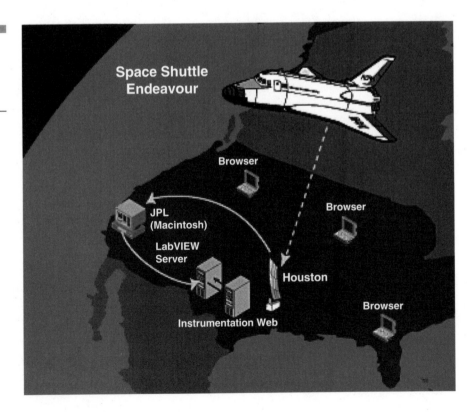

events. Information can be parceled out and delivered in custom formats to scientists, engineers, managers, and the public—in real time. In addition, previously only small teams of scientists or engineers had access to the data, with the public seeing it six months to a year later. The Web provides everyone potential access to the data. And, after all, because the public is paying for it, shouldn't the public see it?

This application also provides an example of a seamless transition from ground support to flight. The same ground support equipment that was used to test and characterize the flight hardware for over a year was then simply disconnected from the flight hardware and reconnected to Mission Control and used during the flight. (Not exactly that easy—nothing ever is—but close.) Advantages include robust software, real-time data reduction and display evaluated during ground usage, and savings in time and cost.

Showing the data on the Web was an afterthought—a bonus, if you will. We had planned to send the data back to JPL for analysis by members of the science team who could not be at mission control in Houston. When we realized that we could get it to JPL, we figured, "Why not put it on the Web?" Because the system we developed uses LabVIEW and was operating on a Macintosh, I got in touch with National Instruments and Apple computer to see if they would like to host a Web site. Both eagerly agreed and demonstrated technology cooperation between JPL, NI, and Apple. In fact, Apple was about to kick off a new science and technology home page. What better way to do so than with real-time data from the shuttle? (This is a good example of the old saying, "Better to be lucky than good"!)

The BETSCE Experiment

Brilliant Eyes Ten-Kelvin Sorption Cryocooler Experiment (**BETSCE**) (Bard et al. 1996) is a space shuttle technology demonstration experiment designed to show that cryocoolers of this type, called *sorption coolers*, can operate in the weightless vacuum environment of space. Sorption coolers have essentially no vibration, require very low input power in this extremely cold temperature range, and can operate reliably for over 10 years. This was the first ever space flight of chemisorption cryocooler technology.

The BETSCE demonstration measured and validated critical microgravity performance characteristics of a hydride sorption cryocooler designed to cool long-wavelength infrared and sub-millimeter-wavelength detectors to 10 K and below. The flight validation data provided by BETSCE will enable use of this novel refrigeration technology in a number of planned future precision-pointing astronomy, Earth observation, and surveillance space satellite applications (Fig. 11.2).

BETSCE successfully validated sorption cooler operation in a microgravity environment. It produced solid hydrogen at 10 K in its first attempt on-orbit, cooling down from 70 K to 10 K in under 2 minutes and sustaining a 100-mW load for 10 minutes, thus meeting the primary system performance objectives. A total of eight quick-cooldown liquid hydrogen cycles were completed, achieving a minimum temperature of 18.4 K and a maximum cooling duration of 32 minutes. Total cycle times ranged from 8 to 11 hours, depending on Shuttle orbiter attitude. Flight data obtained for a total of 18 compressor cycles demonstrated the ability

Figure 11.2
Brilliant Eyes Ten-Kelvin Sorption Cryocooler Experiment (BETSCE) demonstrated the feasibility of chemisorption cryocooler technology in space.

to consistently recompress the hydrogen refrigerant fluid to the same high pressures as achieved in ground testing.

Figure 11.3 shows the system block diagram. Two Macintosh computers were used: the primary computer for telemetry down from and commands up to the shuttle, and a secondary computer for data display, analysis, and Ethernet to JPL and the World Wide Web. Additional computer stations (Analyst and CSR) were used for data analysis and display.

There is always the security risk that someone from the outside will try to hack into what must be a hacker's nirvana—NASA's Shuttle Mission Operations. In fact, only when we could demonstrate that the system using Ethernet was physically uncoupled from sending commands were we allowed to use it.

That leads into another aspect of the Internet and World Wide Web: *responsibility.* Simply because you *can* put information on the Web does not mean that you *should.* Even though the Cold War is over, the United States is in a "war" to remain competitive with the rest of the world. Information that can give another country an unfair advantage hardly belongs on the Web. There is a difference between showing data and showing enabling technology. You can show that something was done without giving away how it was done. Existing export laws may apply to disclosure of

Figure 11.3
Computer system block diagram for the BETSCE experiment.

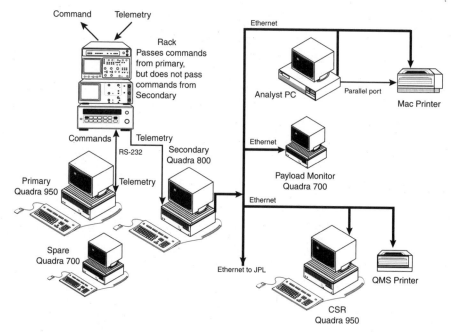

information. Discretion is just the flip side of all the freedom the Web permits.

The original system goes back five years. It was developed to acquire data (on a Mac) for the ground system proof-of-principle experiment. It handled the user interface and archiving of 64 channels of temperature, pressure, and flow data with direct connections through a plug-in board, an external multiplexer, and signal conditioners. Utilities provided post-processing analysis. There were no control outputs, although the manual controls were monitored as inputs.

The system then transitioned into a system to test and characterize the flight experiment using the serial port as the connection to the up-/downlink. It provided the only user interface for the principal investigators to the flight experiment by uplinking immediate commands or command sequences to be operated on later, and recording and displaying all the downlinked data from the experiment. It also provided utilities for calibration, converting spreadsheet command sequences to machine code for uplinking, and postprocessing of recorded data. It was then moved to Mission Control in Houston, where it provided exactly the same functions, the only difference being the "length of the serial cable" (in effect, extending to the orbiting shuttle). One more function was added (transparently) to echo the downlinked data to a similar system at JPL so that a *shadow site* could operate without impacting the critical operations of the principal investigators.

An additional system, the Payload Monitor, was a result of a safety meeting: Certain channels of the telemetry had to be monitored by the support people at JSC, but their system was not flexible enough to make modifications close to launch. We provided an additional LabVIEW screen detailing certain channels of our telemetry using Ethernet. It provided an excellent example of the flexibility that graphical programming provides compared to text-based programming. The additional system was modified and delivered in about one day.

Figure 11.4 is an example of the LabVIEW user interface screen displayed to the science team. It shows valves opening and closing, as well as the locations, types, and values for the approximately 100 sensors used in the experiment. It also shows graphs for three user-selected sensors. The identical data was sent to JPL for display, and from there a subset of data was sent to the National Instruments Web site. This complex display meets the needs of the scientists, but it's not one you would normally present to the inexperienced operator or to the public.

National Instruments created a special server that can take pictures of any LabVIEW VI and place the image on the Web. Also developed was a

Figure 11.4
User interface screen for the science team.

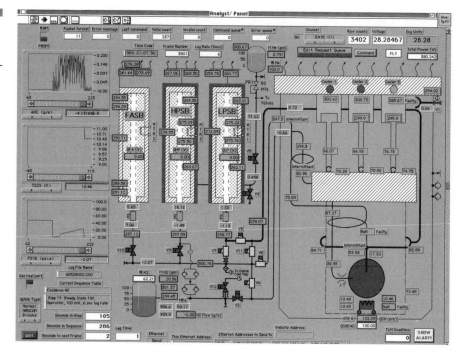

VI capable of receiving data from JPL and displaying it in a form a wide audience could understand. Those VIs evolved into the **LabVIEW Internet Toolkit,** available from National Instruments. It's a painless way to publish and view data and even remote-control your VIs over the Web.

BETSCE successfully achieved its primary objectives of (1) proving a thorough end-to-end characterization and performance validation of a hydride sorption cryocooler in the 10 to 30 K temperature range; (2) acquiring the microgravity database needed to provide confident engineering design, scaling, and optimization; (3) identifying and resolving interface and integration issues; and (4) providing hardware qualification and a safety verification heritage that is extremely valuable for future missions.

The ground support achieved its objectives of flexibility in configuration and modification; reduced software and system development cost and schedule by a factor of 4 to 10; and reduced system development, configuration, documentation, training, and operating costs. Besides that, the ground support provided an excellent example of how quickly and easily information can be made available to the public. It demonstrated that the new world of "instant global" data acquisition and tools such as the Internet and World Wide Web need to be considered as part of any current data acquisition system.

Mars Sojourner Rover

The **Data Monitoring and Display Subsystem** (DMD) in NASA's Jet Propulsion Laboratory is a very large conglomerate of computers and software designed to service many different types of space programs. It is connected to a worldwide array (the Deep Space Network) of dish antennas listening to space probes throughout the solar system. Each probe has its own requirements for data display. The DMD handles these different requirements through a set of text files that the various end users create to tell the DMD how to interpret and display the data coming from each spacecraft. It works fine for the usual "flying" type of spacecraft, where the users are most interested in the latest state of the spacecraft and where things change rather slowly because of the very long travel times and orbital periods. For the Pathfinder Rover mission, however, it became necessary to extend the DMD's capabilities in the recovery of the history of rapidly changing data over a short period of time.

Because the Rover operates on solar power, because a day on Mars is just under 25 hours, and because the Rover only communicates with Earth at the beginning and end of each daylight period, the operators on Earth have precious little time to analyze each day's data and plan a sequence of activities to send to the Rover for the next day. The operators needed a set of utilities that were customized for their specific display requirements in as near to real time as possible. Although these utilities could have been produced with just about any programming language, we believed that the ease of programming in LabVIEW was the only solution that was feasible in the short time allocated for the task. Of course, with more time, more money, or simpler requirements, other approaches could have succeeded, but in this era of *better, faster, cheaper,* a tool that has a proven record of high productivity was the only viable alternative.

The approach taken was to use the DMD to create a growing file of data as it was received from Pathfinder. The same configuration files that the DMD uses are also read by the LabVIEW program. The LabVIEW program then monitors the data file, and whenever new data is read it is inserted in its proper place with the previously collected data and displayed in a variety of different formats ideal for each of the Rover specialists. Many of these displays are text-based and are similar to those provided by the DMD except that they can quickly and easily display old data. Some of the text-based displays are vast improvements over the DMD's displays in that they group data in a more convenient manner and they allow the operator to click on particular fields to cause some operation to happen. For example, the operator can click on an error flag to bring up an explanation (like a help window). Or the operator can click on a button to immediately scroll a very long text display to the next or previous occurrence of a missing or skipped command. Some fields are color-coded for easy recognition and alarm conditions are shown in yellow or red.

Some of the displays are graphic when that provides a clear advantage over text. For example, there is a map of the terrain the Rover traverses showing the vehicle's every move and the detection of rocks and valleys with its proximity lasers (Fig. 11.5). The display in Fig. 11.6 shows the orientation of the Rover and its six wheels as it progresses. The four corner wheels independently steer and all six wheels are independently driven and suspended. In addition, this display shows the condition of the contact sensors around the Rover's periphery that light up whenever it bumps something. It also shows the position of the soil sampler on the Rover's rear as it moves down like a little crane to detect who knows what in the Martian dirt. Figure 11.7 shows the thermal profile of the Rover. The graphic on the left is in an actual temperature scale, while the right graphic shows which temperatures (red or yellow) are in the alarm condition.

Here is a sample of a line from the data file we used when designing the LabVIEW program:

```
1997-188T23:10:51.153,R-0552,Heading,56960,312.881,
1247008258.054,U,,,,,1997-093T16:48:25.791
```

The file is an ordinary text-based comma-separated spreadsheet-type file consisting of twelve fields. The first field is the spacecraft day and time at which the measurement was made. Next is the channel ID followed by the channel name. Next is the raw data value followed by the engineering unit value. After that is the spacecraft internal clock value, which we ignore. Next is a single letter designating the numeric type—in this case *U* stands for an unsigned number. The next four fields are where alarm conditions appear when present. The last field is the day and time at which the data was received on Earth, another value that we ignore.

When the LabVIEW program reads a line of data, it first looks at the channel ID beginning at character position 22 to see if it's one of a predefined list of channel IDs of interest. If it's not, we simply ignore the line and go on to read the next one. If we are interested in the line, we pass the entire line to a subVI that reads the first field to get the time of the data and the fifth field to get the engineering unit value of the data. In case there is no engineering unit conversion for a particular channel, the fifth field will be empty and the subVI will read the fourth field, the raw data,

Figure 11.5
The Rover's path is
displayed graphically.

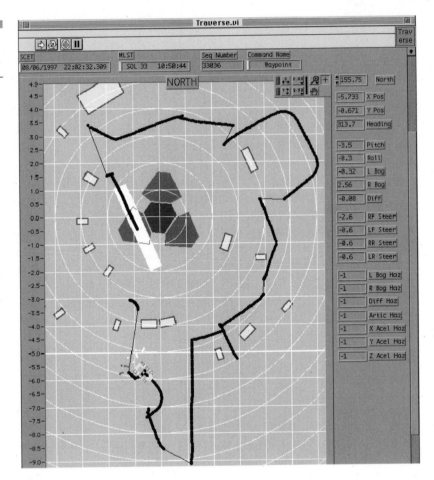

instead. The time and data are returned by the subVI as double-precision numbers. The subVI also checks the alarm fields and returns a code of 0 if they are empty, 1 if only a yellow alarm is present, or 2 if a red alarm is present.

As you can see by examining the sample line of data and understanding the meaning of the fields, the subVI that parses the line is really very simple and could easily have been written in any programming language. An early version of the LabVIEW program successfully read a previously created data file and plotted user-selected channels. When we first attempted to use this same program to read a real-time data file that was being generated by the DMD, however, the graphs plotted garbage. Yet, when the file was finished being filled and we went back and read it again with the same LabVIEW program, it worked perfectly.

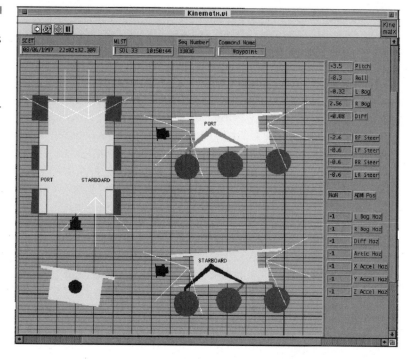

Figure 11.6
Details on the Rover's wheel positions and various sensors are shown in this intuitive display.

Here we have a real-world programming problem, something that we could never have anticipated or prepared for. The question is: How do you diagnose the problem? In LabVIEW there are a great many diagnostic tools built in, the most useful being the very nature of subVIs that provide visibility of the parameters passed in and out through controls and indicators. You can even turn on the data logging feature so that a history of every call is saved for later viewing, either manually in an interactive

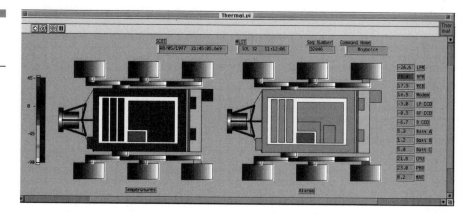

Figure 11.7
Temperature profiles on the Rover.

way or by writing another program to automatically search through all the parameters for a particular set of conditions. Another feature is the ability to observe the data flowing through a program as it is executing. All sorts of breakpointing, single-stepping, and probing of data are available as standard features of LabVIEW.

In our case, the problem was quickly identified by simply watching the parameters passed to the subVI that parses the line of data. We saw that one of the fields—the channel name—was missing. As a result, the spacecraft's internal clock was being interpreted as the data value, truly a good way to get garbage. We asked the DMD experts how this was happening and they explained that the entire file was first written in real time without the parameter names and then rewritten with the parameter names inserted in their proper place on every line just before the file was closed. Since our LabVIEW program had to work correctly under both conditions, we solved the problem in just a few minutes by counting the number of fields in the data line and using that number to determine which fields contained the data and alarm conditions. The whole process of testing the program for the first time with real-time data, observing the garbage, finding the problem, and fixing it took less than one hour. This ability for quick diagnosis is really important in an environment where other people are involved in running a test, not just because it avoids wasting a lot of their time, but because it creates a real sense of cooperation among them when they see how quickly and easily problems are identified and corrected. Sometimes they even participate in the diagnostic process because they can readily see the parameters being processed by subVIs. LabVIEW has a tendency to draw newcomers in.

Another problem that was discovered as a result of a feature that was added to the LabVIEW program was a bug in the Rover's program that resulted in some data being ignored. This feature was an error flag that reported any line number of the data file that contained a repeated time stamp for a given channel. It turned out that in rare cases when the Rover saved up data because it did not have real-time communication with the Pathfinder lander, it could attach the same time stamp to two different sets of data that were actually acquired at different times. Although this bug was not catastrophic, it was fixed and a patch was uploaded to the Rover during its trip to Mars. It is doubtful that this bug would have been discovered if any other programming language were being used for data display because, in our opinion, only the bare minimum ever gets programmed under tight time constraints with other programming languages. The luxury of having error reports "just in case," along with all kinds of other "bells and whistles," is very easy to achieve in LabVIEW.

The DMD runs on Sun workstations and LabVIEW runs on them just as well under X-Windows. However, sometimes all the workstations were tied up in testing with the Earth-based Rover in the outdoor *Mars Yard* or the indoor *Sandbox*. In those and other cases, program development progressed just as easily, with the LabVIEW programs being sent to a Mac or PC via FTP. The cross-platform feature of LabVIEW proved to be a big asset in this endeavor.

Summary

These examples show how LabVIEW has been used for complex and critical tasks involving space missions. Key areas such as telemetry display and flight hardware testing have been demonstrated. All have resulted in savings of time and money as well as satisfied customers, which in this case includes the American public. In Chap. 12, "Advanced LabVIEW Applications for Space Missions," we'll look at some additional large-scale systems with a focus on development approaches such as rapid prototyping, and at issues encountered in these larger projects.

Bibliography

S. Bard, P. Karlmann, J. Rodriguez, J. Wu, L. Wade, P. Cowgill, and K. M. Russ, "Flight Demonstration of a 10 K Sorption Cryocooler," *9th International Cryocooler Conference*, Waterville Valley, NH, June 1996.

G. Wells and E. C. Baroth, "Telemetry Monitoring and Display using Lab-VIEW," *Proceedings of National Instruments User Symposium*, Austin, TX, March 28–30, 1993.

12

Advanced LabVIEW Applications for Space Missions

Ed Baroth, Ph.D., and George Wells

Measurement Technology Center (MTC), Jet Propulsion Laboratory, California Institute of Technology

The Measurement Technology Center (MTC) evaluates commercial data acquisition, analysis, display, and control hardware and software products that are then made available to experimenters at the Jet Propulsion Laboratory. In addition, the MTC acts as an internal systems integrator to deliver turnkey measurement systems that include software, user interfaces, sensors (such as thermocouples and pressure transducers), and signal conditioning, plus data acquisition, analysis, display, simulation, and control capabilities. The MTC also supports flight projects at JPL by supplying a variety of ground support equipment.

A variety of applications related to space missions have been developed by the MTC. They include the Galileo mission discussed in this chapter, as well as the BETSCE experiment and Mars Sojourner Rover mission described in Chap. 11, "Data Acquisition from Space via the Internet." Some additional remarks will be made regarding applications of LabVIEW for flight code itself.

This chapter is not a programming tutorial, but rather a demonstration of the capabilities of LabVIEW in signal analysis and troubleshooting. If you have any doubts regarding the applicability of graphical programming and personal computers to mission-critical systems, this article should put them to rest.

LabVIEW Supports the Galileo Spacecraft

The original Galileo software application discussed here was created as the result of parallel development competition between a graphical programming team and a text-based (C) programming team (Wells and Baroth 1993, 1995). Although not a scientific study, it was a fair comparison between different development methods and tools. With approximately eight weeks of funding over a period of three months, the graphical programming effort was significantly more advanced, having gone well beyond the original requirements. In contrast, the C development effort did not complete the original requirements. For our purposes, this application verified that using visual programming can significantly reduce software development time.

As a result of this initial effort, additional LabVIEW follow-on work was awarded to the graphical programming team. This chapter documents that follow-on work, which amounted to four years of work and a budget of over $500,000. The work was begun using LabVIEW 2 and continued in that version even when later versions became available.[1]

Galileo Mission Background

The Galileo spacecraft arrived at Jupiter in December 1995. Six months before encounter it released a probe. A timer in the probe activated its radio transmitter just before arriving at the planet. The original plan called for a real-time relay of the probe radio signal by the Galileo spacecraft to Earth, but this was impossible because Galileo's high-rate dish antenna failed to open fully. Instead, the Galileo computer was reprogrammed to strip out the overhead and housekeeping bits in the data stream coming from the probe. The important data sent by the probe transmitter was stored in the limited onboard memory for later downlinking to Earth. This downlinking occurred sometime during the first orbit using the low-gain omnidirectional antenna at a much lower bit rate than if the high-gain antenna had been fully functional.

Upon encountering Jupiter, the spacecraft was put into a highly elliptical orbit with a period of about three months. Each orbit was modified slightly to allow the spacecraft to encounter a different moon or feature of Jupiter. For a few days during these close encounters, intense data acquisition was performed and the data was logged to the onboard tape recorder. During the remainder of each three-month orbit, while the spacecraft was relatively far from Jupiter, the computer subsystems were involved in compressing and compacting the tape data and downloading it to Earth.

The MTC supported a software redesign of the computer system aboard the Galileo spacecraft, including the probe (Wells and Baroth 1994). To assure that every byte was correctly downloaded, the ground-based *Test Bed* setup of the computer subsystems (which mimics the computers aboard the spacecraft) and the emulation hardware for the instruments were monitored. The performance of any new software was assessed by the LabVIEW code by checking the telemetry for accuracy.

Before orbit insertion, the onboard tape recorder began showing signs of an anomaly. A command to rewind never resulted in the recorder reaching the end of tape. After analysis of the spacecraft data, it was determined that the tape was sticking to one of the tape guides. The cause and, more importantly, the cure for the tape-sticking anomaly needed to be determined. LabVIEW provided a quick look into the tape recorder

---

[1]For space missions, the fear of new bugs easily outweighs the lure of new features.

anomaly problem (Wells, Baroth, and Levanas 1996). It was already being used for testing the compression and compaction routines of the computer subsystems. Although other acquisition software or logging hardware could have been used for this application, the advantages of using LabVIEW—custom data display and presentation capability, quick configuration time, and ease of modification—were keys to a successful application and a satisfied customer.

Now we'll take a detailed look at three aspects of the LabVIEW development projects: probe telemetry, Galileo telemetry, and the tape recorder anomaly.

Galileo Probe Telemetry Simulator and Analyzer

The task of the computer redesign was complicated by the fact that there are actually two redundant probe radio receivers and several computer subsystems with their own memory partitions on the orbiter. A *Configuration Table* was set up to specify which receiver(s) would be the source of the data and which sections of which subsystems would be the destinations of the stripped data.

LabVIEW software was developed to perform a stripping algorithm on the emulated probe data used in the test, and, using the Configuration Table, to create a *Predict Table* of the data to be downloaded (Fig. 12.1). A probe analyzer program was developed to monitor the telemetry from the Test Bed, decommutate the memory readout data, compare it to the Predict Table, and display the progress of the test. After the test was over, utilities de-

Figure 12.1

Block diagram of the ground support sequence of data flow from the Galileo probe.

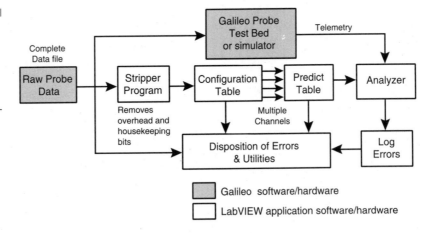

veloped in LabVIEW were used to disposition any discrepancies, including incorrect or missing bytes, and relate them to the original expanded data to determine the nature of the problem. A necessary additional component was a Test Bed simulator that enabled all of the other programs to be developed and debugged before connection to the actual Test Bed.

LabVIEW running on a Macintosh Quadra constituted the programming environment. The advantages LabVIEW provides include the ease with which the customer can communicate requirements to the programmers and understand the operation of the program so that changes can be suggested. Gains in productivity are attributed to the communication among the customer, developer, and computer that is facilitated by the visual syntax of the language. (See Chap. 1, "LabVIEW Enables the Interactive Communication Process.") LabVIEW proved exceptionally capable in providing an integrated environment to manage all aspects of the telemetry test, from pretest data setup to posttest discrepancy resolution, as well as running the test in several simulator modes or with the Test Bed.

The creation of the Predict Table was performed in two steps. First, files containing the simulated raw data from the two radio receivers had to be stripped using the same algorithm that would be programmed into the Galileo computers. The fact that the processors are different is considered to be a check on the programmers' understandings of the algorithm. Second, the Configuration Table determined where the stripped data would be stored in the onboard memory of the Test Bed and in the Predict Table of the analyzer program. The Stripper program, Configuration Table, and Predict Table are LabVIEW emulations of the identical operations performed in the Test Bed, except that instead of the bytes being stored in various subsystem memories, as occurs in the Test Bed, they are saved to the Predict Table disk file.

If the test mode required that the simulator actually generate the telemetry, the two analog output channels of a plug-in DAQ board were initialized to generate a pair of continuous signals. One of them is a square wave of a frequency specified by the operator and the other is the data. Both have 0- to 5-V swings. If the test mode does not require real telemetry, then the data bit stream is saved in memory. The simulator is used for debugging or demonstration purposes only.

Figure 12.2 is the user interface for the simulator program. It displays the names of the subsystems along the top and the rates at which frames are generated. The user can also generate errors of various types. The subsystem type for each frame is displayed as a mark on a scrolling strip chart.

Figure 12.2
Telemetry simulator
user interface.

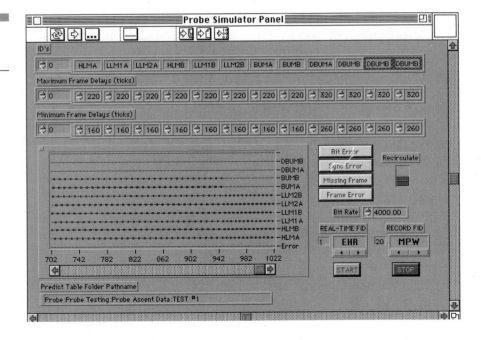

If the test mode requires the analyzer program to read the real teleme-try signal, the DAQ board is initialized to take continuous readings on a single analog channel synchronized by a hardware clock signal. If the test mode does not require real telemetry, then the requested bits come from the memory saved by the simulator. In either case, the analyzer program will wait until the requested bits are available.

During initial development, the simulator and analyzer communicated directly through a common memory software routine on the same Mac-intosh computer. Later, the simulator generated a real clock and data stream on one Macintosh that the analyzer read on another Macintosh using DAQ boards. This two-computer configuration was so close to the real Test Bed configuration that, when it came time to connect the analyzer to the Test Bed telemetry stream, it was operating within a few hours.

During the course of simulated or actual monitoring of the telemetry signal, the memory readout contents were compared with locations in the Predict Table as specified by the Configuration Table. As long as the con-tents match, only the subsystem name and address are saved, but in the event of an error, the entire 80 bytes for both the Predict Table and the telemetry stream are saved. Also, a count of the number of times each byte in the Predict Table is read is maintained, along with a flag indicat-ing whether any byte was read in error. A counter displays the remaining number of bytes from the Predict Table that have not yet been read. A bitmap displays a pixel for each byte in the Predict Table and turns black if it has been read correctly. Thus, it is very easy to monitor the progress of the test.

Figure 12.3 shows the analyzer in operation and generally reflects the same subsystem patterns as the simulator but is delayed in time. The *Predict Tables* and *Downloaded* indicators show the actual hex bytes whenever there is a discrepancy. Other indicators display various errors or status.

To better analyze any errors that may occur during a test, additional utilities were developed to pinpoint the location of the error in the Predict Table and trace it back to the corresponding error bits in the original raw data files. One of these utilities would display the raw and the stripped data as defined by the Predict Table and as defined by the Galileo telemetry so that the system and nature of the error could be identified. Without these utilities it would have been virtually impossible to determine the source of the errors within any reasonable time. Typically, however, tests of this nature have been run in the past without such utilities, simply because of the difficulty and cost of developing them and because of the optimistic hope that they would never be needed.

HIGH PRODUCTIVITY MEANS MORE FEATURES Since Lab-VIEW promoted high programmer productivity, the customer had plenty of time to suggest new features such as the ability to log the raw telemetry

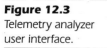

Figure 12.3
Telemetry analyzer
user interface.

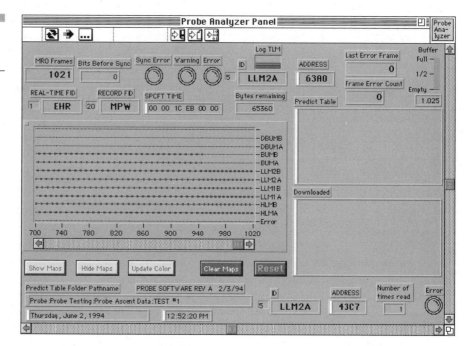

stream to a disk file and then simulate the telemetry stream from disk so that a test could be repeated without incurring the cost of rerunning the actual test using the Test Bed and support personnel. This was a simple modification of the original implementation using the simulator and analyzer on the same Macintosh and proved to be valuable because, as it turned out, during the actual first run of the Test Bed an incorrect Configuration Table was used, which generated a large number of errors. When the test was rerun from the logged disk file with the correct Configuration Table, there were no errors, saving a costly rerun using the Test Bed personnel.

Another suggestion that was implemented was the ability of the analyzer to "read" telemetry from the TCP/IP port instead of a disk file. This allowed communication between the analyzer and a Test Bed emulator that was written on a Sun workstation. The Sun provided the Galileo programmers with an easier and faster platform on which to develop their code. (The Galileo CPUs are ancient 1802 8-bit processors.)

GRAPHICAL VERSUS TEXT-BASED PROGRAMMING During the course of program development, it became necessary to generate the source files for the probe receivers based on data that had previously been downloaded from the Galileo spacecraft telemetry in a test mode. A C programmer who was familiar with the file structure was assigned this task. As a backup, the task was also given to a LabVIEW programmer. The application was developed in LabVIEW by one programmer in less than two weeks. For the one data file on which the routine was written to operate, no errors were found in the input data.

After spending approximately one month on the task, the C programmer delivered a product that was advertised as being complete. The C programmer noted that when the program ran, it found errors in the input data. Since the customer already had the LabVIEW version (with no errors), the raw data was compared with the two sets of output files and it was discovered that a bug in the C code caused it to find bad data where none existed. The C programmer spent a week or so making changes to the code, but was still not able to process the data correctly. The customer then decided to halt the C programming effort.

Galileo Telemetry Simulator and Analyzer

Two separate tasks were performed in support of Galileo: Phase I, a minor reprogramming effort to support a backup data path for the tape recorder, and Phase II, a major reprogramming of the telemetry format of the flight computers.

Figure 12.4 shows the ground support sequence of data flow from the instruments to the analyzer. The purpose of this effort was to test the compression algorithms plus the commutation of the data into packets. Using LabVIEW, software was developed to perform the various compression algorithms to be used on the different science instruments. Each instrument has multiple modes of compression to take into account the relative value of the data at differing times in the mission. The compressed data for each of these modes for each instrument are stored in files called Predict Tables, similar to those used on the probe simulator.

A necessary additional component was a telemetry simulator/emulator so that the analyzer program could be developed and debugged before connection to the Test Bed. It ran on a Macintosh IIfx and used a DAQ board (National Instruments NB-MIO-16X) to create a telemetry stream.

During a test, the Test Bed reads the raw instrument data, performs the updated compression and commutation algorithms, and generates a telemetry stream. The analyzer discussed here monitors the telemetry from the Test Bed, decommutates the data, compares it to data in the Predict Tables, and displays the progress of the test. The following sections will give you an idea of the complexity of the underlying telemetry data formats and the related software challenges.

DETAILS OF THE TELEMETRY ANALYSIS The telemetry from the Low-Gain Antenna Mission of the Galileo spacecraft contains data from 15 instrument sources. The sources are assigned mnemonics and each has from two to seven types of data or modes of operation that extend the mnemonic names by a single digit. There are 56 of these instrument types and each is assigned an application identification (*App ID*) code. The data from these App IDs is independently collected into packets of up to 511 bytes and then appended to a header of 3 to 8 bytes as depicted in Fig. 12.5.

Figure 12.4

Block diagram of the ground support sequence of data flow from the Galileo main spacecraft.

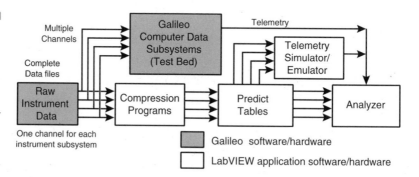

Figure 12.5
Packet structure for
Galileo telemetry.

Time incl flag	App ID	Packet size	Packet Sequence number	Format ID	Packet time (optional)	Instrument science data and status
						Content defined by instrument
Bits:						
1	7	9	7	0, 4 or 8	24, 28 or 32	

Packet header (3 - 8 Bytes)　　　　　Packet data (2 - 511 Bytes)

The packets are then assembled into Virtual Channel Data Units (VCDUs), which always contain 4 bytes of header and 442 bytes of packets with provisions for allowing packets to roll over from one VCDU to a later one as shown in Fig. 12.6. Four VCDUs (a total of 1784 bytes) are then assembled into a *frame* with a 2-byte frame number, an 8-byte pseudonoise (PN) synchronization word, and 254 bytes of Reed-Solomon error correction codes applied in eight unequal-size groups. This 2,048-byte frame is then run through convolutional encoding that doubles the number of bytes, producing 4,096 bytes (32,768 bits) of telemetry. Figure 12.7 is a schematic of the frame structure.

The testing of the telemetry stream involves a reverse process so data from the individual packets assigned to each of the App IDs can be recovered and compared to predicted values. The first step is to capture the telemetry in real time. The telemetry stream from the Computer Data Subsystem of the Test Bed consists of a clock line and a data line, both

Figure 12.6
Virtual Channel Data
Unit (VCDU) data
structure.

VCDU ID	VCDU Sequence number	First packet pointer	Remnant of prior packet from instrument	First full packet	Full packet(s)	Partial packet
Bits:						
3	20	9				

VCDU header (4 Bytes)　　　　　VCDU contents (442 Bytes)

Figure 12.7
Structure of a com-
plete telemetry
frame.

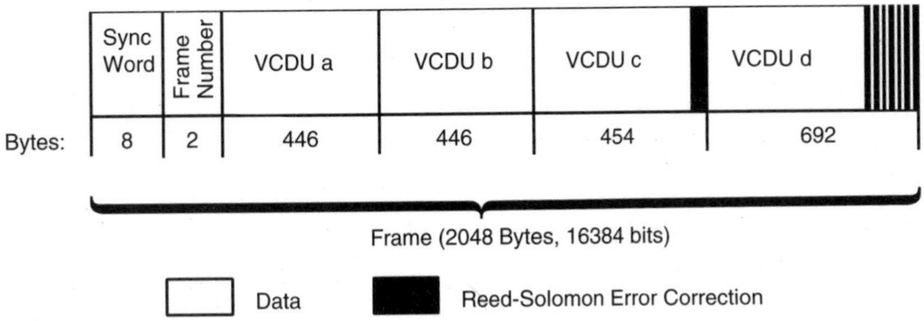

Sync Word	Frame Number	VCDU a	VCDU b	VCDU c	VCDU d
Bytes: 8	2	446	446	454	692

Frame (2048 Bytes, 16384 bits)

☐ Data　　　■ Reed-Solomon Error Correction

swinging 0–5 V. The clock line is connected directly to the *sample* input on a data acquisition board. On each low-going transition of this clock line, the voltage on the data line is measured and stored in memory using the double-buffered data acquisition mode of the LabVIEW DAQ library that provides continuous sampling of an input voltage. The sampled voltages are compared to a threshold (set at 2.5 V) producing a single data bit for each clock pulse.

The second step is to run these bits through a deconvolution process that purposely does not correct errors but produces two independent bit streams. The 8-byte pseudonoise sync word is searched for in both of these streams until it is found in one of them, at which point the other one is ignored. The next 2040 bytes are then assembled into a 2-byte frame sequence number, 254 bytes of Reed-Solomon error correction codes, and four VCDUs of 446 bytes each.

The full screen (21-inch monitor) user interface (LabVIEW Front Panel) is shown in Fig. 12.8. It gives you an idea of the complexity of the user interface required to display the analysis. Extra boxes and numbers have been drawn on the panel to help explain it in detail.

The area marked as number 1 in Fig. 12.8 displays the number of bits occurring before the synchronization word was found, the frame num-

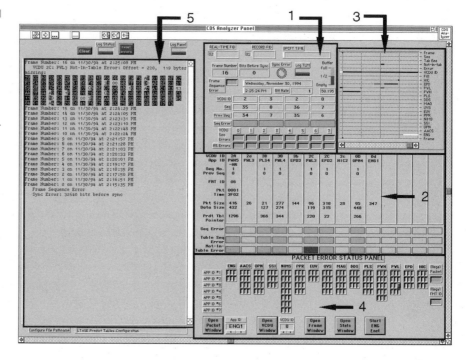

Figure 12.8
User interface for the Galileo telemetry analyzer. Highlighted zones marked 1 through 5 are discussed in the text.

ber and whether it is out of sequence, and whether the eight groups of Reed-Solomon (RS) codes are incorrect (no corrections are applied). These RS errors are displayed in red in the frame in which they occur and change to yellow on subsequent frames. The operator can click on these latching error indicators, changing them to green. The *buffer* indicator displays the status of the real-time buffer. The *Log TLM* switch allows the operator to save the raw telemetry stream to a disk file for later analysis.

The third step is to check the headers of the four VCDUs (depicted in Fig. 12.6). These headers contain 3 bits defining a VCDU ID type (0–7), 20 bits defining a sequence number, and 9 bits used to handle the rollover of packets between VCDUs. Each of the eight VCDU IDs keeps track of its own sequence number and can contain packets only from certain App IDs. Errors are again displayed in latching red, yellow, or green indicators.

The fourth step (Fig. 12.8, number 2) is to partition each VCDU into packets, temporarily storing any partial packet at the end and recombining any remnant packet at the beginning with its previously stored partial. The analyzer displays the sequence of packets within the four VCDUs contained in each frame in two different ways. First, a series of vertical text windows identifies information in each packet with three red/green error indicators below them. The top line of the text window displays the VCDU ID number followed by a letter signifying the position of the VCDU within the frame. Lowercase letters (a, b, c, or d) are used for partial packets at the end of a VCDU and uppercase letters (A, B, C, or D) are used for complete packets and for remnant packets at the beginning of VCDUs that have been combined with their previously stored partials.

The three error indicators below each packet text window are turned off (shown in gray) for the partial packets at the end of each VCDU because errors are not processed until the partial is combined with its remnant. The second line of the text window displays the App ID mnemonic and number. Further down the text window is the packet size, which includes only those bytes within the current VCDU. The sum of the packet sizes for all the packets (including remnants and partials) within each VCDU will equal 442.

The second way the packets within the four VCDUs in each frame are displayed is in a scrollable strip chart (Fig. 12.8, number 3). The frames are delineated with marks at the top and bottom of the strip chart. The VCDUs are delineated with vertical gridlines, separating the frame into four parts. The first part (on the left) corresponds to the VCDU with the letter *A*, the next one *B*, then *C*, and finally *D* on the right. The VCDU numbers are indicated by the colors of the stripes labeled *VCDU ID* on the strip chart. White, for example, corresponds to VCDU ID 0. The instrument subsystems are listed on the strip chart. The positions of the striped segments making up the lower two-thirds of the strip chart indicate the App ID mnemonics within each VCDU. Their colors indicate the App ID numbers and their lengths indicate their sizes. The errors are indicated by red stripes at the top of the strip chart. This strip chart is a compact and intuitive way of displaying a large amount of diffuse and diverse data.

The fifth step is to display the packet header information in the text window (Fig. 12.8, number 2). The current and previous sequence numbers are displayed and the corresponding error indicator below the text window turns red if the packet is not in sequence. Some App ID types allow for a format ID of 4 or 8 bits that is used to interpret the data. These bits are displayed on the format (*FMT ID*) line as one or two hex nibbles. The time of the packet (in spacecraft clock units) can be optionally included in the header. A *Time Included* bit in the header signifies whenever this happens. The actual number of bits of time varies depending on the App ID; it is between 20 and 32 bits and is displayed as five to eight hex nibbles if present. When there are less than 32 bits, the more significant bits are discarded.

The sixth step is to analyze the packet data. The size is displayed on the *Data Size* line in the text window (Fig. 12.8, number 2). Each App ID has associated with it a file containing the predicted telemetry bytes, called its Predict Table. When each packet is received (including a remnant attached to a partial), it is searched for in its predict table. If it is found, its location is indicated in the text window at the *Predict Table* (*Prdt Tbl*) *Pointer* and the next expected location is saved in memory. The next time the same App ID occurs, if the data in the packet is not found at the expected location, the *Table Seq Error* indicator will show red. If the data cannot be found in its predict table, the *Not-In-Table Error* indicator shows red. The three error indicators below each packet text window are not latched; that is, they always show status for the current frame.

The seventh step is to update the small latched error indicators in the *Packet Error Status Panel* (Fig. 12.8, number 4). Each App ID has a set of three indicators corresponding to the three indicators below the packet text windows. The one on the left is *Seq Error*, the center one is *Table Seq Error*, and the one at right is *Not-In-Table Error*. Any new errors during the current frame appear as red and change to yellow on subsequent frames. The operator can clear any of these indicators by clicking on them individually or all of them at once by clicking the *Reset Errors* button.

The eighth step is to update the large text window (Fig. 12.8, number 5) that provides details on the errors. In addition to the information included in other places on the panel, offending packets are dumped so that post analysis can be performed. This text window can also be written to a file by turning on the *Log Status* switch.

The last step involves controlling other diagnostic windows under control of the operator, including packet windows that display all the data for a particular App ID, VCDU windows that display all the data for a particular VCDU type, a frame window that displays the entire unprocessed frame, and a statistics window that displays the current sequence number, the current format ID, and the latest included time for each App ID.

To give you a sense of scale, the total number of controls and indicators on the front panel is 475, it has 100 subVIs, and it requires 7 MB of disk space as implemented in LabVIEW 2. The diagram is shown in Fig. 12.9. Again, it is quite large, an often unavoidable fact of life with complex user interface applications.

Galileo Tape Recorder Anomaly

As part of the analysis of the sticking tape recorder, a data acquisition and postprocessor system using a Macintosh and LabVIEW was connected to a duplicate of the Galileo flight tape recorder at JPL using a test box sup-

Figure 12.9
Diagram for the telemetry analyzer main VI. It's large and quite complex, as is often the case in applications of this scale.

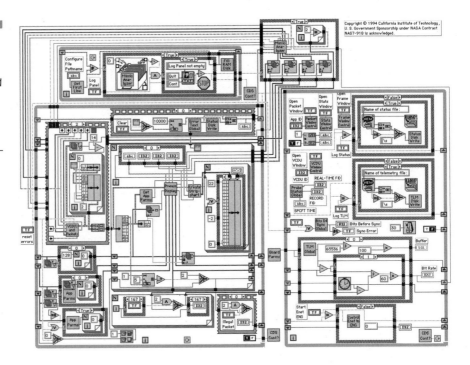

Copyright © 1994 California Institute of Technology, U. S. Government Sponsorship under NASA Contract NAS7-918 is acknowledged.

plied by the tape recorder manufacturer. The tape recorder is a sealed unit with electrical interfaces. The tester box has knobs, buttons, and test jacks and is used to exercise and monitor the tape recorder's performance. Two of the test signals were connected to a National Instruments NB-MIO-16X board and sampled at 2500 scans per second for several hours at a time.

The first channel is a signal that signifies when the tape recorder servo is *in lock* (9 V) or *out of lock* (0 V). The second channel is related to the amplitude of the signal on the read head and can have five discrete levels between 0 and 5 V at 1.25-V intervals. Five volts represents full strength and the lower levels represent varying degrees of dropout caused by the contaminants on the tape.

The purpose of the tests was to learn whether driving the tape over the contaminants degrades it. To reduce the amount of data saved to disk, only changes that exceed a specified threshold, along with relative time, are logged. The postprocessing program counts the accumulation of dropouts at each of the four signal levels below full strength on each pass of the tape. What is innovative about using LabVIEW for this application is the ease with which data can be analyzed in real time to save only the significant events to disk. This reduces the data-to-disk storage by 3 or 4 orders of magnitude.

Figure 12.10 shows the front panel of the logger program before it is run. The user would typically set the threshold for channel 0 (the in-lock signal) to 1 V since it swings between 0 and 9 V. The threshold on channel 1 (the read head amplitude) is set to 0.2 V because the intervals are just over 1 V. These thresholds are not critical, as long as they are greater than the noise level and less than half of the intervals. The user is prompted for

Figure 12.10
Tape recorder logger panel.

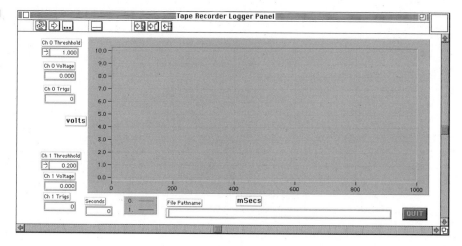

a file name when the VI is run and it immediately starts logging. The user then starts the tape recorder and returns hours later after the end of tape has been reached. The graph shows the two channels of data in the normal voltage-versus-time display.

Figure 12.11 shows the postprocessor program that reads the data file created by the logger. It allows the user to discard data points at the beginning and end outside the range within which the tape recorder was in lock. The top graph shows the two channels, again as a normal voltage-versus-time (in seconds) display. Points were discarded at the start and the end. The next graph counts the in-lock events and shows the tape recorder going in lock at about 90 s and remaining there throughout the test. A digital display to the right of the graph indicates that there was one event of this type (called Event 0).

The bottom five graphs are similar in that they show a count of events versus time but are all related to channel 1 (read head signal strength). Every time this channel drops below 5 V (as indicated by the circles on the top graph), an event of type 1 through 4 is counted, along with total

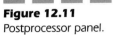

Figure 12.11
Postprocessor panel.

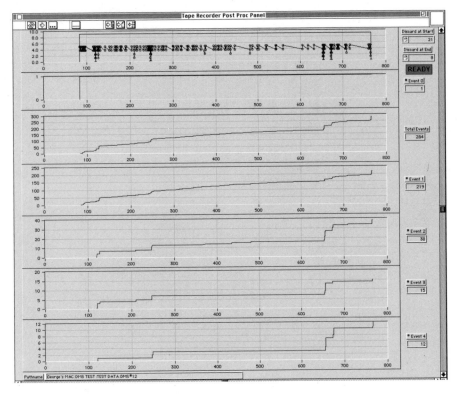

events. These are displayed as a function of time on one of the four bottom graphs along with the total events graph.

Most data analysis software shows a time or frequency domain display, but LabVIEW made it easy to customize the display to provide a unique display and give the customer exactly what was wanted.

Another task involved analyzing telemetry data from the spacecraft tape recorder power supply current as the tape was moved from one end to the other. This data required a great deal of processing because it used a generic memory dump mode. Figure 12.12 shows the current slowly increasing as more torque was required to pull the tape from one reel to the other. The data were collected in 17 blocks of 165 samples, and FFTs were performed on each block and displayed in a waterfall plot and averaged on the bottom plot. Two peak frequencies are clearly discernible and correspond to similar frequencies measured on the duplicate tape recorder on the ground.

The team at JPL has agreed on the best approach to operate the tape recorder. They determined that the tape sticking is simply a problem that will occur when the tape recorder is stopped. They also believe they can always unstick the tape and that there is no danger of the tape breaking.

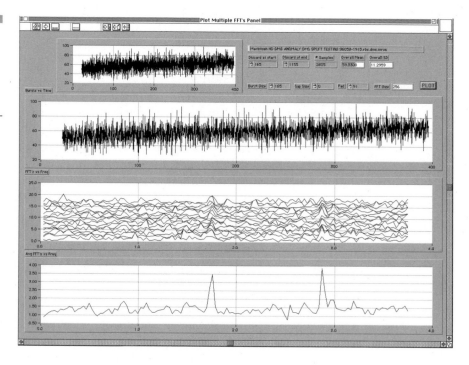

Figure 12.12
Analysis of spacecraft tape recorder data. This panel actually occupies a 19-inch screen.

Furthermore, the data provided by the LabVIEW-based data acquisition system shows that the tape is not degraded by continued use. The tape recorder will be used for encounters and the anomaly is not expected to degrade any of the scientific objectives of the mission.

Conclusions from the Galileo Task

A commercial visual programming language—LabVIEW—using a Macintosh computer was able to perform a series of tasks for the Galileo space mission. This included the capability to simulate, test, and display a telemetry stream. It provided easy visibility into the decommutation process modified by the Galileo programming support team. The time needed to write and modify the code using visual programming was significantly less than that required using text-based development in C.

This task showed that it is possible to use visual programming for realistic and relatively complicated programming applications. It demonstrated a dramatic increase in productivity and reduction in schedule. The end user believes that no other programming approach could produce this level of output.

Other advantages demonstrated were in the areas of prototyping and verification. Different approaches can be demonstrated and evaluated quickly using a visual programming language. Verification can be demonstrated more easily using the graphical user interface features available in a visual programming language than using conventional text-based code.

As stated, the gains in productivity are attributed to communication between the customer, developer, and computer facilitated by the visual syntax of the language. The advantages LabVIEW provides include the ease with which the customer can communicate requirements to the programmers and understand the operation of the program so that changes can be suggested. With this communication, the boundaries between requirements, design, development, and test appear to collapse.

One final note: Even with a successful reprogramming effort to compensate for the failure of the high-gain antenna to open properly, the effort to open the antenna has not stopped. To that end, tests to exercise the antenna ribs are being conducted on the flight spare antenna at JPL to determine what exactly caused the ribs to stick. Two hardware limit switches were placed on the antenna, but, as an additional backup, another software timeout limit was written, simply because it was easy to do in LabVIEW. When the first limit switch failed (mechanically), it failed in such a way as to cause the second limit switch to fail. The LabVIEW time-out limit did not fail and kept the antenna from serious damage.

LabVIEW as Flight Software

Existing flight software is expensive and the current NASA environment requires lower cost and a shorter development cycle. Graphical programming, such as LabVIEW, has been demonstrated to reduce software development time and overall cost of system integration for ground-based systems. LabVIEW software is used by NASA Principal Investigators (PIs) in ground-based studies in preparation for future flight experiments. The natural question is: Why not use LabVIEW as flight software? The current answer is that it does not run on flight-based processors and real-time operating systems.

If LabVIEW did run on embedded flight processors, it would allow a seamless transfer of ground to flight software in that the same software developed for ground-based algorithms could be directly applied to the flight software. It would not replace the efforts of flight software developers. In fact, it does the opposite: It gives these developers a highly productive class of tools (graphical programming) that previously have been limited to ground-based applications.

Other advantages would include enhanced communication between algorithm developers (scientists and Principal Investigators) and flight software developers, productivity improvements (4 to 10 times), real-time requirements discovery, decreased development and maintenance efforts, fast prototyping for user interface, and the use of a "standard" laboratory language.

Concerns include precise hardware control, which includes timing (submillisecond control), CPU register access, and so forth, as well as interface issues: command and telemetry (remote operation) versus monitor and keyboard/mouse operation. Other issues include choice of platform, hardware drivers, and operating system support, plus issues of fault protection, that is, how to achieve maximum performance with expected parts failures. Finally, issues such as autonomy need to be considered as well, as newer missions with restricted communications opportunities will require smarter decisions about the data being taken.

National Instruments has teamed with JPL to develop a version of Lab-VIEW for flight software. This would be useful in a wide variety of NASA missions, military missions, and industrial automation applications. The main objective of this task will be to develop a version of LabVIEW software compatible with a Lockheed Martin RAD 6000 flight processor. This task will be accomplished by combining the flight software capability at JPL with the graphical programming development expertise at National Instruments. The goal of this collaborative effort is to develop and test a real-time, multithreaded version of LabVIEW ported to a RAD 6000 real-time flight processor within a year of this writing.

The new flight version will initially be evaluated for use in Low Temperature Microgravity Physics Facility (LTMPF) experiments on the International Space Station (ISS) in 2003. LabVIEW software is now being used for data acquisition and analysis in ground-based studies on Dr. Martin Barmatz's Microgravity Scaling Theory Experiment (MISTE) flight definition experiment. The JPL MISTE low-temperature laboratory will be used to evaluate the initial LabVIEW flight versions. The success of this could lead to important follow-on activities for LabVIEW applications in a large number of NASA flight projects.

Bibliography

G. Wells and E. C. Baroth, "Telemetry Monitoring and Display using Lab-VIEW," *Proceedings of National Instruments User Symposium*, Austin, TX, March 28–30, 1993.

G. Wells and E. C. Baroth, "Use of a Commercial Visual Programming Language to Simulate, Decommutate, Test and Display a Telemetry Stream," *Proceedings of the International Telemetering Conference*, San Diego, CA, October 1994.

G. Wells and E. C. Baroth, "Using Visual Programming to Simulate, Test, and Display a Telemetry Stream," *MacSciTech's SEAM '95 Conference*, San Francisco, CA, January 8–9, 1995.

G. Wells, E. C. Baroth, and G. Levanas, "LabVIEW Saves Galileo Data—Again, or, Using LabVIEW to Diagnose the Galileo Tape Recorder Anomaly," *Proceedings of National Instruments User Symposium*, Austin, TX, August 6–8, 1996.

13

Software Engineering Primer*

Gregg Fowler
National Instruments

Software engineering is the field of study related to defining the best processes for developing software, and the main goal of this chapter is to help LabVIEW users apply these techniques to G code development. Most of the techniques developed in software engineering apply to graphical programming languages just as well as they apply to textual programming languages.

Some people think that you have to be a formally trained computer scientist to apply the principles of this field. On the contrary, software engineering is based on common sense that anyone can understand, and you can (and should) take a *graded approach* to its application. For instance, an extensive design and testing process is desirable when your software controls a potentially hazardous system, whereas for a quick benchtop test program, you need not bother.

This chapter works in conjunction with Chap. 14, "LabVIEW Software Quality Assurance Guide and Toolkit," which describes another fundamental aspect of software engineering: **quality management**. You should also consider acquiring a copy of the *Professional G Developers Toolkit* from National Instruments; it contains many useful development tools and recommendations for large projects. This chapter was derived from the manual included with that toolkit.

Development Models

G, the graphical programming language of LabVIEW and BridgeVIEW, makes it easy to assemble components of data acquisition, test, and control systems. Because it is so easy to program in G, you might be tempted to begin developing VIs immediately with relatively little planning. For very simple applications, such as quick lab tests or monitoring applications, this approach might be appropriate. However, for larger development projects, good planning becomes vital.

Common Development Pitfalls

If you have developed large applications before, you probably have heard some of the following quotes. Most of these approaches start out with good intentions and seem quite reasonable. However, these approaches are often unrealistic and can lead to delays, quality problems, and poor morale among team members.

"I haven't really thought it through, but I'd guess that the project you are requesting can be completed in . . ."

Off-the-cuff estimates are rarely correct, because they are usually based on an incomplete understanding of the problem. When you are developing for someone else, you might each have different ideas about requirements. To estimate accurately, you and your customer must clearly understand the requirements and work through at least a preliminary high-level design so you understand the components you need to develop. Techniques for estimation are described in more detail later in this chapter, under the heading *Scheduling and Project Tracking*.

"I think I understand the problem the customer wants to solve, so I'm ready to dive into development."

There are two problems with a statement like this. First, lack of consensus on project goals results in schedule delays. Your idea of what a customer wants might be based on inadequate communication. Developing a requirements document and prototyping a system, both described later, can be useful tools to clarify goals. A second problem with this statement is that diving into development might mean writing code without a detailed design. Just as builders do not construct a building without architectural plans, developers should not begin building an application without a detailed design. See the *Code and Fix Model* section later in this chapter for more information.

"We don't have time to write detailed plans—we're under a tight schedule, so we need to start developing right away."

This situation is similar to the previous example but is such a common mistake that it is worth emphasizing. Software developers frequently skip important planning because it does not seem as productive as developing code. As a result, you develop VIs without a clear idea of how they all fit together, and you might have to rework sections as you discover mistakes. Taking the time to develop a plan can prevent costly rework at the development stage. See the *Life Cycle Models* and *Prototyping and Design Techniques* sections for better approaches to developing software.

"Let's try for the whole ball of wax on the first release—if it doesn't do everything, it won't be useful."

In some cases, this might be correct. However, in most applications, developing in stages is a better approach. When analyzing the requirements for a project, you should prioritize features. You might be able to develop an initial system that provides useful functionality in a shorter time at a lower cost. Then, you can add features incrementally. The more you try to accomplish in a single stage, the greater the risk of falling behind schedule. Releasing software incrementally reduces schedule pressures and ensures timely software release.

> **"If I can just get all of the features in within the next month, I should be able to fix any problems before the software is released."**

To release high-quality products on time, maintain quality standards throughout development. Do not build new features on an unstable foundation and rely on correcting problems later. This exacerbates problems and increases cost. While you might complete all of the features on time, the time required to correct the problems in both the existing and new code can delay the release of the product. You should prioritize features and implement the most important ones first. Once the most important features are tested thoroughly, you can choose to work on lower-priority features or defer them to a future release. See Chap. 14, "LabVIEW Software Quality Assurance Guide and Toolkit," for more details on techniques for producing high-quality software.

> **"We're behind in our project—let's throw more developers onto the problem."**

In many cases, doing this can actually delay your project. Adding developers to a project requires time for training, which can take away time originally scheduled for development. Add resources earlier in the project rather than later. Also, there is a limit to the number of people who can work on a project effectively. With a few people, there is less overlap—you partition the project so each person works on a particular section. The more people you add, the more difficult it becomes to avoid overlap.

> **"We're behind in our project, but we still think we can get all the features in by the specified date."**

When you are behind in a project, it is important to recognize that fact and deal with it. Assuming that you can make up lost time can defer choices until it becomes costly to deal with them. For example, if you realize in the first month of a six-month project that you are behind, you could sacrifice planned features or add time to the overall schedule. If, in the fifth month, you find the schedule slipping, other groups might have made decisions that are costly to change.

When you realize you are behind, consider features that can be dropped or postponed to subsequent releases, or adjust the schedule. Do not ignore the delay or sacrifice testing scheduled for later in the process. Estimating project schedules is described in more detail in the *Scheduling and Project Tracking* section.

Numerous other problems can arise when developing software. The following list includes some of the fundamental elements of developing quality software on time:

- Spend sufficient time planning.
- Make sure the whole team thoroughly understands the problems that must be solved.
- Have a flexible development strategy that minimizes risk and accommodates changes.

Life Cycle Models

Software development projects are complex. To deal with these complexities, developers have collected a core set of development principles. These principles define the field of software engineering. A major component of this field is the **life cycle model**. The life cycle model describes the steps you follow to develop software—from the initial concept stage through coding, to the release, maintenance, and subsequent upgrading of the software.

Currently there are many different life cycle models. Each has its own advantages and disadvantages in terms of time to release, quality, and risk management. This section describes some of the most common models used in software engineering. Many hybrids of these models exist, so use the parts you believe will work for your project.

While this section is theoretical in its discussion, in practice you should consider all of the steps these models encompass. You should consider when and how you decide that the requirements and specifications are complete and how you handle changes to them. The life cycle model serves as a foundation for the entire development process. Good choices in this area can improve the quality of the software you develop and decrease the time it takes to develop it.

CODE AND FIX MODEL The **code and fix** model is probably the most frequently used development methodology in software engineering. It starts with little or no initial planning. You immediately start developing, fixing problems as you find them, until the project is complete. Code and fix is a tempting choice when you are faced with a tight development schedule, because you begin developing code right away and see immediate results.

Unfortunately, if you find major architectural problems late in the process, you might have to rewrite large parts of your application. Alternative development models can help you catch these problems in the early concept stages, when it is much less expensive to make changes. Accommodating changes is easier in the requirements and specifications stage of a project than it is after you have written a lot of code.

The code and fix model is only appropriate for small projects that are not intended to serve as the basis for future development.

WATERFALL MODEL   The **waterfall** model is the classic model of software engineering. It has deficiencies, but it serves as a baseline for many other life cycle models.

The pure waterfall life cycle consists of several nonoverlapping stages, which are listed next. It begins with the software concept and continues through requirements analysis, architectural design, detailed design, coding, testing, and maintenance. Figure 13.1 illustrates the stages of the waterfall life cycle model.

- *System requirements*—Establishes the components for building the system. This includes the hardware requirements (number of channels, acquisition speed, and so on), software tools, and other necessary components.

- *Software requirements*—Concentrates on the expectations for software functionality. You identify which of the system requirements are affected by the software. Requirements analysis might include determining interaction needed with other applications and databases, performance requirements, user interface requirements, and so on.

- *Architectural design*—Determines the software framework of a system to meet the specified requirements. The design defines the major components and their interaction, but it does not define the structure of each component. In addition to the software framework, in the architectural design phase you determine the external interfaces and tools that will be used in the project. Examples include decisions on hardware, such as plug-in boards, and external pieces of software, such as databases or other libraries.

- *Detailed design*—Examines the software components defined in the architectural design stage and produces a specification for how each component is implemented. **Computer-aided software engineer-**

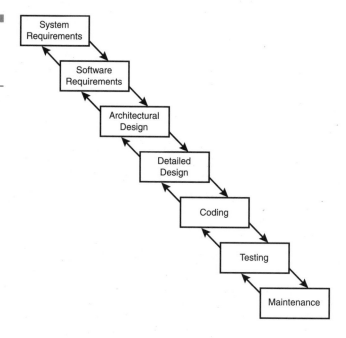

Figure 13.1
The waterfall model
of software
engineering.

ing (CASE) tools may have particular value at this stage to assist you in the design process.

- *Coding*—Implements the detailed design specification.

- *Testing*—Determines whether the software meets the specified requirements and finds any errors present in the code.

- *Maintenance*—Performed as needed to address problems and enhancement requests after the software is released. In some organizations, each change is reviewed by a change control board to ensure that quality is maintained. You can also apply the full waterfall development cycle model when you implement these change requests.

In each stage, you create documents that explain your objectives and describe the requirements for that phase. At the end of each stage, you hold a review to determine whether the project can proceed to the next stage. Also, you can incorporate prototyping into any stage from the architectural design on. See the *Prototyping* section later in this chapter for more information.

The waterfall life cycle model is one of the oldest models and is widely used in government projects and in many major companies. Because it emphasizes planning in the early stages, it helps catch design flaws before they are implemented. Also, because it is very document- and planning-intensive, it works well for projects in which quality control is a major concern.

Many people believe you should not apply this model to all situations. For example, with the pure waterfall model you must state the requirements before beginning the design, and you must state the complete design before you begin coding. That is, there is no overlap between stages. In real-world development, however, you might discover issues during the design or coding stages that point out errors or gaps in the requirements.

The waterfall method does not prohibit returning to an earlier phase (for example, from the design phase to the requirements phase). However, this involves costly rework—each completed phase requires formal review and extensive documentation development. Thus, oversights made in the requirements phase are expensive to correct later.

Because the actual coding comes late in the process, you do not see results for a long time. This can be disconcerting to management and customers. Many people also find the amount of documentation excessive and inflexible.

While the waterfall model has its weaknesses, it is instructive because it emphasizes important stages of project development. Even if you do not apply this model, you should at least consider each of these stages and its relationship to your own project.

MODIFIED WATERFALL MODEL   Many engineers recommend modified versions of the waterfall life cycle. These modifications tend to focus on allowing some of the stages to overlap, reducing the documentation requirements, and reducing the cost of returning to earlier stages to revise them. Another common modification is to incorporate prototyping into the requirements phases, as described in the next section. These compromises represent a means by which you can take a graded approach to software engineering—a simpler process for simpler projects.

Overlapping stages such as requirements and design make it possible to feed information from the design phase back into the requirements. However, this can make it more difficult to know when you are finished with a given stage, and, consequently, it is more difficult to track progress. Without distinct stages, problems might cause you to defer important decisions until late in the process when they are more expensive to correct.

PROTOTYPING   One of the main problems with the waterfall model is that the requirements are often not completely understood in the early development stages. When you reach the design or coding stages, you begin to see how everything works together, and you might discover that you need to adjust requirements.

Prototyping can be an effective tool for demonstrating how a design might address a set of requirements. You can build a prototype, then adjust the requirements and revise the prototype several times until you have a clear picture of your overall objectives. In addition to clarifying the requirements, the prototype also defines many areas of the design simultaneously.

The pure waterfall model does allow for prototyping in the later architectural design stage and subsequent stages, but not in the early requirements stages.

There are drawbacks to prototyping. First, because it appears that you have a working system very quickly, customers might expect a complete system sooner than is possible. In most cases, the prototype is built on compromises that allow it to come together quickly but that could prevent the prototype from being an effective basis for future development. You need to decide early on whether you will use the prototype as a basis for future development. All parties should agree with this decision before development begins.

You should be careful that prototyping does not become a disguise for a code and fix development cycle. Before you begin prototyping, you should gather clear requirements and create a design plan. Limit the amount of time you will spend prototyping before you begin. This helps to avoid overdoing the prototyping phase. As you incorporate changes, you should update the requirements and the current design. After you finish prototyping, you might consider falling back to one of the other development models. For example, you might consider prototyping as part of the requirements or design phases of the waterfall model.

G PROTOTYPING METHODS   There are a number of ways to prototype a G-based system.

In systems with I/O requirements that might be difficult to satisfy, you can develop a prototype to test the control and acquisition loops and rates. For example, you can test DAQ concepts with a VI adapted from the LabVIEW examples. You'll quickly come to understand the real-world performance of complete systems—hardware, computer, driver software, and application software—as compared to specifications in a catalog and avoid promising more performance than is feasible.

Systems with complex user interface requirements are perfect for prototyping. Determining the method you will use to display data or prompt the user for settings can be difficult on paper. Instead, consider designing VI front panels with the controls and indicators you need. You might leave the block diagram empty and just talk through the way the controls would work and how various actions would lead to other front panels. For more extensive prototypes, you could even tie the front panels together; however, be careful not to get too carried away with this process. In I/O prototypes, random data can simulate data acquired in the real system.

If you are bidding on a project for a client, this can be an extremely effective way to discuss with the client how you might be able to satisfy his or her requirements. Because you can add and remove controls quickly (especially if you avoid developing block diagrams), you can help customers clarify their requirements. As described in Chap. 1, "LabVIEW Enables the Interactive Communication Process," this type of live, interactive session with your customer can be highly productive.

SPIRAL MODEL   The **spiral** model (Fig. 13.2) is a popular alternative to the waterfall model. It emphasizes *risk management* so you find major problems earlier in the development cycle. In the waterfall model, you have to complete the design before you begin coding. With the spiral model, you break up the project into a set of risks that need to be handled. You then begin a series of iterations in which you analyze the most important risk, evaluate options for resolving the risk, address the risk, assess the results, and plan for the next iteration.

Risks are any issues that are not clearly defined or that have the potential to affect the project adversely. For each risk, you need to consider two things: how likely it is, and how bad it is for it to occur. You might use a scale of 1 to 10 for each of these, with 1 being unlikely to occur and not bad if it occurs, and 10 being extremely likely to occur and catastrophic

Figure 13.2
The spiral model for software development.

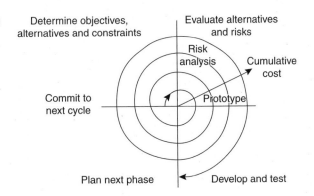

to the project if it occurs. Your risk exposure is the product of these. You can use a table to keep track of the top risk items of your project. See Table 13.1 for an example of how to do this.

In general, you should address the risks with the highest risk exposure first. In this example, the first spiral should address the potential for the data acquisition rates to be too high to handle. After the first spiral, you may have demonstrated that the rates are not too high, or you might have to change to a different configuration of hardware to meet the acquisition requirements. Each iteration might identify new risks. In this example, using more powerful hardware might make high cost a new, more likely, risk.

For example, assume that you are designing a data acquisition system with a plug-in data acquisition card. In this case, the risk is whether the system can acquire, analyze, and display data quickly enough. Some of the constraints in this case are requirements for a specific sampling rate, precision, and system cost.

After determining the options and constraints, you evaluate the risks. In this example, you could create a prototype or benchmark to test acquisition rates. After you see the results, you can evaluate whether to continue with the approach or choose a different option. You do this by reassessing the risks based on the new knowledge you have gained from building the prototype.

In the final phase, you evaluate the results with the customer. Based on customer input, you can reassess the situation, decide on the next highest risk, and start the cycle over. This process continues until the software is finished or you decide the risks are too great and terminate development. You might find that none of the options is viable because each is too expensive or time-consuming or does not meet the requirements.

TABLE 13.1

Risk Exposure
Analysis Example

ID	Risk	Probability	Loss	Risk Exposure	Risk Management Approach
1	Acquisition rates too high	5	9	45	Develop prototype to demonstrate feasibility
2	File format may not be efficient	5	3	15	Develop benchmarks to show speed of data manipulation
3	Uncertain user interface	2	5	10	Involve customer, develop prototype

The advantage of the spiral model over the waterfall model is that you can evaluate which risks to address with each cycle. Because you can evaluate risks with prototypes much earlier than in the waterfall process, you can address major obstacles and select alternatives in the earlier stages, which is less expensive. With a standard waterfall model, you might have allowed assumptions about the risky components to spread throughout your design, requiring much more expensive rework when the problems were later discovered.

Life cycle models are typically described as distinct choices from which you must select one. In practice, however, you can apply more than one model to a single project. You might start a project with a spiral model to help refine the requirements and specification over several iterations using prototyping. Once you have reduced the risk of a poorly stated set of requirements, you might apply a waterfall life cycle model to the design, coding, testing, and maintenance stages.

There are other life cycle models not presented here. If you are interested in exploring other development methodologies, refer to the references at the end of this chapter.

Prototyping and Design Techniques

This section gives you pointers for project design, including programming approaches, prototyping, and benchmarking.

When you first begin a programming project, deciding how to start can be intimidating. A lot of G programmers start immediately with a code and fix development process, building up some of the VIs they think they will need. Then they realize that they actually need something different from what they have built already. Consequently, a lot of code is developed and then reworked, or thrown away unnecessarily.

Clearly Define the Requirements of Your Application

Before developing a detailed design of your system, you should define your goals as clearly as possible. Begin by making a list of requirements. Some requirements are very specific, such as the types of I/O, sampling rates, or the need for real-time analysis. You need to do some research at this early stage to be sure you can meet the specifications. Other requirements depend on user preference (graph styles, for instance) or on compatibility with other applications (for example, file formats).

Try to distinguish between absolute requirements and desires. You *might* be able to satisfy all requests, but it is best to have an idea about what you can sacrifice if you run out of time. Prioritize features in consultation with your customer.

Also, be careful that the requirements are not so detailed that they constrain the design. For example, in designing an I/O system the customer probably has certain sampling rate and precision requirements. He or she is also constrained by cost. Those issues should be included in your requirements. However, if you can avoid specifying the operating system and hardware, you can adjust your design after you begin prototyping and benchmarking various components. As long as the costs are within budget, and the timing and precision issues are met, the customer might not care whether the system uses a particular type of plug-in card or other hardware.

Another example of overly constraining a design is being too specific about the format for display used in various screens with which the customer interacts. A picture of a display might be useful to explain requirements, but be clear about whether the picture is a requirement or a guideline. Some designers go through significant contortions trying to produce a system that behaves in a specific way because a certain behavior was a requirement. In this case, there might be a simpler solution that produces the same results at a much lower cost in a shorter time.

For additional information on developing formal requirements and specifications, see Chap. 14, "LabVIEW Software Quality Assurance Guide and Toolkit."

Top-Down Design

The block diagram programming metaphor used in G was designed to be easy to understand. Most engineers already use block diagrams to describe systems. The goal of the block diagram is to make it easier for you to move from the conceptual system block diagrams you create to executable code.

The basic concept is to divide the task into manageable pieces at logical places. Begin with a high-level block diagram that describes the main components of your system. For example, you might have a block diagram that consists of a block for configuration, a block for acquisition, a block for analysis of the acquired data, a block for saving the data to disk, and a block to clean up at the end of the system.

The choice of an optimum overall architecture for your application can save you time by making the program easier to write, easier to understand, easier to debug, and perhaps easier to upgrade later on. The fundamentals of LabVIEW architectures are discussed in Chap. 4, "Building an Application," in the book *LabVIEW Graphical Programming*.

After you have determined the high-level blocks, create a block diagram that uses those blocks. For each block, create a new *stub VI* (a nonfunctional prototype representing a future subVI). Create an icon for this stub VI and create a front panel with the necessary inputs and outputs. You do not have to create a block diagram for this VI yet. Instead, define the interface and see if this stub VI is a useful part of your top-level block diagram.

After you assemble a group of these stub VIs, determine the function of each block and how it works. Ask yourself whether any given block generates information that some subsequent VI needs. If so, make sure that your top-level block diagram sketch contains wires to pass the data between the VIs. You can document the functionality of the VI by using the **VI Info** dialog from the *Window* menu, and you can document controls and indicators by using the pop-up **Data Operations**>> **Description** tool in LabVIEW and BridgeVIEW. At a minimum, describe the task that the VI performs and how it fits into the overall hierarchy.

In analyzing the transfer of data from one block to another, try to avoid global variables, because they hide the data dependency between VIs and might introduce race conditions. See the "Performance Issues" chapter in the *LabVIEW User Manual* for more information. As your system becomes larger, it becomes difficult to debug if you use global variables as your method of transferring information between VIs.

Continue to refine your design by breaking down each of the component blocks into more detailed outlines. You can do this by going to the block diagram of what was once a stub VI and filling it out, inserting lower-level stub VIs that represent each of the major actions the VI must perform.

Be careful not to jump too quickly into implementing the system at this point. One of the objectives here is to gradually refine your design so you can determine whether you have left out any necessary components at higher levels. For example, when refining the acquisition phase, you might realize that you need more information from the configuration phase. If you completely implement one block before you analyze a subsequent block, you might need to redesign the first block significantly. It is better to try to refine the system gradually on several fronts, with particular attention to sections that have more risk because of their complexity.

Bottom-Up Design

You should usually avoid bottom-up system design, although it is sometimes useful when used in conjunction with top-down design. Bottom-up design is the exact opposite of top-down design. You start by building the lower-level components and then progress up the hierarchy, gradually putting pieces together until you have the complete system.

Because you do not start with a clear idea of the big picture, the problem with bottom-up design is that you might build pieces that do not fit together the way you expect.

There are specific cases in which using bottom-up design is appropriate. If the design is constrained by low-level functionality, you might need to build that low-level functionality first to get an idea of how it can be used. This might be true of an instrument driver, where the command set for the instrument constrains you in terms of when you can perform certain operations. For example, with a top-down design, you might break up your design so that configuration of the instrument and reading a measurement from the instrument are done in distinct VIs. The instrument command set might turn out to be more constraining than you thought, requiring you to combine these operations. In this case, with a bottom-up strategy, you might start by building VIs that deal with the instrument command set.

In most cases, you should use a top-down design strategy. You might mix in some components of bottom-up design if necessary. Thus, in the case of an instrument driver, you might use a risk minimization strategy to understand the limitations of the instrument command set and develop the lower-level components. Then use a top-down approach to develop the high-level blocks.

Designing for Multiple Developers

One of the main challenges in the planning stage is to establish discrete project areas for each developer. As you design the specification and architecture, you should begin to see areas that have a minimal amount of overlap. For example, a complicated data monitoring system might have one set of VIs that displays and manipulates data and another set that acquires the information and transfers it to disk. These two modules are substantial, do not overlap, and can be assigned to different developers.

Inevitably, there will be some interaction between the modules. One of the principal objectives of the early design work is to specify how those modules interact with each other. The data display system must access the data it needs to display. The acquisition component needs to provide this information for the other module. At an early stage in development, you might design the connector panes of VIs needed to transfer information between the two modules. Likewise, if there are global data structures that must be shared, these should be analyzed and defined early in the architectural design stage before the individual developers begin work on their components. Use control **typedefs**, created in the Control Editor, to maintain standardized data types.

In the early stages, each developer can create stub VIs with the connector pane interface that was defined for the shared module. This stub VI might do nothing, or if it is a VI that returns information, you could have it generate random data. This allows each member of the development team to continue development without having to wait for the other modules to be finished. It also makes it easy for the individuals to perform **unit testing** of their modules as described in Chap. 14, "LabVIEW Software Quality Assurance Guide and Toolkit."

As components near completion, you can integrate the modules by replacing the stub components with their real counterparts. At this point you can perform **integration testing** to verify that the system works as a whole.

Front Panel Prototyping

As mentioned previously in the section entitled *Development Models,* front panel prototypes can provide insight into the organization of your program. Assuming your program is user interface intensive, you can attempt to mock up an interface that represents what the user sees.

Avoid implementing block diagrams in the early stages of creating prototypes so you do not fall into the code and fix trap. Instead, create just the front panels, and as you create buttons, list boxes, and rings, think about what should happen as the user makes selections, asking questions such as the following.

- Should the button lead to another front panel?
- Should some controls on the front panel be hidden and replaced by others?

If new options are presented, follow those ideas by creating new front panels to illustrate the results. This kind of prototyping can help solidify the requirements for a project and give you a better idea of its scope.

Prototyping cannot solve all development problems, however. You have to be careful how you present the prototype to customers. Prototypes can give an overly inflated sense that you are rapidly making progress on the project. You have to make it clear to the customer, whether an external customer or other members of your company, that this prototype is strictly for design purposes and that much of it will be reworked in the coding phase.

Another danger in prototyping is that you might overdo it. Consider setting strict time goals for the amount of time you will prototype a system to prevent yourself from falling into the code and fix trap.

Of course, front panel prototyping only deals with user interface components. As described here, it does not deal with I/O constraints, data types, or algorithm issues in your design. Quantifying the front panel issues might help you to better define some of these areas, because it gives you an idea of some of the major data structures you need to maintain; however, it does not address all of these issues. For those, you need to use one of the other methods described in this chapter.

Performance Benchmarking

For I/O systems with a number of data points or high transfer rate requirements, test the performance-related components early, because the test might prove that your design assumptions are incorrect.

For example, if you plan to use an instrument as your data acquisition system, you might want to build some simple tests that perform the type of I/O you plan to use. While the manufacturer's specifications might seem to indicate that the instrument can handle the application you are creating, you might find that triggering, for example, takes longer than you expected, or that switching between channels with different gains cannot be done at the necessary rate without reducing the accuracy of the sampling. Or perhaps, even though the instrument can handle the rates, you do not have enough time on the software side to perform the desired analysis.

A simple prototype of the time-critical sections of your application can help to reveal this kind of problem. The **Timing Template** example VI in the examples/general/timing directory illustrates how to time a process. Because timings can fluctuate from one run to another for a variety of reasons (the initial run might take longer because it allocates buffers; system interrupts, screen updates, and user interaction can also cause it to take longer in some cases), you should put the operation in a loop and display the average execution time. You can also use a graph to display timing fluctuations.

Identify Common Operations

As you design your programs, you might find that certain operations are performed frequently. Depending on the situation, this might be a good place to use subVIs or loops to repeat an action.

For example, consider Fig. 13.3, where three similar operations run independently. This might be a good way to write your code in that the three operations may be able to execute in parallel, depending on the task performed by the subVI. On the other hand, the duplication of nodes on the diagram adds visual confusion and may add to the size of the diagram and compiled code.

An alternative to this design is a loop that performs the operation three times (Fig. 13.4). You can build an array of the different arguments and use autoindexing on the border of the for loop to set the correct value for each iteration of the loop. If the array elements are constant, you can use an array constant instead of building the array on the block diagram. This approach is clear and efficient.

Some users mistakenly avoid using subVIs because they are afraid of the overhead it might add to their execution time. It is true that you probably do not want to create a subVI from a simple mathematical operation such as the Add function, especially if it must be repeated thousands of times. However, the overhead for a subVI is fairly small—on the order of microseconds—and usually it is dwarfed by any I/O you perform or by any memory management that might stem from complex manipulation of arrays.

Figure 13.3
Several instances of the same subVI on one diagram. Good or bad?

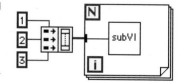

Figure 13.4
Using a loop to call a
subVI with varying
parameters.

Scheduling and Project Tracking

This section describes techniques for creating estimates of development time and using those estimates to produce schedules. Here we also distinguish between an **estimate**, which reflects the time required to implement a feature, and a **schedule**, which reflects how you fulfill that feature. Estimates are commonly expressed in ideal person-days (eight hours of work). In creating a schedule from estimates, you must consider dependencies (one project might have to be completed before another can begin) and other tasks (meetings, support for existing projects, and so on).

Project Estimation

One of the principle tasks of planning is to estimate the size of the project and fit it into the schedule. Most projects are at least partially schedule-driven. Schedule, resources, and critical requirements all interact to determine what you can implement in a particular software release.

Unfortunately, when it comes to estimating software schedules accurately, very few people are successful. Major companies have all had software projects exceed original estimates by a year or more. Poor planning or an incomplete idea of project goals often causes deadlines to be missed. Another major cause of missed schedules is known as *feature creep*—your design gradually grows to include features that were not part of the original requirements. In many cases, the slips in schedule are due to the use of a code and fix development process rather than a more measurable development model.

Off-the-cuff estimates are almost never accurate for the following reasons:

■ *People are usually overly optimistic.* An estimate of two months might seem like an infinite amount of time at first. Then, during the last two weeks of the project, when developers find themselves working many overtime hours, it becomes clear that the estimate is not sufficient.

■ *The objectives, implementation issues, and quality requirements are not understood clearly.* When challenged with the task of creating a data monitoring system, an engineer might estimate two weeks. If the product is designed *by* the engineer *for* the engineer, this estimate might be right. However, if it is for other users, the engineer is probably not considering requirements that might be assumed by a less knowledgeable user but never specified clearly. For example, VIs need to be reliable and easy to use, because the engineer is not going to be there to correct them if a problem occurs. A considerable amount of testing and documentation is necessary. Also, the user needs to save results to disk, print reports, and view and manipulate the data on screen. If he or she has not discussed or considered the project in detail, the engineer is heading for failure.

■ *Day-to-day tasks are ignored.* There are meetings to attend, holidays, reports to write, conferences to go to, existing projects to maintain, and other tasks that make up a standard work week.

Accurate estimates are difficult because of the imprecise nature of most software projects. In the initial phase of a project, complete requirements are not known, and the way you will implement those requirements is even less clear. As you clarify the objectives and implementation plans, you can make more realistic estimates. And prior, relevant experience is of course invaluable.

Some of the current best-practice estimation techniques in software engineering are described in the following sections. All require breaking the project down into more manageable components that can then be estimated individually. There are other methods of estimating development time. See the *Bibliography* section for a list of documents that describe these and other estimation techniques in more detail.

LINES OF CODE/NUMBER OF NODES ESTIMATION   Software engineering documentation frequently refers to **Lines of code** (LOC) as a measurement, or metric, of software complexity. Lines of code as a measurement of complexity is very popular, in part because the information is easy to gather. Numerous programs exist for analyzing textual languages to measure complexity. In general, LOC measurements include every line of source code developed for a project, except for comments and blank lines.

The **VI Metrics** tool, included with the Professional G Developers Toolkit, provides a method for measuring a corresponding metric for

G-based code. The VI Metrics tool lets you count the number of nodes used within a VI or within a hierarchy of VIs. A node is almost any object on a block diagram, excluding labels and graphics, but including functions, VIs, and structures such as loops and sequences.

You can use number of nodes as a method for estimating future project development efforts. For this to work, you must build up a base of knowledge about current and previous projects. You must have an idea of the amount of time it took to develop components of existing software products and associate that information with the number of nodes used in that component.

Armed with that historical information, you next need to estimate the number of nodes required for a new project. It is not possible to do this for an entire project at once. Instead, you must break the project down into subprojects that you can compare to other tasks completed in the past. Once you have broken it down, you can estimate each component and produce a total estimate of both the number of nodes and the time required for development.

PROBLEMS WITH LINES OF CODE AND NUMBERS OF NODES   Size-based metrics are not uniformly accepted in software engineering. Many people favor these metrics because they are relatively easy to gather and because a lot of literature has been written about them. Detractors of size metrics point out the following flaws:

- *Size-based metrics are organization dependent.* Lines of code/numbers of nodes can be useful within an organization as long as you are dealing with the same group of people and they are following the same style guidelines. Trying to use size metrics from other companies or groups can be very difficult because of differing levels of experience, different expectations for testing and development methodologies, and so on.

- *Size-based metrics are also dependent on programming language.* Comparing a line of code in assembly language to one written in C can be like comparing apples to oranges. Statements in higher-level languages can provide more functionality than those in lower-level languages. Comparing numbers of nodes in G to lines of code in a textual language can be inexact for this reason.

- *Not all lines of code are created with the same level of quality.* A VI that retrieves information from a user and writes it to a file can be written so efficiently that it involves a small number of nodes or it can be written poorly with a large number of nodes.

- *Not all lines of code are equal in complexity.* An Add function is much easier to use than an Index Array node. A block diagram that consists of 50 nested loops is much more difficult to understand than 50 icons connected together in a line. Consider using some of the other measurements in the VI Metrics tool to produce your own metrics. For instance, the *number of diagrams* measurement (where the top-level diagram is 1, and each frame of a structure is 1) might be used directly or with a weighting factor in a complexity formula that you develop to suit your needs.

- *Size-based metrics rely on a solid base of information associating productivity with various projects.* To be accurate, you should have statistics for each member of a team because the experience level and effectiveness of team members varies.

Despite these problems, size metrics are used widely for estimating projects. A good technique to use is to estimate a project using size metrics in conjunction with one of the other methods described later in this chapter. Different methods can serve as checks for one another. If you find differences between the two estimates, analyze the assumptions in each to determine the source of the discrepancy.

EFFORT ESTIMATION   Effort estimation is similar in many ways to number of nodes estimation. You break the project down into components that can be more easily estimated. A good rule of thumb is to break the project into tasks that take no more than a week to complete. Tasks that are more complicated are difficult to estimate accurately.

Once you have broken the project down into tasks, you can estimate the time to complete each task and add the results to calculate an overall project cost.

WIDEBAND DELPHI ESTIMATION   You can use **wideband delphi estimation** in conjunction with any of the other estimation techniques to achieve more reliable estimates. For successful wideband delphi estimation, multiple developers must contribute to the estimation process.

First, divide the project into separate tasks. Then meet with other developers to explain the list of tasks. Avoid the subject of time estimates during this early discussion.

Once you have agreed on a set of tasks, each developer separately estimates the time it will take to complete each task, using, for example, uninterrupted person-days as the unit of estimation. The developers should list any assumptions made in forming their estimates. The group then reconvenes to graph the overall estimates as a range of values. It is a good idea to have a person outside the development team lead this meeting and to keep the estimates anonymous.

After graphing the original set of values, each developer reports any assumptions made in determining the estimate. For example, one developer might have assumed a certain VI project takes advantage of existing libraries. Another might point out that a specific VI is more complicated than expected because it involves communicating with another application or a shared library. Another team member might be aware of a task that involves an extensive amount of documentation and testing.

After stating assumptions, each developer reevaluates and adjusts the estimates. The group then graphs and discusses the new estimates. This process might go on for three or four rounds.

In most cases, you will converge to a small range of values. Absolute convergence is not required. After the meeting, the developer in charge of the project can use the average of the results, or he or she might ignore certain outlying values. If some tasks turn out to be too expensive for the time allowed, the developer might consider adding resources or scaling back the project.

Even if the estimate is incorrect, the discussion in the meetings gives a clear idea of the scope of a project. The discussion serves as an exploration tool during the specification and design part of the project so you can avoid problems later.

OTHER ESTIMATION TECHNIQUES   Several other techniques exist for estimating development cost. These are described in detail in some of the documents listed in the Bibliography. The following list briefly describes some other popular techniques.

- **Function-point estimation**—Function-point estimation differs considerably from the size estimation techniques described so far. As opposed to division of the project into tasks that are estimated separately, function-point estimation is based on a formula applied to a category breakdown of the project requirements. The requirements are analyzed for features such as inputs, outputs, user inquiries, files, and external interfaces. These features are tallied and each is weighted. The results are added up to produce a number representing the complexity of the project. This number can then be compared to function-point estimates of previous projects to determine an estimate.

    Function-point estimates were designed primarily with database applications in mind, but have been applied to other software areas as well. Function-point estimation is popular as a rough estimation method because it can be used early in the development process based on requirements documents. However, the accuracy of function points as an estimation method has not been thoroughly analyzed.

- **COCOMO estimation**—Constructive Cost Model (COCOMO) is a formula-based estimation method for converting software size estimates to estimated development time. COCOMO is a set of methods that range from basic to advanced. Basic COCOMO makes a rough estimate based on a size estimate and a simple classification of the project type and experience level of a team. Advanced COCOMO takes into account reliability requirements, hardware features and constraints, programming experience in a variety of areas, and tools and methods used for developing and managing the project.

Mapping Estimates to Schedules

An estimate of the amount of effort required for a project can differ greatly from the calendar time needed to complete the project. You might accurately estimate that a VI should take only two weeks to develop. However, in implementation you must fit that development into your schedule. You might have other projects to complete first, or you might need to wait for another developer to complete his or her work before you can start the project. You might have meetings and other events during that time.

Estimate project development time separately from scheduling it into your work calendar. Consider estimating tasks in ideal person-days that correspond to eight hours of development without interruption.

After estimating project time, try to develop a schedule that accounts for overhead estimates and project dependencies. Remember that you have weekly meetings to attend, existing projects to support, reports to write, and so on.

Record your progress at meeting both time estimates and schedule estimates. Track project time and time spent on other tasks each week. This information might vary from week to week, but you should be able to come up with an average that is a useful reference for future scheduling. Recording more information helps you plan future projects accurately.

Tracking Schedules Using Milestones

Milestones are a crucial technique for gauging progress on a project. If completing the project by a specific date is important, consider setting milestones for completion.

Set up a small number of major milestones for your project, making sure that each one has very clear requirements. Because the question "Did you reach the milestone?" can only be answered "yes" or "no," an answer of "mostly" or "ninety percent of the project is complete" is meaningless! In the case of the 90 percent answer, the first 90 percent might have been completed in two months while the remaining 10 percent will require another year.

To minimize risk, set milestones to complete the most important components first. If, after a milestone is reached, the schedule has slipped and there is not enough time for another milestone, the most important components will have been completed.

Throughout development, strive to keep the quality level high. If you defer problems until a milestone is reached, you are in effect deferring risks that might delay the schedule. Delaying problems can make it seem like you are making more progress than you actually are. Also, it can create a situation where you attempt to build new development on top of a house of cards. Eventually the facade comes crumbling down, and you waste more time and resources than you would have if you had dealt with the problem in the first place.

When working toward a major milestone, set smaller goals to gauge progress. Derive minor milestones from the task list created as part of your estimation.

RESPONDING TO MISSED MILESTONES One of the biggest mistakes people make is to miss a milestone but not reevaluate the project as a consequence. After missing a milestone, many developers continue on the same schedule, assuming that they will work harder and be able to make up the time.

Instead, if you miss a milestone you should evaluate the reasons you missed it. Is there a systematic problem that could affect subsequent milestones? Are the requirements still changing? Are quality problems slowing down new development? Is the development team at risk of burning out from too much overtime?

Consider problems carefully. Discuss each problem or setback and have the entire team make suggestions on how to get back on track. Avoid accusations. You might have to stop development and return to design for a period of time. You might decide to cut back on certain features, stop adding new features until bugs are fixed, or renegotiate the schedule.

Remember that schedules and milestones are *flexible* tools that help plan and map your progress. Schedules should be living documents, not cast in stone for all time. Address problems as they arise, modify the schedule if necessary, and then monitor progress to avoid repeating mistakes or making new ones.

Missing a milestone should not come as a complete surprise. Schedule slips do not occur all at once; they happen little by little, day by day. Correct problems as they arise. Do not wait until the end of the milestone or the end of the project. If you do not realize that you are behind schedule until the last two months of a yearlong project, there probably will not be anything you can do to get back on schedule.

Bibliography

Dataflow Programming with LabVIEW. National Instruments Application Note. A set of perspectives on data flow programming that shows how LabVIEW compares with classical data flow graphs, equations, and block diagrams.

Dynamics of Software Development. Jim McCarthy, Microsoft Press, Redmond, WA, 1995, ISBN 1-55615-823-8. Another look at what has worked and what has not for developers at Microsoft. This book is written by a developer from Microsoft and contains numerous real-world stories that help put problems and solutions in focus.

LabVIEW Data Acquisition VI Reference Manual. A useful sample of quality documentation for libraries of VIs. (Included in the LabVIEW manual set.)

LabVIEW Graphical Programming. Gary W. Johnson, McGraw-Hill, New York, 1997, ISBN 0-07-032915-4. An excellent overview of how to apply LabVIEW to real-world problems.

LabVIEW Instrument I/O Reference Manual. Detailed information for developers of instrument drivers. (Included in the LabVIEW manual set.)

LabVIEW Technical Resource. Editor: Lynda P. Gruggett, LTR Publishing, Dallas, TX, phone (214) 706-0587, fax (214) 706-0506, www.ltrpub.com. A quarterly newsletter and disk of VIs featuring technical articles about all aspects of LabVIEW.

Microsoft Secrets. Michael A. Cusumano and Richard W. Selby, Free Press, New York, 1995, ISBN 0-02-874048-3. In-depth examination of the programming practices Microsoft uses. Whether or not you are interested in Microsoft, this book contains interesting discussions of what they have done right and what they have done wrong. Includes a good discussion of team organization, scheduling, and milestones.

Rapid Development. Steve McConnell, Microsoft Press, Redmond, WA, 1996. Explanation of software engineering practices in a very down-to-earth fashion with many examples and practical suggestions.

Software Engineering. Merlin Dorfman and Richard Thayer (Eds.), IEEE Computer Science Press, Piscataway, NJ, 1996, ISBN 0-8186-7609-4. Collection of articles on a variety of software engineering topics, including a discussion of the spiral life cycle model by Barry W. Boehm.

Software Engineering—A Practitioner's Approach. Roger S. Pressman, McGraw-Hill, New York, 1992, ISBN 0-07-050814-3. A detailed survey of software engineering techniques with descriptions of estimation techniques, testing approaches, and quality control techniques.

Software Engineering Economics. Barry W. Boehm, Prentice-Hall, Englewood Cliffs, NJ, 1981, ISBN 0-13-822122-7. Description of the delphi and COCOMO estimation techniques.

Visual Programming Using Structured Data Flow. Jeffrey Kodosky, J. Mac-Crisken, and G. Rymar, Proc. IEEE Workshop on Visual Languages, 1991. (Also available from National Instruments.) Description of some of the theory behind the graphical programming paradigm of LabVIEW.

LabVIEW
Software Quality
Assurance Guide
and Toolkit

Gary W. Johnson
Lawrence Livermore National Laboratory

Tell me now: Would you buy a new car with full knowledge that it was built without written plans? How about a car whose entire testing and inspection phases consisted of no more than a quick road test as it rolled out of the plant? Well, that's exactly what we do every day in the software industry. Programmers like us sit down and write programs in LabVIEW and other languages without so much as a scrap of paper listing the requirements. We do some debugging runs and patch the thing up until it (apparently) works. And we rarely bother writing a user manual. Is there something amiss here?

As a LabVIEW developer, your objective is to deliver the highest-quality product. That means analyzing (and meeting) the user's requirements, spending some time in the design phase, and doing the coding, testing, and documentation according to some accepted standards and practices. These standards and practices are elements of **software engineering**, as described in Chap. 13, "Software Engineering Primer." They represent the path to software quality and to *added value* in your software. If the extra effort does not add value, you are either (A) an incredible programmer who in fact does not need any of this, or (B) only going through the motions, filling out the paperwork, and not taking any of this to heart.

I've struggled with this quality business for some time now and have concluded that there are measurable payoffs to the application of modern software engineering techniques and quality standards such as ISO 9000 to the development of LabVIEW applications. For instance, I found that multiplatform portability is a snap if you write and follow a clear list of design rules. An initial investment of time in the design phase and the creation of some standards documents saved many hours later on. Also, formalized testing uncovered numerous bugs and suggested improvements at all phases of the project. These are examples where value was added because the programming team decided to invest the required time and effort up front. And our customers are very, very happy.

When you're first confronted with the prospect that your next Lab-VIEW application has to meet the strict quality standards prescribed by ISO 9000 or other standards, you may feel overwhelmed, or at least a bit uncertain about what to do. This chapter will help you take that first step into the world of formal **software quality assurance** (SQA). The tools supplied here are applicable not only to ISO 9000, but to many other SQA standards as well. Realize that quality software comes from *good software engineering practices;* the type and quantity of QA paperwork you generate is secondary. A working knowledge of software engineering methods is important to your success, and the quality management tools spring directly from those methods. The only thing here that has been customized for ISO 9000 in particular is the format of a few documents.

You should use this chapter and the referenced tools as a starting point for your own quality program. Modify the documents and VIs to meet your needs and let the quality and value added to your software speak for itself. Designing and using an effective SQA program is not easy or cheap, especially the first time through. You, the developer, must be determined to become the best software engineer in the marketplace, to put together an effective quality program, and to proudly display the results to your customers.

Toolkits to the Rescue

There's no reason to start from scratch in the SQA business, because there are several good toolkits available. National Instruments offers two packages that you will find valuable, and this chapter will help you as well.

■ The **Professional G Developers Toolkit** is the most important tool for quality LabVIEW software development. In fact, I consider it an absolute requirement for major projects. Costing about $700, the toolkit helps you manage large projects with multiple developers. It includes source code control (SCC), software metrics to measure G code complexity, tools for printing VI hierarchies, tools for managing VI libraries, a style guide, and a documentation package that discusses software engineering techniques. I'll talk more about its capabilities in this chapter. Also, you can expect more features in the toolkit as time goes on; software products are far from static!

■ The **Unit Test and Validation Procedures Toolkit** helps you with the testing phase of your project by supplying semiautomatic test frameworks and LabVIEW-based logging of test results. It was originally written by Ken Lisles of Instrument Systems because his project had to meet the QA requirements of the Food and Drug Administration (FDA). The package also includes a style guide with recommendations for designing your code for testability.

■ This chapter includes a package I call **LV9000**, which consists of a set of model documents for working under an ISO 9000-grade quality program and includes all phases of a project from proposal through testing to delivery.

Depending upon the size, scope, and requirements of your project, you may use any or all of the these toolkits. I strongly recommend that you read this chapter and consider reviewing some of the references cited. Please note that LV9000 is *not* a complete, corporate-level ISO 9001 quality plan. See the bibliography for information in this very broad area. LV9000 is intended primarily for the small LabVIEW shop—those with one, or just a few, developers. You need a jump start in the quality assurance business, and this is it!

About LabVIEW and ISO 9000

In this section, we'll look at the relevant aspects of ISO 9000 quality standards from a LabVIEW developer's perspective. Also mentioned here is the topic of software engineering and how the information in Chap. 13, "Software Engineering Primer," is at the root of quality software development. Finally, I'll give you some tips on using the LV9000 package, the Professional G Developers Toolkit, and the Unit Test and Validation Procedures Toolkit.

ISO 9000 in a Nutshell

The intent of the International Organization for Standardization (ISO) is to unify standards from many nations in many industries in the interest of improving the worldwide trade situation. The 9000 series of ISO standards deals with quality management and quality assurance in the most general sense. You will find that the actual documents are mercifully brief and to the point, having been distilled from the quality guidelines of many countries. In turn, each country has its own way of referring to the ISO 9000 standards. For instance, in the United States, the series has been adopted as the American National Standards Institute (ANSI)/American Society of Quality Control (ASQC) Q9000 series. If you are required to use a standard different from ISO 9000, this chapter should still be of value because of the degree of interrelation among standards-setting bodies. In fact, there is a long-term trend toward *harmonization* of all the various quality standards worldwide, which may one day reduce confusion for those of us who work under such auspices.

The difficulty comes in interpreting the standards and implementing a quality program for your particular business—in this case, LabVIEW software development. Table 14.1 summarizes the overall structure of the

TABLE 14.1

ISO 9000 at a
Glance

Type	Name	Description
Guidelines	ISO 9000 (1987)	Guidelines for selection and use
	ISO 9000-2 (prospective)	Guidelines for application of ISO 9001, ISO 9002, and ISO 9003
	ISO 9000-3 (1991)	Guidelines for the application of ISO 9001 to the development, supply, and maintenance of software
	ISO 8402 (1986)	Quality vocabulary
Quality systems (contractual models)	ISO 9001 (1987)	Model for quality assurance in design/development, production, installation, and servicing
	ISO 9002 (1987)	Model for quality assurance in production and installation
	ISO 9003 (1987)	Model for quality assurance in final production and test
Quality management and quality system elements	ISO 9004 (1987)	Guidelines
	ISO 9004-2 (1991)	Part 2: Guidelines for services
Guidelines for auditing quality systems	ISO 10011-1 (1990)	Part 1: Auditing
	ISO 10011-2 (1991)	Part 2: Qualification criteria for quality auditors
	ISO 10011-3 (1991)	Part 3: Management of audit programs

ISO 9000 standards. The ones we are interested in are **ISO 9001**, which covers all aspects of product development, and **ISO 9000-3**, which tells you (in general terms) how to apply ISO 9001 to software applications. Curiously, software is the only industry singled out by the ISO folks. Perhaps they've gotten wind of the fact that most software development is performed without the use of formal engineering practices! More on this important topic later.

In a nutshell, ISO 9000 requires that you

- Plan what you're going to do (and write it down)
- Manage the process by which you do it
- Verify in writing that you did it

The standards ask that you follow commonly accepted engineering practices, in this case *software* engineering practices. That's where you actually spend the time to plan in significant detail what your LabVIEW program has to do, plan how you will structure it, and plan how you will test it. You should do all of this *in writing*. If that sounds like a lot of work, it's because you've been operating like a casual hacker—quality *un*controlled. Of course, you're in good company, because there are surprisingly few software development firms of any size that really do the job right.

The standards also say that you must have a clear management structure, and that management is involved at every step of the process. For the small developer, this means you must clarify the responsibilities of your customer, your subcontractors, and any others who work on your project. Who will write the initial requirements document? Who will update it? Who can propose and approve the changes? Who will do the testing? Who signs off on the final deliverables? Each of these issues must be defined in order to avoid confusion, defective products, and lots of finger-pointing when things go awry.

Quality, in the eyes of the ISO 9000 auditors, implies many things. Here are a few of the relevant aspects of quality and their translations to LabVIEW development.

- *Quality means that the engineering process is well defined.* You apply accepted software engineering methods to your LabVIEW projects. You analyze the problem and write down the requirements. Then you take the time to design the application, perhaps using specialized software tools, before doing any serious programming. You follow VI standards that clarify your diagrams and simplify the debugging and testing process through modularization.

- *Everything is under control.* You have a schedule that everyone agrees to follow. Changes to the customer's requirements are documented, designed, and applied in an orderly fashion. Obsolete documents don't accidentally get used in the production process. Your hard disk directories make sense.

- *You verify (test) your work.* You test your software at several stages. During development, you might build a test VI that exercises your latest module. Keep that test VI, and use it during formal **unit test** software testing. Design for testing by keeping your code modular and standardized. For example, use a standard connector pane layout for common controls and indicators such as error cluster I/O and file refnums. Write and use test procedures. If you can't write a procedure, you probably have no means of verifying whether or not your programming *really* works correctly. As the project nears completion, perform **integration testing** to show that collections of VIs work properly together, and finally perform **system testing**.

- *You validate your work.* You can show that your program satisfies the customer's requirements. Keep the requirements document handy and keep looking it over as you do your design and coding. Check things off as you address them. Always discuss problem areas with the customer early; don't sweep things under the rug.

- *You have a system for configuration management.* Versions of documents and software are stored in a safe and consistent manner. New versions are not released without formal testing and sign-off by responsible persons. Keep a running list of software modification requests and check the items off when you implement them. When you modify a VI, don't immediately overwrite the master copy; work on a duplicate instead. Keep double backups. Use the **source code control** (SCC) features available in the Professional G Developers Toolkit, particularly to handle sharing of VIs among multiple developers and to control access.

- *A system for multiple levels of review is in place.* You may have formal **design reviews**, especially on big projects. You show your customer your designs before you implement them. Do this by creating prototype panels and simplified "dummy" VIs for demonstration. Discuss trade-offs such as cost versus performance or memory requirements versus speed and explain how those aspects influenced your design. Invite the customer to review your work early on, at the *alpha* testing stage, and issue *beta* test software in stable, usable condition.

- *All operations are documented.* Keep written records of all important decisions and deliveries. Keep copies of all quality documents (requirements, designs, test procedures, etc.) on disk or in printed form. This is particularly important if you or your customer are subject to formal audits.

About ISO 9000 Registration

Companies can elect to become **ISO 9000 registered**. To do so, they must assemble a detailed quality management plan backed by a formalized management structure, policy, and procedures that make it all work. The company must apply standards, specifications, and clear methodologies that help build quality products that meet the needs of its customers. And of course, everything has to be documented to show that the policies are working effectively. When the in-house assessment process is completed and all the systems of documentation and management are ready, a certified ISO 9000 auditor is hired to review the quality system. With hard work and real commitment, any company can register—even yours. But it's your decision as to whether it's worthwhile. For instance, are you doing lots of work for the European Community (EC)? That's a hotbed of competition where ISO 9000 registration carries a lot of weight. Are you supplying regular consulting services to clients who demand formal software quality assurance under other standards, such as the Food and Drug Administration (FDA) or the military? Do you plan to grow your company significantly? If so, you might consider registration. Registration also implies ongoing surveillance visits every six to nine months by your certification body. They will expect to see your quality system evolve along with your company, which only makes sense.

But for the rest of us—the small LabVIEW developers—registration is not really necessary. Under the standards, it is up to the registered company (your client) to verify that its subcontractors (you) are doing your work in a forthright fashion. The registered company will establish the quality assurance requirements up front, and will ask for proof that you know what you're doing and are capable of meeting the requirements. By proof, I mean procedures and documentation. That's where LV9000 can help: by supplying you with some proven LabVIEW software quality management tools that meet specific ISO 9000 registered customer needs.

Software Engineering—It's the Law

One hazard of developing in LabVIEW is that it's so easy and fun to do that we are tempted to write the code without any planning or design. While this may be acceptable for the simplest, most informal applications, you are sure to get in trouble when developing complex systems—and the ISO 9000 police will *not* be happy.

Software engineering techniques and software life cycle models are effective tools for controlling quality, managing risk, and helping to guarantee delivery time and cost on your projects. Even a simple waterfall life cycle model—analyze, design, code, and test—is a big improvement over the quick hack. Your goal is to address the needs of your customer, sometimes refered to as meeting the "-bilities": testability, maintainability, reliability, expandability, and usability. Chapter 13, "Software Engineering Primer," contains an overview of software engineering, as does the manual included with the Professional G Developers Toolkit. I encourage you to read these guides, and perhaps their references, to gain a working knowledge of good development practice.

Working with an ISO 9000 Registered Client

Your ISO 9000 registered clients are serious about the quality of their products and they expect you to produce equally high-quality results in LabVIEW. Besides your own technical competence and experience, there are several things you can do during the early phases of the project that will make the process easier and better.

- *Establish a management structure.* Who's in charge at the customer's location? At your company, who's in charge of which aspects of your development effort? For large projects, management tasks may include budget, schedule, and other business matters, quality management (the person responsible for administering the quality plan and keeping everyone on track), and some kind of management hierarchy for the software development project in particular.

- *Establish lines of communication.* In the Information Age, you have many communication options: telephone, fax, e-mail, FTP, express shipments, face-to-face meetings, and so forth. Put together a list of contacts for both the customer's side and your side of the project. Find out who the major players are. Who do you call when there is a low-level hardware interface problem? Who is the QA manager? Where do you send the bill? Write it all down on one page and send a copy to everyone.

- *Agree on documentation formats and procedures.* For some projects, the customer expects you to supply a final user manual that is nearly camera ready. That's a lot of work! On the other hand, the customer may only want a plaintext document with a few simple figures. Agree on electronic formats. Decide on the platform, the word processor and/or graphics programs, page layout programs, and so forth. Does the customer have a style guide for corporate documents that you need to follow? You might need to hire a subcontractor to handle page layout, illustration, and/or editing. How will you submit the final documents? Choose a convenient medium, and get in touch with the person who will work with you on the publishing of your great literary tome.

- *Will special equipment be required?* Who will supply it? Don't get stuck having to locate, design, fabricate, or purchase expensive test equipment or exotic cables. If your customer can loan you the necessary items, make arrangements up front. If the project is likely to generate much follow-on work, decide how you will arrange to borrow the equipment again at a later date. Software maintenance may be difficult if you can't obtain the right hardware. Sometimes it's worthwhile buying the items if they can be buried in the cost of the contract.

■ *Make provisions to ensure that customer-supplied software is tested.* Customer-supplied software, be it source code or embedded firmware, can arrive in any condition. I've had some really interesting experiences with commercial instruments! Be cautious if you are receiving partially written LabVIEW code. Who wrote it? Is it well designed and documented? Will you have to test it? This is a very risky area; avoid it when possible. Also, don't overlook embedded code (the internal program that runs a modern GPIB or serial instrument is an example). For instance, when writing a driver for a new instrument, you may find that *you* are debugging *their* firmware. Make sure that you are not responsible for any problems or delays induced by such unpredictable events. At the very least, make sure you get paid for the extra work.

■ *Who generates the requirements?* Most often, it's a cooperative effort. The customer has a wish list and some vague requirements. You have experience in LabVIEW development and customers fully expect you to chime in and tell them what's reasonable. Offer suggestions for improvement in any areas in which you feel competent. Above all, make sure everyone agrees to both the spirit and the letter of the requirements document before you do any development.

Plan your quality assurance strategy. If your project is designed with the intent that each VI will be subject to formal testing, you will take a rather different approach to your coding. For instance, VI formatting standards are no longer just recommendations, but fairly rigid visual inspection templates. The good news is, after you write a few VIs subject to these standards, the process becomes second nature.

Working with Unregistered Suppliers

Turning the picture around, if your company is ISO 9000 registered and you hire an unregistered subcontractor or parts supplier who is inexperienced in the ways of SQA, expect difficulties. In this case, *you* are ultimately responsible for the outcome of the project and all of the quality management issues. Indeed, the ISO 9001 standard includes a section on purchasing that encompasses supplier and subcontractor control. Where possible, choose ISO 9000 registered subcontractors and suppliers, or at least keep a list of acceptable suppliers with whom you have had positive experience. When it comes to hiring contract programmers, plan on educating your subcontractor and making sure that the important quality mechanisms listed earlier are in place.

Quality is literally in the hands of everyone on the project. Is all this effort worthwhile? Only if it adds value to the final product.

Using the LV9000 Toolkit

The LV9000 toolkit consists of a set of documentation templates and style standards. In this section, we'll step through the entire LabVIEW development process from planning to delivery with the toolkit providing help along the way.

It's impossible to provide a set of magic documents that cover every conceivable need. Instead, LV9000 supplies some generic documents and checklists that you should modify to suit your particular project. You should create stationery documents in a word processor, especially for the test procedures since there are likely to be a large number of them. Design a format that you are happy with. Include "boilerplate" paragraphs where appropriate. Put in instructions or reminders to the document editor. For instance, if you always forget to update the footer or header, insert some big, bold text that says, "*Update the header, dummy.*"

What's on the CD-ROM

Here is a list of the items you will find in the LV9000 directory on the CD-ROM:

 \LV9000

Delivery Letter Document

Development Proposal Document

Driver VI Test Procedure Document

Get VI Info and History.vi

Software QA Plan Document

Software Requirements Document

Software Test Plan Document

Standard VI Template (Standard VI.vit)

Style Guide Document

User Interface VI Test Procedure Document

VI Inspection Checklist Document

VI Standards Document

File Formats

Regarding files in the LV9000 directory on the CD-ROM, Microsoft Word binary version 6 format is used for all documents and LabVIEW 4.1 for VIs. Word is fairly universal, so no other format is supplied. If you have difficulty with these documents, contact the author (e-mail address: johnsong@llnl.gov) and I will try to meet your needs.

Planning and Designing Your Project

The business of project management, which is required for any quality-oriented process, begins with fact-finding, proposing, and planning your project. Then you add the other elements of software engineering: analysis of the problem, designing a solution, coding, and finally testing it out. Figure 14.1 gives an overview of the documents and tools that make up a software development project with comprehensive quality management.

Proposals and Quotes

\LV9000\ Development Proposal.doc

Writing my first work proposal was awkward. What to say? How much to charge? The sample proposal included with LV9000 can help you get organized. Even if you already have significant experience quoting work, look over the **Development Proposal Document** and see if it gives you any more ideas. Or, if you're a relative novice, feel free to plagiarize the text. What is important is *content*. Show that you understand the customer's requirements by explaining them in your own words. Explain in general terms how you intend to solve the problem. Refer to standards or other documents, such as ISO, ANSI, or IEEE, where appropriate (but only if you actually intend to follow them!). Convince the customer that you are

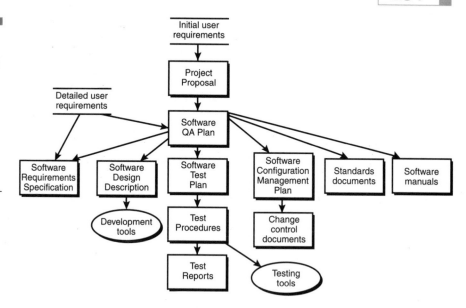

Figure 14.1
A large number of documents and tools may be required to satisfy the requirements of formal software development projects with comprehensive quality management. This is a road map.

skilled in software engineering, system integration, LabVIEW development, and any other relevant areas. I usually attach a company profile or resume to address those issues.

Some guidelines on project estimation are included in the Professional G Developers Toolkit and its references. Your most important guide is prior experience in LabVIEW development. That's why I mention the need for keeping records, such as VI metrics, from prior projects. An additional factor to consider is that formal software quality assurance requires significantly more time and effort than quick hack development. I've found that projects take about 2 to 3 times longer when full formal software testing is required. If a highly detailed software engineering process is contemplated, even more time will be needed. Above all, be sure that you clearly list all of the important deliverables. Don't get caught underbidding a project because you and your customer didn't agree on deliverables.

Initial Phase: Planning

As early as possible in your project, you should generate a **development plan** (Fig. 14.2) to organize the effort. The contents of this plan will later be used as the basis for a software quality assurance plan (SQAP), so your efforts serve double duty. The plan should include:

■ A project definition—state the objectives (major deliverables) and name the supplier and purchaser

Figure 14.2
A development plan will help you organize your project as well as satisfy the guidelines of almost any quality management system.

Gary W. Johnson ▸ *Electronics Engineer*
K. Decker Johnson ▸ *Scientific Illustrator*

Project Plan

Lorem ipsum dolor sit amet, consectetuer adipiscing elit, sed diam nonummy nibh euismod tincidunt ut laoreet dolore magna aliquam erat volutpat. Ut wisi enim ad minim veniam, quis nostrud exerci tation ullamcorper suscipit lobortis nisl ut aliquip ex ea commodo consequat.

I. Background
Lorem ipsum dolor sit amet, consectetuer adipiscing elit, sed diam nonummy nibh euismod tincidunt ut laoreet dolore magna aliquam erat volutpat. Ut wisi enim ad minim veniam, quis nostrud exerci tation ullamcorper suscipit lobortis nisl ut aliquip ex ea commodo consequat.

II. Objectives
Lorem ipsum dolor sit amet, consectetuer adipiscing elit, sed diam nonummy nibh euismod tincidunt ut laoreet dolore magna aliquam erat volutpat. Ut wisi enim ad minim veniam, quis nostrud exerci tation ullamcorper suscipit lobortis nisl ut aliquip ex ea commodo consequat.

III. Deliverables
A. Lorem ipsum dolor sit amet, consectetuer adipiscing elit, sed diam nonummy nibh euismod.
B. Tincidunt ut laoreet dolore magna aliquam erat volutpat. Ut wisi enim ad minim veniam.
C. Quis nostrud exerci tation ullamcorper suscipit lobortis nisl ut aliquip ex ea commodo consequat.

IV. Organization

V. Schedule

Task	Jan	Feb	Mar	Apr	May
Requirements doc.					
Developer training					
Test plan					
Prototype design					
Design review					
Coding					
Documentation					
Beta test					
Formal test					
Release					

■ Project organization—show the team structure and responsibilities

■ A schedule with milestones—describe the phases of the project

■ Project management structure—show who is responsible for what

■ Development methods and tools—state the tools, techniques, and standards you will use for development

■ A list of related documents, such as a configuration management plan, test plan, and so forth

Be concise—the plan only needs to be a page or two for a small-scale project, but it will make you think about the project organization and goals. The items in the plan will probably appear in any written proposals you present to your customer, so the plan serves double duty. Start by interviewing the customer. Talk to the most knowledgeable people on the project that you can find. Acquire as many documents as you can, particularly equipment manuals and written design requirements. Consider these important topics:

I. *Understand the problem.* If you can't write down a definition of the problem at hand in clear and concise terms, you certainly won't be able to write a suitable program to solve the problem. Learn about the physical system, instrument, or hardware and the expected modes of operation, and find out who will operate the system.

II. *Do not sign up for something you cannot handle.* This may seem like common sense, but many have violated this rule, especially when desperate for work. If all else fails, try to get help from someone else who really knows the area of interest. Consider subcontracting part of the work.

III. *Make a clear list of deliverables.* What, exactly, is it that you are going to deliver? This list helps determine the scope of the project. Important items to list are:
   A. Software modules or packages
   B. Documents, such as manuals
   C. Hardware items, such as custom cables or interface devices
   D. Training
   E. Long-term maintenance and support

IV. *Use a checklist for features.* Such a list is useful when interviewing your customer. Divide the list broadly into categories and build an outline. Eventually, you can make it into an interview form with checkboxes for standard features. Here are a few favorite topics:
   A. Hardware
      1. Sensors and controls
      2. Computer interfaces
      3. Computer
   B. User interface
   C. Operating modes
   D. Data collection and storage
   E. Performance specifications

V. *Draft the Test Plan early.* Software testing plays a major part in meeting ISO 9000 requirements. Reach an agreement with your customer as to how detailed the testing should be (for instance, will absolutely every subVI be formally tested, or just the higher-level ones?) and what the written reporting requirements will be. LV9000 will certainly help you here, but there's no need to go overboard if the customer does not have relevant needs.

VI. *Use previous project experience as a model—learn!* Every project is a little easier than the one before. Build a knowledge database for project planning and execution. Save your old proposals, checklists, and other documents for reuse on new projects. Use the **VI Metrics Tool** (Fig. 14.3) from the Professional G Developers Toolkit to measure complexity of your VIs and quantify the cost of development. In the long run, these efforts will save you time and add value to your work.

Software Requirements Specifications

\LV9000

Software Requirements.doc

Perhaps the most fundamental and most difficult document to prepare for any project is the **requirements** specification. In this document, you must be very precise and very thorough in describing what the software must do. There is no limit to the amount of detail that can be included, because this document is the immediate precursor to the actual VIs that you write at all levels from drivers to user interface. On the CD-ROM is a

Figure 14.3
The VI Metrics tool quantifies the complexity of a LabVIEW hierarchy. Here, it's showing details about the diagram, such as number of nodes, structures, and number of sub-diagrams and nesting levels.

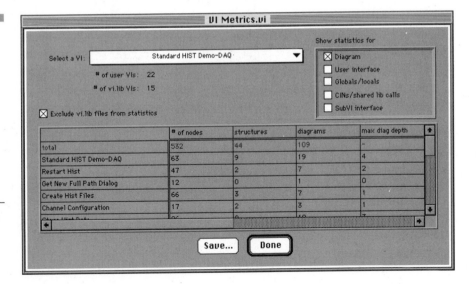

sample **Software Requirements** document that you might use as a starting point. The IEEE software standards have guidelines for writing requirements documents, and I've loosely followed them here. The standards are, as usual, highly detailed and somewhat redundant, so consider the sample document a practical implementation that meets the *spirit* of the standard. Major topics to discuss in a requirements document are:

- Purpose and scope—the overall system and its purpose
- Acronyms, abbreviations, terms, and references—all the reference material a developer might need to know about (try to eliminate any confusion)
- General functionality—what the software must do from a high-level point of view
- Constraints—limitations you expect to deal with
- Assumptions and dependencies—such as assuming that LabVIEW works as advertised
- Specific functional requirements—the body of the requirements document, where you go through the functionality of each mode or module of software in minute detail

As with any important design document, your customer must review the requirements document and agree to its contents in writing. Ian Riley of Brill Engineering in England (a National Instruments Alliance member) says that Brill has experienced some difficulty in obtaining customer sign-off. As a security measure, the company's policy gives customers two weeks in which to return signed documents. No response automatically implies agreement. This might be another item of *fine print* for your standard contract.

Software Quality Assurance Plan

\LV9000\
**Software QA
Plan.doc**

The purpose of a **software quality assurance plan** (SQAP) is to define all the steps you will use to manage your software development project from requirements through coding, testing, and maintenance. If you've already written a development plan, your SQAP is probably half done. The **Software QA Plan** document on the CD-ROM will be a big help. I've adapted it from a collection of large and small projects that I've been associated with over the years. As such, it's comprehensive and is overkill for most projects. At its core, any SQAP, even the simplest, addresses the following major topics:

- Purpose—what the document covers and why
- References—primarily national references that will apply to the project
- Management—who is responsible for what
- Required software documentation—all the associated documents, including the requirements document, design documents, and test plan
- Standards and metrics—standards that apply to VI development and metrics you will use to assess adherence to standards as well as performance
- Reviews—major design review steps
- Testing plan—the means by which you will test the software
- Configuration management—your strategy for managing changes and keeping source code in order through the life of the software
- Techniques—the methods you will use in software development

An important fact to remember when preparing a SQAP is: *Never say you're going to do something unless you are actually prepared to do it!* It's easy to say you will follow the IEEE software specifications, but those are very complex documents and it is highly unlikely that the average programmer will survive the requirements phase, let alone the testing and documentation phases. Who are you trying to please—somebody who thinks word count equals quality? Rather, I hope you're trying to please your customer. It's much better to simplify the plan to the barest minimum that will assure a *quality product with enhanced value.*

Cross-Platform Considerations

While LabVIEW generally makes it easy to port your code to other platforms, there are many details that need your attention early in the development process. A valuable tool in this area is the **VI Standards Document**. If you set the standards with the intent of platform independency, and then follow these standards right through formal testing, much time will be saved later on. The many details of LabVIEW portability are outlined in the *LabVIEW User Manual.* Incorporate key items into your VI standards. For instance, don't use Macintosh-specific characters or fonts if you plan to move your VIs to Windows, and vice versa. Instead, use only the standard fonts (System, Dialog, and Application) as defined by LabVIEW.

The **source code control** (SCC) tool of the Professional G Developers Toolkit includes some cross-platform support. Specifically, if you want to support a project that contains nonportable features, such as Code Interface Nodes (CINs), the SCC tool allows you to link each platform with its associated VIs. When you build your distribution sets, you'll know that the right modules will be included.

Library Control Systems

The ISO 9000 standards require you to keep track of all important documents, tools, and versions of your code. Keeping your records in order not only satisfies requirements but smooths the flow of work and provides a safety net in case a disk crash destroys a few days' work. Keep a master list of all documents and use revision letters with dates and change logs as a part of each document. This will help prevent accidental use of outdated information, which is even more important in team environments. The SCC tool permits you to add extra files, such as documentation and CIN source code, to your project. This *Extra Files* feature is accessed through the Project >> Source Code Control >> Project...dialog.

You can use notebooks with partitions to keep current documents and reference materials handy. Previous generations may reside in a file cabinet or on a file server. In most cases you only need to keep older versions until the project is completed.

Program Prototyping and Design

After agreement is reached on requirements and work processes for your project, the design phase begins. There are many methods and formal software engineering concepts that you can use in this phase. Here are a few important ideas.

- *Prototyping* is an integral part of many design processes. There may be uncertainty regarding performance that can only be reduced by writing a test VI. Also, user interfaces with simulated I/O are easily created for customer feedback. LabVIEW architectures can be prototyped to validate conceptual models. In fact, rapid prototyping is a particularly strong feature of LabVIEW that departs from traditional software development models and is well worth exploiting.

- *Modeling and design tools* can clarify and expedite your overall design. At the very least, you should consider a top-down design approach.

More sophisticated models—object models, state transition diagrams (Fig. 14.4), and data flow models—can be used where appropriate, assuming you know how to use them. Data flow models are especially useful, considering the fact that G is a data flow language.

- *Computer-aided software engineering* (CASE) tools can organize all aspects of software design. Most CASE tools include several different graphically defined software models and all the associated documentation devices that go with them, such as a data dictionary. Automatic code generation is available for some languages; perhaps there will be a such a tool for LabVIEW some day. That would allow you to jump directly from design to testing!

As I've already stated, software engineering is at the foundation of quality LabVIEW development. You don't need college-level training to use the formal methods, either; I've picked up most of what I know by working with experienced computer scientists, reading, experimenting with CASE tools, and doing large-scale development. For more information, consult the Professional G Developers Toolkit and its references.

Coding Your Project

Ah, the coding phase. Now that you have finished slaving over all those requirements, designs, prototypes, and standards documents, you may begin this most enjoyable phase of LabVIEW development. Good code is written by someone who has been trained in the language, has practical experience, understands the elements of good style, and cares about writing a high-quality product. With these personal traits and the appropriate software engineering tools, you can't miss.

Figure 14.4
Models from a CASE tool (Mac A&D). *Left:* an entity relationship diagram. *Right:* a state transition diagram. Such design tools are valuable with any programming language.

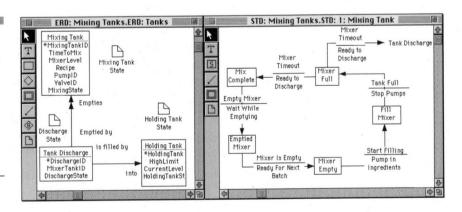

LabVIEW Style Guides

All projects, and especially large multideveloper projects, will benefit from a standardized LabVIEW style guide. Whether you use one of the existing documents or create your own custom version, each developer on your team should review the style guide before coding begins. If your company has special requirements and practices, they should be added to the document. Such reference documents are required in ISO 9000-3 under *Implementation*.

\LV9000
Style Guide
3.1.doc

The classic style guide, *LabVIEW with Style*, is included on the CD-ROM as an editable document for your convenience. This style guide contains recommended practices for LabVIEW development and addresses areas such as front panel design, elements of good data flow programming, program design, and debugging techniques. A detailed checklist for front panels, diagrams, and other VI attributes is readily incorporated into any QA plan. Feel free to modify the style guide to suit your purposes.

A condensed version of the classic style guide appears in the manual for the Professional G Developers Toolkit. Another style guide, entitled *LabVIEW Application Programming and Style Guide Standards for the Industrial Programmer*, is included with the Unit Test and Validation Procedures Toolkit. In it, Ken Lisles covers concepts of software engineering as it applies to LabVIEW, design strategies, hierarchical organization, good code design practices (particularly design for testing), and documentation standards. Again, all of these style guides are good starting places for your own custom document.

Using the VI Standards Document

\LV9000\VI
Standards.doc

The **VI Standards** document is an embodiment of the style guide as a practical VI design and quality assurance tool. It contains concise lists of characteristics and features that must be incorporated into each VI. During the coding phase, you should refer frequently to this document to make sure that all important attributes of your VIs meet the standards. When you perform formal software testing, you will use the **Inspection Checklist** document (which is derived from the VI Standards document) to assure that each VI is visibly correct. Using standards early in the coding phase will save you much time later on by forcing you to design uniform VIs that meet all the "-bilities."

To make the VI Standards document more readable, paste in screen shots of important graphical features including standard front panel details, icons, and dialog boxes such as the VI Setup dialog with its many selections.

Like all quality documents, this one should be controlled. That means using the cover sheet with revision letters, dates, and descriptions of the changes that were made. A revision control sheet is included as the first page of the sample document.

Using the Standard VI Template

**\LV9000\
Standard VI.vit**

Another handy tool for developers is the **Standard VI** Template. The one included with LV9000 (Fig. 14.5) demonstrates many of the requirements listed in the VI Standards document, and it's annotated in red text for instructional purposes. A good template works like a stationery document: You open it, save it with a new name, and begin editing. If you're using LabVIEW 4.1 or later, add the suffix .vit to tell LabVIEW that the file is a template and it will open the VI untitled. Place it in vi.lib\user.lib for instant access from the LabVIEW function palette.

Plan on designing more than one standard VI. For instance, you may want one for drivers and one for user interface VIs. Include as many stan-

Figure 14.5

The Standard VI Template helps you make all your VIs look and operate the same.

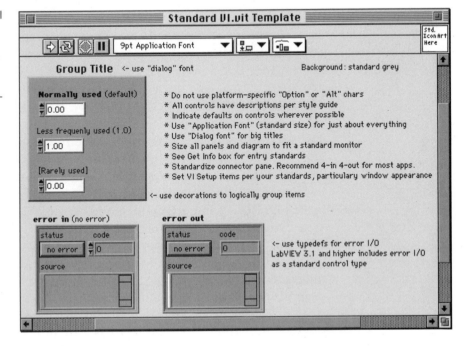

dard items as you can. It's much faster to delete a few extra items on the panel or diagram than it is to locate, copy, and paste them in. (Don't leave all the extra text on the panel; it's superfluous after the initial instructional period.) Some items to consider including are:

- Standard controls, especially typedefs
- Standard graphical elements for the panel, especially if you have some custom graphics
- Standard icon and connector pane
- *Boilerplate* text, such as copyright information or developer credits, in the Get Info box
- Frequently used code for the diagram, such as the error I/O Case structure or a While Loop with a timer

Working in a Team Environment

While the synergy of teamwork is valuable, conflicts sometimes arise when two or more developers edit the same VI without synchronizing their work. You might overwrite someone else's work unless you have a formal agreement regarding shared code or documents. To avoid such conflicts, I highly recommend **Source Code Control (SCC)** tool in the Professional G Developers Toolkit, in which a VI is checked out for editing by only one programmer at a time. It also tracks changes in the code and maintains historical backup copies. For higher levels of security, you can use Microsoft SourceSafe with the SCC tools (Windows only). It adds passwords, file compression, and other security measures not provided by the built-in SCC engine.

A centralized file server is the preferred place to store the master version of the code and all other project resources. Network or modem connections make the server a convenient repository, but only administrative controls can make it a *conflict-free* repository. Here are some ideas for avoiding conflict:

- *Never mix temporary test versions in with the main project.* Keep test versions on your own private disk. Test versions have a way of acquiring the same file names as the "real" versions, which invites confusion.
- *Apply security measures to stable parts of the code.* Once a portion of the code has passed testing, place it in a directory that can't be accidentally overwritten. Programmers should be forced to enter passwords to overwrite code that is under **configuration control**. You can

assign one person to manage this aspect of the development process—call him or her the librarian—and make everyone go through that person to update the master files. Configuration control is also enforced if you use the SCC check-in/check-out features.

■ *Split the working directories among specified programmers.* Try to divide the work in such a way that each programmer is assigned to a clearly specified portion of the code. Don't edit code in someone else's department. Instead, handle changes by telling the appropriate person what needs to be done.

■ *Use a directory resolver or backup application to update files* rather than simply overwriting everything with a copy command. There are many applications available that look at two directories and attempt to synchronize them. Dates and locations are checked and you can receive warnings when something unexpected crops up. You might consider one of the applications intended for synchronizing files between portable and desktop machines available for both Macintosh and Windows. Using the code checkout features of the SCC prevents routine file update clashes, but won't prevent a system administrator from overwriting an entire directory.

LabVIEW undergoes frequent upgrades. When an upgrade is issued, decide on an appropriate time to make the change, then be sure to upgrade all members of your project team simultaneously. Don't forget the people at your customer's site. If you are developing a project for widespread distribution, remember that not every user will necessarily have the latest version of LabVIEW. I generally wait several months after a major release before converting our published applications. Also, keep in mind that the act of recompiling under a new version may invalidate any software testing performed under the old version. This subject must be addressed in your development plan.

Using the LabVIEW VI History Feature

Beginning with LabVIEW 3.1, a **VI history dialog** is available for tracking changes to each VI. Through the LabVIEW Preferences (Fig. 14.6), you can have the history feature log changes under various scenarios. This is especially important in a team environment because it may be the only way to tell who made the latest changes. If you turn on one of the automatic history logging modes, such as *Add an entry every time VI is saved,* you are guaranteed to have at least a minimal history of who made the

Figure 14.6
The VI history preference box (part of the LabVIEW Preferences) lets you define which items will be recorded in each VI's history log.

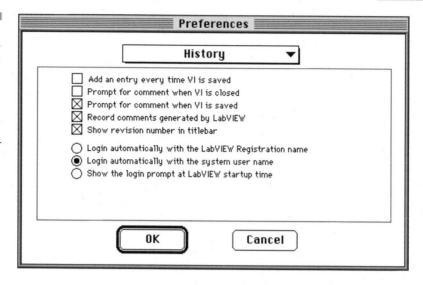

change and when. It is up to the programmer to fill in the *what*. Even a very brief description of the change is helpful. You should also record important milestones for a VI, such as *Completed testing. V1.03*.

If you're using the Source Code Control tools, you will receive an automatic prompt for a new history entry each time you check in a modified VI. You can read VI history text through the View History option in the Project >> Source Code Control >> Advanced dialog box. A utility, **Get VI Info and History.vi**, is available on the CD-ROM for programmatically extracting the VI history text (and the VI description text) from any VI.

\LV9000
Get VI Info and History.vi

Code Backups

Back up your code on a regular basis. This includes all programs you have written, documents, software tools (LabVIEW or CASE tools included), and vital data that you need for development and testing. Try copying the entire project directory to another hard disk partition. It's fast and painless. For a master backup (perhaps weekly), you can also use removable media that you can keep somewhere else, such as a fireproof safe. File servers are very effective for backups of all types. If you're using the SCC tool, it can automatically maintain previous versions of each VI on the server. If you don't have a fancy network, consider a modem-based system. For instance, Mac users can run AppleTalk Remote Access (ARA) over modems on a single-user basis with little effort.

Testing Your Project

Software testing—the validation phase—is a key quality management step in any process. ISO 9000-3 concisely describes the process as it applies to software under *Testing and Validation*. The IEEE software engineering standards and various texts also discuss this topic in great detail. Testing is best performed continuously: during initial coding and debugging, during the construction of the VI hierarchy, during the in-house alpha test phase, and of course during the formal test phase. If done properly, the formal test phase is just that: a formality. It proves (in writing, of course) that your program functions as expected under controlled conditions. The act of writing the test procedure typically requires you to exercise your program in a realistic fashion, thus testing as you write.

Remember that you don't *test* the quality in, you *build* the quality in. That's why we go through a design phase and use VI standards and good coding practices. A well-designed program with consistent, neat, and accurate diagrams will surely be a higher-quality product than one where you cross your fingers and hope to catch all the bugs at testing time. Yes, testing is a big job (the writing part is really depressing to most programmers), but I've found that the discipline that formal testing instills helps me produce better products. And *that* is what quality is all about.

What Should You Test?

Initial software testing is carried out at the **unit** level. A convenient unit for LabVIEW is a single VI, generally in the lower or middle levels of a hierarchy. **Integration** testing is performed next. You exercise the complete program, though you may be using simulated hardware or other tools. Then, a **system** test is performed with real hardware if possible. It's sometimes called **system integration** testing because the two may be fairly close in scope. Finally, you may have to undergo **acceptance** testing by the customer, probably at the customer's plant. Each flavor of testing should be addressed by written procedures.

In addition to the various *phases* of testing, there are different *kinds* of testing, such as functional, boundary, performance, inspection, and usability testing. Most familiar is **functional** testing, where you verify the outputs or results in response to a set of input conditions. In turn, functional testing can be broken down into **white box** and **black box** testing. In white box testing, you use your detailed knowledge of how the program works to devise the tests and to observe the behavior of the VI. An example would be adding a debugging probe to a critical value in a state machine, or displaying the value of a global variable while the VI runs. Black box testing assumes nothing about the underlying program and merely compares expected results with actual results. **Boundary** testing is a particular kind of functional test where the input conditions are at or near a critical limit value. For instance, some calculations fail when an argument is 0. Once you've determined that the VI is functionally valid, you might measure its **performance** under specific conditions. This might include speed and memory usage with large and small data sets. A simple, but effective, testing step involves visual **inspection** of panels, diagrams, VI setups, and so forth. You generally use a checklist, make sure that the developer has followed all the guidelines, and see that the diagrams make sense. **Usability** testing can be a little more nebulous in that you are attempting to quantify the user's perception of your application. Important usability tests might include an evaluation of user interactions when an error is detected, or an evaluation of consistency and simplicity among user interface VIs.

The number of controls (inputs) and modes of operation are major factors that determine the number of tests you have to perform. Even for apparently trivial VIs, there may theoretically be *billions* of possible test cases. That's why we like white box testing, because knowledge of the VI's innards can quickly reduce the list of required tests to something practical. For instance, you don't have to try every possible numeric value in evaluating the correctness of a comparison function; only a few values near the "trip point" are required. The theory behind software testing is really deep; there are many books, research papers, and conferences devoted to the subject. For most purposes, you can rely on common sense and an understanding of the program to tell you which situation to test.

To be thorough, each VI should have a written **test procedure**. I occasionally skip some of the simplest subVIs in large applications if they are trivial in nature and if a higher-level VI exercises them in a meaningful fashion. The trick is to decide what is trivial and meaningful, and what the cost/benefit ratio is. Consider the amount of work you will have to do to generate the required documents, and compare that with the likelihood of a bug going undetected. When in doubt, formally test to the best of your ability.

It is probably impractical to extend your quality testing to LabVIEW itself in an explicit manner. Instead, LabVIEW can be implicitly tested by virtue of the fact that it is omnipresent in all of the programs you write and test.

Writing the Test Plan

\LV9000\
Software Test Plan.doc

An overall **test plan** describes how you will manage and perform the software verification phase of your project. This document is one of those higher-level quality management plans that the customer may want to review and approve. At the very least, the customer will want to know the general methods you use for testing. On the CD-ROM, I've included a **Software Test Plan** that you can use as a starting point. It meets the requirements of ISO 9000, and most other quality systems, as well.

The test plan begins with an overview of the project and methods you plan to use: purpose, scope, references, and approach. These sections help team members as well as outsiders to understand what you're planning to do and how it relates to the software product. The next part discusses those all-important **responsibilities**—who will do what. Though it seems a trivial exercise, we've all seen what happens when people aren't held accountable and tasks are left for "someone else." Instead, address everything in writing.

The outline of a standardized test procedure is then discussed (more on that in a minute), followed by a list of **deliverables**. Finally, you include an index to the individual test procedures. When you're preparing the index, you decide which VIs you will test. Such an index is a management tool that helps with overall project organization, and it comes in handy when it's time to check that you've tested everything you said you were going to test.

Writing All Those Test Procedures

Once you've decided which VIs need procedures, the burdensome task of writing the procedures begins. I found that while it's possible to write detailed test procedures during the coding phase, much reworking is often required after revisions are added during beta testing. A compromise is to draft a procedure that addresses basic functions that you're sure will survive future editing. During beta testing, there is usually some slack time to revise and complete the procedures. Testing tools such as dummy data files, top-level test programs, automated test code, and special hardware that are developed at any time during the project can and should be retained for formal testing.

\LV9000\
User Interface Test Proc.doc

The **User VI Test Procedure**, included with LV9000 on the CD-ROM, is an example of a procedure that you might write for a high-level interactive VI. In this case, the user is expected to manipulate controls and observe the results of each action. Later in this chapter, we'll consider automatic testing, where you write a top-level VI to test a particular VI or part of a hierarchy. If you're using automation, the number of steps in the test procedure quickly collapses. You may also want to use the Unit Test and Validation Procedures Toolkit (also described later), which provides a semiautomatic test tool with built-in record keeping. In that case, the test procedure is again simplified and, as a bonus, the test report is created automatically.

Look over the structure and content of the example procedure. I used the table features in Microsoft Word to construct the body of the procedures. A spreadsheet might also be suitable. You can modify the document and make test procedure stationery from it for reuse.

Using the VI Inspection Checklist

\LV9000\VI Inspection Checklist.doc

Being a graphical programming language, LabVIEW is most amenable to *visual* inspections. For this reason, I designed a **VI Inspection Checklist** that you use as an early step in formal testing. The checklist is derived from the VI Standards document, which tells the developer how a VI should look and how it should be set up. For that reason, it's important that you harmonize the inspection checklist with your standards document early in the project.

For each VI subject to inspection, you print a copy of the checklist, fill in the VI name and the date, and enter your name. Proceed through the various categories, carefully inspecting each item for conformance to the standards. I've found many small errors during inspections, most of them minor and easily corrected. It helps if someone besides the original coder does the inspection to obtain a fresh view. If one person on your team is fanatical about graphical presentation, or is a stickler for detail, he or she is the one to assign to this task.

Automated or Manual Testing?

Most user interface VIs have to be tested manually, one control at a time, because you need to record visual responses to your actions. I am not aware of any significant time-saving tips for such VIs. Automated testing, which is most practical for lower-level subVIs, requires development of additional test VIs, but may save you effort in the long run. Several scenarios illustrate this payoff. In one case, I worked on a large project for which the team had to port the application from the Macintosh to Windows. That entailed a complete retesting of the entire hierarchy, but the automated test capability made verification a breeze. Each time the application was upgraded, testing was again required. And when a new version of LabVIEW was released, we had to do some minor surgery on the application and…test it again. By that time, we were really glad we had spent time developing test automation!

Number-crunching subVIs are logical candidates for automated testing. For simpler cases, you can usually write your own test VIs in just a few minutes. For inputs, use preinitialized arrays, strings, or tables, and put the VI under test inside a For Loop. Compare the VI outputs with other preinitialized arrays containing expected results as shown in Fig. 14.7.

Printed test results are sometimes required for the final software test report. In that case, you could modify the simple test VI to include a formatted result string that is written to a file. The string may also include the name of the VI, the time and date, and perhaps the input data as well. On the other hand, maybe all you need to do is run the automatic tester and write *pass* on a line in the test report.

For the ultimate in flexibility, you can store the input and expected output data in a file (perhaps maintained with a spreadsheet), have the test VI load and parse the test data, and finally print a report. It's a generic approach, but much programming effort is required to parse the data, which is probably different for every VI under test.

Using the Unit Test and Validation Procedures Toolkit

The Unit Test Toolkit takes a broad, generalized view of testing individual VIs. It assumes real-world scenarios where a VI acts not just on simple internal data flows (like an arithmetic operation) but also on external data. External data I/O includes global variables, files, hardware I/O devices, and

Figure 14.7
This is a simple example of an automatic test VI. In the long run, automation can save you time.

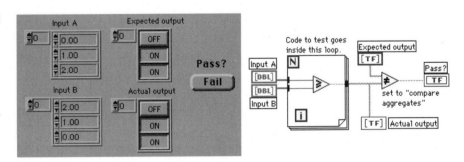

access to operating system resources. During testing, these external sources can complicate the heck out of things! For instance, access to a serial port implies that you would like to independently verify data that is read or written, and that may not be easy. Global variables are another potential confusion factor because they break the well-understood data flow chain. The toolkit has some good ideas for taming these difficult situations. In particular, global variables can be read or written before running the VI unit under test (UUT), and then read again after running to verify proper results.

There are two main tools in the toolkit: a **VI Group database manager** (VIG) and a **VI Test container** (VIT). The VIG is based on a table control into which you enter information associated with each VI in a group or hierarchy. Items in the table include VI name, revision number, reference to an associated VIT test file, and results of various tests. You can save the contents of the table to a spreadsheet file and read them back in at a later time. The diagram for the VIG VI is easy to understand and modify, so you can customize it for your application. It's a good tool for the LabVIEW developer because you don't have to leave LabVIEW to record your test results. I always had reams of paper piled up and wrote directly on the forms. The VIG concept certainly reduces the clutter factor.

The VIT is a template (Fig. 14.8) VI where you install a UUT. Like the VIG, this test container VI maintains a database with a comprehensive list of test conditions and results for each step, or case, of the testing process. Each test **case** is defined by entries typed into an array that describes the purpose of the test case and pass/fail criteria for output data, external events, and user interactions for interactive panels. Required input data (**test vectors**) can be assembled into arrays (probably having one element

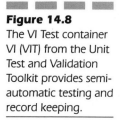

Figure 14.8
The VI Test container VI (VIT) from the Unit Test and Validation Toolkit provides semi-automatic testing and record keeping.

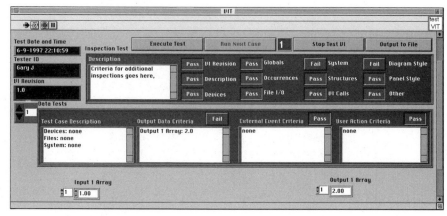

per step), and outputs can be observed in various indicators pasted into the panel of the VIT. The UUT and any global variables are wired into the diagram of the VIT. After configuring the VIT, you save it with a name that associates it with the UUT. Testing proceeds manually, one step at a time, and results can be directed to a spreadsheet file. You could certainly modify the VI to add automation. As with any good LabVIEW toolkit, there aren't any fundamental limitations.

Record Your Results

Quality records are part of your deliverable package. Records include such items as inspection and test reports, test results, change orders and reports, and defect logs. Some of these may be informal, but they are useful as a measure of the quality of your product. For instance, a defect log can be maintained during both informal and formal testing to show what problems cropped up and how you fixed them. This requires honesty and hard work, which may explain why defect logs are hardly ever seen!

Delivery and Support

When the testing is complete, it's time to make the final delivery or distribution of your software project. Beyond delivery, you will probably be liable for some kind of short- or long-term support based on your business agreement with the customer. (You *did* remember to include support in the contract, didn't you?)

What to Deliver

The primary deliverable is the software in the format that you've agreed upon—diskettes, CD-ROM, or some other medium. The list of possible documentation begins with a user manual, an item that every customer will surely ask for. (See Chap. 4 in *LabVIEW Graphical Programming* for recommended practice on writing user documentation.) Next on the list is a programmer's reference manual that covers internal details about your software. I generally write such a document for complex applications where the overall structure requires explanation, and to assist other developers in understanding data structures, program flow, tricky parts in the code, and tips on modifying the application. Finally, all those QA documents that you spent so much time writing must also be delivered. Each document should be delivered in printed form, and many on disks as well.

\LV9000
\Delivery
Letter.doc

To complete the package, write a professional-looking **delivery letter**. The letter included with LV9000 is pretty generic, but it does contain one important paragraph you will want to include to document the fact that you executed the test procedures:

> The Test Plan for the XXX software product, as listed in the XXX Software Text Plan, Rev. A, was executed by John Programmer at HisTown, CA, from October 3 to October 9, 1994. I certify that the Test Plan for XXX has been completed successfully and submit the attached test results for your review and acceptance.

The letter also includes an itemized list of the package contents.

Maintenance and Service

After formal release of a version of your software, you enter the **maintenance** phase of the project. A formal **service plan** may be needed for large projects. State clearly what, if any, routine maintenance is required in order for your product to stay healthy. Include operating system maintenance recommendations, and address issues of routine LabVIEW upgrades.

Perhaps the biggest decision is defining how bugs will be reported and how changes will be requested. In your software quality management plan, you may include a **software change request form**. This is the most formal and explicit way to communicate issues regarding software defects and requests for new features, because both you and the customer are forced to work through those issues in writing. Tasks can be graded according to their importance, severity, or impact on the overall project, and then assigned to a specific person. When the issue is resolved, the form is completed, the affected software is retested and distributed, and the form becomes a permanent part of the quality records. The obvious drawbacks to this method are that it is tedious and time consuming almost to the point of ridiculousness. More often, you can simply agree to handle bug reports and change requests by the usual telephone and e-mail routes that we're all familiar with. Just maintain a project log to keep track of customer requests and resolutions.

A service plan—no matter how simple—can save you trouble. Consider: How fast does the customer want you to respond? Determine who will do what when a defect is discovered. How much will it cost and how will you be paid? Don't wait until catastrophe strikes in the form of a midnight phone call!

Bibliography

You are also encouraged to consult the excellent list of references included with the Professional G Developers Toolkit Reference Manual.

ANSI/ASQC Q9000 Series Standards. The American versions of the ISO 9000 standards are available from ASQC, 611 East Wisconsin Avenue, Milwaukee, WI 53202.

Handbook of Walkthroughs, Inspections, and Technical Reviews: Evaluating Programs, Projects, and Products. Daniel P. Freedman and Gerald M. Weinberg, Dorset House, New York, 1990. ISBN: 9-932633-19-6. An excellent, down-to-earth discussion of how to conduct design and code reviews with many examples of things to look for and the best practices to follow during a review.

LabVIEW Graphical Programming, 2d Ed. Gary W. Johnson, McGraw-Hill, New York, 1997. ISBN 0-07-032915-4. Practical guide to LabVIEW applications in instrumentation and control.

ISO 9000: Meeting the New International Standards. Perry L. Johnson, McGraw-Hill, New York, 1993. ISBN 0-07-032691-6. A general introductory guide to ISO 9000. Easy to read and informative.

ISO 9000.3: A Tool for Software Product and Process Improvement. Raymond Kehoe and Alka Jarvis, Springer-Verlag, New York, 1996. ISBN 0-387-94568-7. Describes what is expected by ISO 9001 in conjunction with ISO 9000.3 and provides templates for documentation.

The ISO 9000 Documentation Toolkit. Janet L. Novak, Prentice-Hall, Upper Saddle River, NJ, 1995. For development of quality documentation at the corporate level. Includes document templates on disk.

The ISO 9000 Handbook. Robert W. Peach, Irwin, Chicago, IL, 1997, ISBN 0-786307-86-2. A very good general guide. Includes some information on software quality. Good appendices listing ISO 9000 consultants, training services, and registration information. Includes complete text of the main standards.

ISO 9000 for Software Developers. Charles H. Schmauch, ASQC Press, Milwaukee, WI, 1994. ISBN 0-87389-246-1. Primarily dedicated to ISO 9000 registration and audits. Little information regarding the mechanical details of applying the standards to real software projects.

LabVIEW Code Extensions

Brian Paquette
SensArray Corporation

Even though LabVIEW provides you with broad functionality, times may arise when you would like to do something that isn't possible with Lab-VIEW's included feature set. If you couldn't extend LabVIEW's capabilities, at best you might work around the lapse, and at worst you might glumly abandon your idea. The developers of LabVIEW at National Instruments foresaw this dilemma and included means to broaden Lab-VIEW's reach. These are the **Code Interface Node** (CIN) and the **Call Library Function**, collectively referred to here as **code extensions**. With these doorways, you can add your own conventional text-oriented code, access the operating system, and incorporate libraries provided by other programmers.

National Instruments has provided good documentation on CINs and the Call Library Function. Rather than parroting information that Lab-VIEW's own documentation already records, I am going to provide additional information here to broaden your understanding of this subject. In learning how to use CINs and the Call Library Function, be very sure to study the LabVIEW documentation, especially the *LabVIEW Code Interface Reference Manual.* Excellent overviews exist in that documentation. Be sure to read the CIN Common Questions Section; LabVIEW 4 and 5 users can also get details of CIN functions in the LabVIEW on-line documentation available through the Help menu.

Descriptions

We'll start off by looking at the methods available for accessing code extensions from LabVIEW: CINs, Call Library Functions, and Shared Libraries. At the core of this discussion is which kind of code extension makes sense in a given situation.

Code Interface Nodes

CINs are block diagram nodes (Fig. 15.1) that allow you to include in your LabVIEW applications code produced from conventional programming languages. An external module, typically written in C, is written and compiled with an appropriate compiler. That object code is then linked into your LabVIEW program through a Code Interface Node on the diagram. Parameters are then passed to and from the external module when you run the VI.

Figure 15.1

Figure 15.1
A Code Interface
Node wired into a
LabVIEW block
diagram.

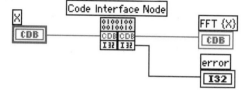

Why would you use a CIN? One reason would be to optimize lengthy calculations. I wrote a test VI comparing array element replacement where LabVIEW diagram execution speed was compared to CIN execution speed. The VI begins with an input array containing random numbers between 0.0 and 1.0 as shown in Fig. 15.2. It then goes through the array replacing all elements having values between 0.0 and 0.5 with the value 0.0. On the computer used for the test, the CIN (see Fig. 15.3) executed 6.0 times faster than the diagram code. Keep in mind that this example is contrived. In other instances, the block diagram may execute as fast as (or conceivably faster than) a comparable CIN.[1]

Another reason to use CINs would be to access the underlying operating system in ways not provided for by LabVIEW. Programmers have used

[1]The VI in Fig. 15.2 makes optimal use of a LabVIEW technology called *inplaceness*—the ability to perform operations on data structures such as arrays while avoiding data duplication and thus minimizing memory management. A more "obvious" version of this VI, using autoindexing of the arrays on the boundaries of the For Loop, ran 2.6 times slower than the optimized version.

Figure 15.2
Performance of this
VI was compared
with a CIN version
(listing appears in Fig.
15.3). The CIN was
6.0 times faster in this
particular example,
but results can vary
widely depending
upon what actions
the code performs
and the particular
computer system.

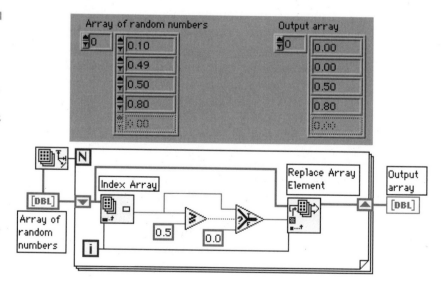

Figure 15.3
This bit of C code performs the same array replacement operation as the VI in Fig. 15.2.

```c
typedef struct {
    int32 len;
    float64 val[1];
    } dblArray;
typedef dblArray **dblArrayHdl;

CIN MgErr CINRun(dblArrayHdl array)
    {
    int32 i;
    double *thisVal;
    for (i = (*array)->len, thisVal = (*array)->val;
        i != 0; i--, thisVal++)
        if (*thisVal < 0.5)
            *thisVal = 0.0;
    return noErr;
    }
```

this to implement such diverse features as setting the computer's time, security mechanisms, and digital movie creation. After searching fruitlessly through LabVIEW's manuals for hours, you may finally come to the conclusion that LabVIEW just won't let you accomplish your desired end. In many such cases, you can include your own text-oriented code that does what you want. (For Windows, Call Library Functions may be a better choice for accessing the operating system, as discussed later in this text.)

Memory constraints can also indicate the use of CINs. When you are operating on extremely large datasets, the copies of the dataset produced by some LabVIEW diagram operations can rapidly consume your memory budget. You can use CINs to perform various operations in-place on your data, eliminating the need for an expensive copy of your dataset. String handling is another area where LabVIEW performance suffers due to the memory management operations required for every string manipulation. With external code, you can usually eliminate such overhead.

CINs also allow the inclusion of "legacy" source code, where you directly include software routines already developed in your application, thus avoiding the need for sometimes lengthy conversions to block diagrams. Data analysis frequently offers such opportunities. In fact, the bulk of LabVIEW's own advanced analysis functions utilize CINs to take advantage of widely available algorithms and to enhance performance.

Call Library Functions

Often, libraries of software functions are available that you would like to access from your LabVIEW application. The Call Library Function lets you do so. The libraries you can access must be of a type that links dynamically while your application runs. These are called **Dynamic Linked**

Libraries (DLLs) under Windows and **Shared Libraries** on the Macintosh and UNIX. You cannot use so-called static libraries that link to a program at build time with Call Library Functions.

The example in Fig. 15.4 was adapted from a useful package written by Thijs Bolhuis at the University of Twente (t.bolhuis@el.utwente.nl). The library is called sndblexm.llb (SoundBlaster Examples) and is available from ftp.pica.army.mil. Bolhuis implemented a general-purpose multimedia control interface (the **MciSendString VI**) by using a Call Library Function that sends text commands to the Windows95 multimedia system. With this VI you can use numerous multimedia functions like playing and recording sounds, Musical Instrument Digital Interface (MIDI) files, playing Microsoft Audio Visual Interface (AVI) movie files, or controlling the CD player. The only trick is that you have to know the string commands. You can find these commands in the Windows System Developer Kit from Microsoft.

Figure 15.4 also shows the configuration dialog for the Call Library Function. You access this dialog by popping up on the function and

Figure 15.4
The Call Library Function is a convenient way to access external, precompiled code.

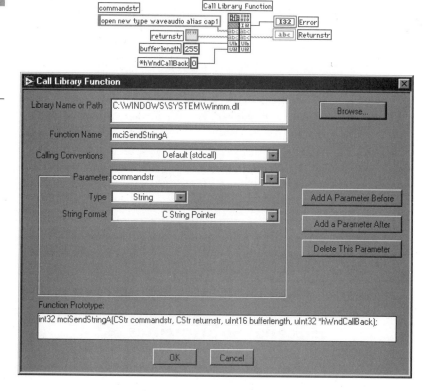

selecting *Configure*. There is a clear correspondence between the inputs and outputs on the Call Library Function and the actual function prototype, visible at the bottom of the configuration dialog.

Shared Libraries are a relatively new development for the Macintosh, and you may not find many of use to you. DLLs exist in greater numbers for Windows. Under Windows, the Call Library Function provides even greater value, as the operating system itself comprises DLLs that you can call directly in many cases. The Call Library Function offers a simpler route to the operating system's features than does a CIN.

Hardware manufacturers frequently provide DLLs for their devices, and often these DLLs can be accessed from Call Library Functions. In some cases, even though the DLLs can be accessed, proper operation requires more than simple function calls. In such cases, a CIN may be a better bet. Here's a case in point:

> Buffered acquisition can prove unwieldy at best via Call Library nodes. Buffered acquisition operates by setting up a memory buffer into which the DLL places data in the background. Generally, your calling program must allocate and provide the buffer to the DLL.
>
> Try *that* with a Call Library node, and you should brace yourself for the resounding crash of your program. No reliable method exists from the LabVIEW diagram to allocate a block of memory for use by the DLL. Yes, you could pass in a block, by passing an array or a cluster, but when you return from the library call, you have no right to expect that block to remain available for the DLL.
>
> What does this mean? Well, LabVIEW could (and probably will) decide to reuse that block of memory for something else. Then, when the DLL tries to write into it, at best, some data will get corrupted. At worst, you could cause a hard, unrecoverable crash of your application.
>
> (You could generate a suitable memory block with a CIN, then use that block in a library call. You'd need to write your own CIN for this and would need to dispose of the memory block when your DLL no longer requires it. Frankly, if I were doing it, once I pulled out the compiler for that much of the job, I would knock out the whole thing in C code for a cleaner solution. Also keep in mind that this problem would only arise if you were planning to use a third-party vendor's hardware. National Instruments' hardware works just fine with LabVIEW without these painful convolutions.)

External Subroutines

External subroutines are only callable from within CIN code resources. They provide a way to share code among several CINs. (*Note:* External subroutines are not supported on the Power Macintosh. National Instruments recommends using shared libraries as a cleaner mechanism for sharing code.) An example is the FFT algorithm provided with LabVIEW. Take a look in your LabVIEW\vi.lib\analysis\lvsb directory, and you'll see the ReFFT.lsb (LabVIEW subroutine) and several others. If these routines are documented, you can call them from your own CINs.

If you are just learning about CINs, then you should avoid external subroutines until you are comfortable with CINs themselves. Think of external subroutines as an advanced CIN feature. When you feel ready to tackle external subroutines, consult the very adequate *LabVIEW Code Interface Reference Manual* for implementation details.

Not for the Novice

LabVIEW typically forgives many programming errors, such as division by 0. It also insulates a programmer from memory usage and addressing issues as well as operating system details. In other words, you can blithely get away with things in LabVIEW's civilized environment that would thoroughly crash a conventionally written program. Further, you need little knowledge of the underlying operating system.

Entering the world of LabVIEW code extensions, you leave behind those comfortable surroundings and cross over into the land of fatal errors. Programming mistakes can *kill* here. Instantly, in some cases. In others, a bug may lurk quietly in your code, until the dark day when conditions align to trigger complete software devastation. Dazedly, the user stares at a blank screen wondering where the application went. This reveals no flaw in LabVIEW. You've left the realm that LabVIEW protects and must now yourself shoulder the robustness of your code.

Don't let this scare you. But do take care with your code extensions. Ensure that you understand how your code works. Verify that you are passing parameters properly. Test thoroughly. Include good error checking and handling. And save, save, save your work, *before* you test your code extension, in case you get a failure that blows LabVIEW out of the water, along with all of your VIs.

Start with the Examples

National Instruments provides examples of CINs and Call Library Functions in the LabVIEW\examples\cins directory. They are referenced in the manual and you should take a look at these as part of your learning process. Also, examine the analysis and data acquisition subVIs that Lab-VIEW provides. Many of these call CINs. Observe how the programmers used **wrapper VIs**, discussed later in this chapter, to insulate the CINs. (A wrapper VI simply provides a VI shell within which a single CIN is placed.)

Another source of information and examples is the CIN Corner department of the *LabVIEW Technical Resource* (LTR). (See References.) Take a look at some of the back issues and you'll find examples such as setting the system time, locating system directories, fiddling with cursors, and probing memory. All source code and example VIs are on a diskette with each issue.

Pros and Cons of Code Extensions

This section considers the advantages and disadvantages of each type of code extension. Given a choice, you may want to use one type in preference to another based on the material provided here as well as on your own experience.

Pros for All Types of Code Extensions

- You can reuse previously existing "legacy" source code or libraries with little or no modification.
- You can greatly extend LabVIEW's functionality, particularly in areas that are highly specific to hardware add-ons and operating system features.

Cons for All Types of Code Extensions

- Buggy or ill-designed code extensions can fatally crash LabVIEW.
- In LabVIEW 4 and prior versions, code extensions execute synchronously. Ordinarily, LabVIEW can execute separate portions of your block diagrams simultaneously. However, when your application enters either a CIN or a Call Library Function, only that code extension can execute, pausing the rest of your application. When the code extension executes for a long time, this can cause an apparent applica-

tion lockup, or data acquisition problems, among other troubles. Keep this synchronicity in mind when implementing your code extension. Don't just submerge into a code extension and stay down there.

LabVIEW 5 solves this synchronicity problem to a degree by permitting you to run CINs in a separate execution *thread,* courtesy of your operating system. (A thread is a preemptively scheduled path of code execution managed by the operating system.) Your CIN runs in parallel with the rest of your LabVIEW application (including the rest of the diagram upon which the CIN resides). Note that older CINs must be recompiled with some modifications to take advantage of multitasking. *Mac users note:* As of this writing, MacOS 8 does not support true multitasking; you will have to wait for a future operating system and an updated version of LabVIEW for Macintosh.

- Code extensions don't allow the use of LabVIEW's powerful and friendly debugging tools. Consequently they may be more difficult to get running correctly.

- You must purchase, learn, and maintain yet another software package: the compiler for the code extension.

Pros Specific to CINs

- In various cases, CINs can execute more rapidly than equivalent block diagram code.

- In some cases, CINs can bring excessive memory requirements under control through the use of explicit memory management.

Cons Specific to CINs

- CINs make your application nonportable because the code accessed by the CIN comprises instructions specific to the machine you are running on. Portability is one of LabVIEW's great strengths. CINs affect this portability, as you need a CIN specific to each platform upon which you wish to run. Handle this in the same manner as used by LabVIEW for its own CINs: separate out the VIs that call CINs and prepare additional versions of the VIs using CINs native to the platform to which you wish to port.

■ You must have some understanding of conventional programming languages, ordinarily the C programming language.

Pros Specific to Call Library Functions

■ When code exists in an already-built dynamically linkable library, the Call Library Function offers the simplest way to access the functions of that library.

■ For the Windows platform, the Call Library Function allows direct access to many of the operating system's features.

Cons Specific to Call Library Functions

■ Shared libraries are not as prevalent on non-Windows platforms (Macintosh and UNIX).

■ When calling a library function that requires a complicated data structure for a parameter, you may have difficulty constructing the parameter. In some cases, you may not be able to construct it at all. A parameter that requires a pointer to a struct (cluster) poses real problems, especially if any of the elements of the struct are pointers.

■ You need to understand the workings of libraries you want to call. This means correct documentation should be available for the library.

■ Call Library Functions are even more nonportable than CINs. You can simply recompile most CINs for a different platform. When you are using Call Library Functions, you basically guarantee that you won't be able to call the same library on another platform, as the library most likely doesn't exist as such on the second platform.

Pros Specific to External Subroutines

■ If you use the same functions in many CINs, you can reduce overall code size and memory requirements by placing duplicated functions in external subroutines.

■ Once you've debugged the functions in an external subroutine, you are done debugging them. In contrast, if the same functions exist independently and repeatedly within various CINs, you may have to debug them for each CIN.

Cons Specific to External Subroutines

- Reloading new code resources from external subroutines can be bother if multiple CINs link to the external subroutine. To relc new code resource, you need to get *all* of the calling CINs out memory first; otherwise, the original external subroutine cor resource never unloads. To do this, locate each instance of t' pop up on each one, and select *Purge Bad Code Resource*.

- You cannot store external subroutine code resources in I libraries. They are stored as distinct file objects.

External Code versus LabVIEW Diagrams

When should you use a CIN? A Call Library F'
diagram programming? Simpler is better, so if
code with a LabVIEW block diagram, then c
efficiency or memory consumption require
effort to upgrade. But if absolutely no m'
code with a LabVIEW diagram, then star'

Determining whether you should us
tion requires analysis of what you are
typical programming problems and w

- Getting to the operating system i
  Library Function.

- Getting to the operating syster

- Optimizing inefficient code-
  improved, then ... CIN.

- Optimizing memory cons
  improved, then ... CIN.

- Utilizing legacy source

- Accessing third-party

- Accessing third-part'
  code resource is bu'
  CIN with these, b'

■ Crashing your computer—if that's what you want to do, choose either! Remember: code extension users work on the "cutting edge"; be sure to save your work, so you don't cut yourself!

A distant relative of these code extensions, ActiveX (OLE Automation), is covered in Chap. 9. In the case of ActiveX, the external code is part of another application rather than a stand-alone fragment of code. ActiveX gives you access to methods (functions) and data inside other applications without requiring you to do any low-level coding of your own. That's a pretty handy concept. On the other hand, if you want to create a new function, you have to write a new application and have it running along with LabVIEW.

Tips, Suggestions, and Cautions

The LabVIEW manuals, as I've already indicated, are vital to your success in calling external code. This section will amplify some key points and hopefully provide some wisdom regarding the pitfalls we all encounter during development.

Common Issues

For all types of external code, there are common problems and concepts you need to know about, particularly dealing with parameter passing, memory management, and the architecture of calling VIs.

MEMORY PROBLEMS When using code extensions, you interact directly with the internal data structures of LabVIEW. As an example, consider working with arrays on the block diagram. If you attempt to replace an element past the actual end of the array (e.g., index 100 for an array of 10 elements), LabVIEW will catch this and will do nothing. On the other hand, within a CIN, the same operation can corrupt other data unless you have also implemented error checking to detect this condition. As a worst case, you might even fatally crash your application.

With the Call Library Function, sometimes you may need to provide a memory buffer to the library routine you are calling. You normally create an array of the appropriate type on the LabVIEW diagram and make sure that it contains enough elements. But if the buffer is too small or even empty, the library routine can trash memory just like a CIN with an out-of-bounds pointer.

The difference between **pointers** (addresses to memory structures) and **handles** (addresses of pointers to memory structures) can trip you up in CINs, unless you are familiar with them and realize what you are working with. Pointers are used to pass scalar values such as numerics and Booleans, and they're pretty easy to work with. Handles are used with structured types, particularly arrays and strings. The C statements to access data from handles can be rather convoluted. Be sure to study the memory manager section of the *LabVIEW Code Interface Reference Manual*.

The LabVIEW memory manager includes special functions for dealing with memory allocation—you don't use the C memory functions, such as **malloc()**, nor do you directly call the memory manager for your operating system. As an additional precaution, if you pass an array into a CIN, do not dispose of it within the CIN, as LabVIEW will expect the array to still exist after the CIN is done with it.

WRAPPER VIs AND SEPARATE VI LIBRARIES FOR CODE EXTENSIONS Wrapping your CINs and Call Library Functions in a lightweight VI that contains the code extension node can make your diagrams much cleaner and easier to understand. On the diagram that uses the code extension, having a regular subVI present (along with its connector terminals and information visible in the help window) provides better understanding of your program than would simply plunking down a vague-appearing Code Interface Node or Call Library Function. The front panel and diagram of a typical wrapper VI are shown in Fig. 15.5. Error clusters, refnums, and other familiar controls are usually included. You might include some information about your external code in the Get Info dialog or in diagram comments, or perhaps even include a program listing if it's not too long.

Further, by compartmentalizing your code extensions in wrapper VIs and placing them in their own VI library (or libraries), you ease portability issues. Platform-specific code extensions can be developed for each target platform. Make copies of the wrapper VIs for each platform, and load them with the appropriately complied CIN object or link to the proper DLL. Then, when porting, you simply substitute the VI library containing the correct code extensions for each platform.

PASSING PARAMETERS Another advantage of a wrapper VI is that the data types for each control and indicator are fixed by the VI. You should never change the data type for any terminal connection on a code

Figure 15.5
Wrapper VIs encapsulate a cryptic CIN or Call Library Function, providing a well-defined but minimal interface to the calling LabVIEW diagram.

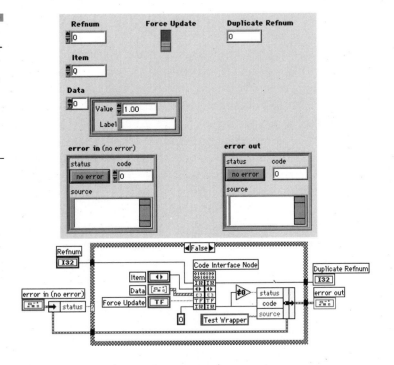

extension node unless the underlying code is recompiled to reflect the change. Ignoring this causes many crashes! Be very thorough when verifying how parameters are passed in and out of your code extensions. Be sure the parameters that are actually passed match what the code extension expects, with particular attention to pointers and handles. Also, take care when passing in string and array buffers. If a buffer needs to be a certain size, be sure to size it first. If you need to pass in the buffer size, be sure to pass in the *correct* size.

CINs

Code Interface Nodes have their own peculiar pitfalls and tricks, in addition to the fact that you'll probably be banging your head against a C compiler. Here are some tips.

LabVIEW MANAGER FUNCTIONS   LabVIEW provides many functions for use within your CINs. These include memory management, file I/O, and data conversion. The LabVIEW manuals and help files document these functions, and you should use them instead of operating-system-specific functions wherever possible. This facilitates recompiling your code for another platform. The LabVIEW CIN functions exist for all platforms and are called identically, whereas operating-system—specific functions require rewriting for each platform (along with debugging the rewritten code).

ACCESSING OPERATING SYSTEM FEATURES   For platforms other than Windows, you will probably need CINs to access the operating system. You can also use CINs for Windows operating system calls, though the Call Library Function streamlines the process and should be used preferentially. (Accessing the operating system through a CIN poses greater challenges on 16-bit Windows 3.1 than on any other system, and you really should use the Call Library Function for that platform.)

When calling the operating system, be sure you know precisely what parameters you need to pass, along with their exact data types. Further, be sure you understand what the operating system is going to do, along with any additional requirements. You obtain this information from documentation specific to your operating system. For the Macintosh, get the Inside Macintosh books. For Windows, you can get the official Windows Programmer Reference Manuals. For each platform, CD-ROMs are also available that include descriptions of the functions, along with much additional information. In fact, both the Microsoft Developer Network Library CD-ROM and the Inside Macintosh CD-ROM cost less than the hard-copy manuals, while offering search capabilities and scads of supplementary documentation. Information about the Microsoft Developer Network is available at www.microsoft.com. Information about Apple Developer Programs is available at www.devworld.apple.com.

DETERMINING WHEN A CIN WILL BE FASTER   No hard-and-fast method exists to evaluate whether replacing block diagram code with a CIN will help your application. One thing to keep in mind: You should only optimize code that consumes a large percentage of the overall execution time. If a routine is called once and executes briefly, you will gain little by converting to a CIN. However, if something executes repeatedly and takes a good amount of time to complete, it is a prime candidate for optimization. (This recalls the old programmer's rule of thumb, *Hand-code the innermost loop.*) But remember that there are trade-offs: Do you want to lose the ease of LabVIEW diagrammatic debugging tools? Are you willing to sacrifice transparent portability?

CLONE YOUR LabVIEW MAKEFILES AND PROJECTS   The *LabVIEW Code Interface Reference Manual* details the construction of LabVIEW **makefiles** and **projects** for various compilers. Rather than rebuilding a new makefile or project each time, generally it is simpler to make a copy of an existing one and then edit it to reflect your new CIN. Be sure to correctly edit *all* of the necessary portions!

USE REGULAR PROGRAMMING TECHNIQUES   There is nothing magical about CIN source code; good programming techniques always apply. Though it should be obvious, remember to use meaningful names for functions and variables, and to generously insert comments in your code.

DEBUGGING   Once your application execution enters a CIN, you can no longer use the convenient LabVIEW debugging features to observe variables or the progress of execution. LabVIEW includes the **DbgPrintf()** function as documented in the *LabVIEW Code Interface Reference Manual*. This function works similarly to the usual C library **printf()** function. You can use it to track execution of your CIN by strategically locating DbgPrintf() statements at various points within your code. You can also use it to trace the values of variables (again, by placing it within your code where you wish to see what the variables are doing).

You must include the DbgPrintf() calls in your source code. That is, you can't dynamically insert them while running the calling VI. Luckily, compiling code for CINs generally goes very fast, so you can stop your application, insert some DbgPrintf() statements, rebuild, and then get running again in short order.

Some useful items to consider printing include:

- *Values of variables.* Be sure to use a formatting code appropriate to the data type you're printing; otherwise you may display garbage.

- *"I got here!" messages.* For instance, you may want to verify that an if-then-else structure is going the appropriate way.

- *Error codes.* Most external routines that you may invoke (from the operating system or the LabVIEW toolbox, for instance) return error codes. Actually, it's best to return these error codes through your function definition so that the calling VI can interpret the error.

SOURCE LEVEL DEBUGGING UNDER WINDOWS NT   Under Windows NT (and possibly Windows 95), you can use the source level debugger available with your compiler to debug your CINs. The *LabVIEW Code Interface Reference Manual* contains instructions for implementing this.

DEBUGGING ON MACINTOSH   On the Macintosh, you can (and should) use an assembly level debugger. **MacsBug** is the traditional tool, and it works for both 68000 and Power PC processors. MacsBug and its user manual are available from Apple Computer through its Web site at www.devworld.apple.com.

DON'T USE THE SAME NAME FOR MULTIPLE CINs Just as you cannot have more than one VI with the same name in memory at the same time, neither can you have more than one code resource (within a CIN) with the same name. Bear this in mind, and be sure to name each code resource uniquely!

On the other hand, this means you could place multiple copies of your CIN on the diagrams of your application. (By this, I mean multiple copies of the Code Interface Node itself, rather than multiple copies of any wrapper VI.) Use this technique with caution. LabVIEW allocates only one data space for globals and static variables even if multiple instances of a CIN exist. Modifying a persistent variable at one instance of the CIN will modify it for all others. (A per-instance data space can also be accessed by your CIN. The "CIN Advanced Topics" section of the *LabVIEW Code Interface Reference Manual* describes how this works. Bear in mind that unfamiliarity with CIN programming could lead to trouble when implementing advanced features. Start with the easy stuff, and work up to the fancy items.)

64k LIMIT ON MACINTOSH On the Macintosh, due to operating system constraints, a CIN's code resource has an upper size limit of 64k. Luckily, most code resources are far smaller than 64k. If you need more than 64k worth of code in a CIN, you will have to put some of it in an external subroutine. Instructions for the development and use of external subroutines are similar to those for CINs and are in the *LabVIEW Code Interface Reference Manual*. (*Note:* This 64k limit is on the object code size, not the source code size.)

A PSEUDOASYNCHRONOUS CIN FRAMEWORK As I mentioned before, in LabVIEW versions prior to 5.0, CINs are executed synchronously—without interruption—and this can hang up your entire hierarchy. Even in LabVIEW 5, where CINs can execute in their own multitasking thread, multiple CINs can delay one another's execution. To circumvent these problems, you can write a pseudoasynchronous CIN.

Let's say you have a large array of values upon which you wish to do complex and computationally intensive processing. If you were to just send the data down into a CIN, you would pause execution of your entire application (or at least the CIN thread) until the CIN completed. For various reasons (a desire to keep the user interface operable, interfacing to I/O lines, etc.) you may find such a pause indefensible.

You can process through such a large array in a pseudoasynchronous fashion by calling your CIN from within a While Loop. After the CIN calculates every row or so, it can return to its calling VI, and the calling VI then calls a Wait function to allow other portions of the LabVIEW application to execute. After the Wait expires, the CIN is called again to process the next portion. Internally, the CIN must keep track of progress in its calculation or other status information. Alternatively, you could pass the status information back to LabVIEW and have it recirculate to the CIN through a shift register.

The **CIN Take Breath VI** (Fig. 15.6) and its C source code, **Breathe.c**, are included on the CD-ROM. Use them as a template for your own pseudoasynchronous CINs.

**\Asynch_
CIN**

Keep in mind that this tricky technique requires a certain attention to detail. Study the example VI and CIN source code to see how each of them perform initialization.

It is best not to make the VI reentrant. In other words, if you are going to use multiple instances of the VI within your program, ensure that each VI instance must complete before another instance of it begins execution. (LabVIEW makes VIs *not* reentrant as a default case, so you need do nothing. What I am saying here is do not change the VI's setup to reentrant.)

When you set up VIs as reentrant, each instance of the VI can execute simultaneously. This can confuse the CIN: The first instance initializes and begins iterating, then the second instance initializes, causing any global information stored for the first instance to become lost. (Remember, this only occurs when you have set the VI to be reentrant. Under the normal VI setup, this problem does not occur.)

You could make the CIN more involved to handle multiple reentrant cases, but that exceeds the scope of this book. Approaches would include

Figure 15.6
The CIN-based Take Breath VI is an example of a way to implement pseudo-asynchronous CINs.

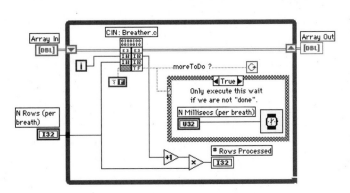

ensuring that you do not use any global data or using per-instance data storage space for the CIN if you feel you must have global storage. (For information on per-instance data storage space for CINs, consult the LabVIEW CIN manual.)

Also, you should not use this technique under LabVIEW 5 (unless you are working on a Macintosh). For non-Macintosh applications, LabVIEW 5 provides its own native multithreading support for CIN asynchronicity, leveraging the operating system's features. Where possible, you should utilize these native services because they help keep your own application simpler and more trouble free.

GLOBAL VARIABLES IN CINs Now that you've started programming with code extensions, you have two types of global variables. You can use the regular LabVIEW diagram globals, and you can also implement global variables in your CIN.

Why should you use globals in a CIN? After all, you cannot get to them from the LabVIEW diagram. (Let me also point out you cannot access LabVIEW globals from a CIN, unless you pass them in as function parameters.)

One reason might be for persistent storage between calls to your CIN. For example, in the pseudoasynchronous application previously discussed, state information could be stored in CIN globals.

Other methods could also be used for persistent storage: for instance, repeatedly passing in the same value as a function parameter to the CIN and the use of *static* variables (variables declared within a specific C function whose value persists from one call of the function to the next).

If you want to access the value stored in CIN's global variables from the LabVIEW diagram, you will have to pass the variables out as function parameters. Also remember that, as with all global variables, you must initialize them before use. The CINLoad() function is the usual place to do this, because it runs when the CIN is loaded into memory. For more information, see the section on global variable usage in the *LabVIEW Code Interface Reference Manual.*

Call Library Nodes

Unlike the CIN, the Call Library Node does not require you to do any external code development, so long as you're calling an existing DLL or Shared Library. Also, the pop-up configuration dialog on the Call Library Node makes it easy to specify parameters for most situations. Here are a few tips for special occasions.

LOCATING OS FUNCTIONS IN DLLs   As mentioned, the Call Library Function excels in accessing operating system functions on the Windows platform. But a catch exists: Of the myriad of DLLs in the Windows directories, how do you know which one contains the function you want? You might use the process of elimination: LabVIEW will complain if it cannot find the function when you tell it which library to use. Checking each system DLL until you locate your function would be painful at best.

Generally, you can locate the DLL containing a particular function by checking what **import library** would be required if calling the function from regular C code. Import libraries provide information to the C/C++ linker that indicates which DLLs should be used for what functions. The import libraries normally match the names of the container DLLs (at least with Microsoft's compiler), with the difference that the DLL file extension is .dll and the import library's file extension is .lib.

For instance, if your documentation indicates that you would use user32.lib for some function (if you were writing C code), then the function would be contained in user32.dll. Typically, the operating system DLLs exist in the SYSTEM or SYSTEM32 directories under the operating system's main directory. That is, if you install your OS into C:\WINNT, then look for the DLLs in C:\WINNT\SYSTEM32 or C:\WINNT\SYSTEM. If you are using the Microsoft Developer Network CD-ROM, most versions will provide the names of import libraries for your functions. Examine the documentation included with your specific version of the CD-ROM for details.

PASSING CLUSTERS AS PARAMETERS   The Call Library Function does not have a setting for cluster parameters (called **structs** in C programming). Luckily, structs are stored in memory with the elements arranged contiguously. So if you are trying to pass a cluster containing two 32-bit integers and a 64-bit float, simply specify two 32-bit integers (I32) and a double (DBL) as parameters as shown in Figure 15.7. Clearly, ordering of parameters is important.

Some functions you may want to call might require a cluster passed in by address (pointer). This is problematic, as simply passing in the elements themselves differs completely from passing a cluster by address. To get around this, you can allocate a byte array of the same size as the cluster and place values into it manually. This technique is error prone, so be sure to save your work frequently. Also, if a cluster passed by pointer must itself contain pointers, you have entered the *stumper zone*. At that point, the only thing to do is whip out a compiler and build a CIN to make your call.

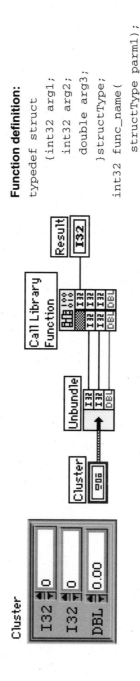

Function definition:

```
typedef struct
    {int32 arg1;
     int32 arg2;
     double arg3;
    }structType;
int32 func_name(
        structType parm1);
```

Figure 15.7
Passing a cluster to a Call Library Function.

TWO TYPES OF STRINGS UNDER Win32 Win32 supports two types of strings: **normal** (or ANSI) strings, where each character is represented by a single 8-bit value, and **wide** strings where each character is represented by a 16-bit value. The wide strings are used for character-rich written languages such as exist in Japan.

Consequently, when a Win32 operating system function takes a string as a parameter, two separate versions of the function exist: one that takes normal strings and one that takes wide strings. The names of the function differ: Normal string functions have an *A* suffix (for ANSI), and wide string functions have a *W* suffix (for wide). You will not locate the function in a DLL under the name without a suffix. (*Note:* Under some Win32 operating systems, only the normal string function may exist. It will still have the *A* suffix.) For example, the MessageBox function (which puts up an *alert* dialog), is found under 16-bit Windows 3.1 simply as MessageBox. However, under Windows NT, you would find MessageBoxA and MessageBoxW instead. Since you will only be passing in normal strings from LabVIEW, you specify the *A*-suffixed variant in these cases.

Summary

Code Interface Nodes and Call Library Functions offer tremendous opportunity for the LabVIEW programmer, but they also leave the programmer unshielded from the hazards of routine programming. When using code extensions, be sure that using one makes sense, and then be very thorough when developing the extension to ensure robustness. And don't forget to save your work!

Bibliography

LabVIEW Technical Resource (LTR), a quarterly publication available from LTR Publishing, 6060 N. Central Expressway, Suite 502, Dallas, TX 75206. Phone (214) 706-0587, fax (214) 706-0506, www.ltrpub.com.

16

LabVIEW and Serial Interfaces

George Wells

Measurement Technology Center (MTC), Jet Propulsion Laboratory,

California Institute of Technology

This chapter is about using serial ports to interface with various data acquisition devices and controllers collectively called **serial instruments**.[1] Virtually all computers have serial ports intended for connection to modems or printers and, as such, have excellent operating system support. Despite the simplicity of this interface (there are only five basic serial functions and VIs in LabVIEW), many people are confused about how to hook serial ports up, so we begin with a description of the hardware layer.

RS-232

The usual specification for serial ports is RS-232, although this standard is rarely fully complied with. Our interest is in understanding how to successfully connect a computer to a device that claims to be RS-232 compatible, even if both the computer and the device are not in full compliance with the standard. The standard is written from the point of view of connecting a computer to a modem (Fig. 16.1). This means that all the terminology for the two data lines and the six handshaking lines (Tables 16.1 and 16.2) assumes that a modem is being used, which is generally not the case with serial instruments.

The manufacturers of these devices have therefore had to bend the specification in different ways as seemed reasonable to each one of them. For example, since a modem connects to a telephone line, it has a handshaking

---

[1]It is not about using the serial ports with SCXI, for which everything will be taken care of for you if you simply run NI-DAQ FieldPoint also has its own software.

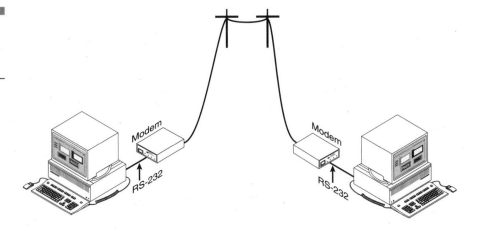

Figure 16.1
The original concept for RS-232: computers and modems.

TABLE 16.1

RS-232 DB-25 Pin
Connections

Computer	Abbreviation	Direction	Name	Modem
1 and 7	Gnd	—	Ground	1 and 7
2	TxD	→	Transmit Data	2
3	RxD	←	Receive Data	3
4	RTS	→	Request to Send	4
5	CTS	←	Clear to Send	5
6	DSR	←	Data Set Ready	6
8	DCD	←	Data Carrier Detect	8
20	DTR	→	Data Terminal Ready	20
22	RI	←	Ring Indicator	22

TABLE 16.2

RS-232 DB-9 Pin
Connections

Computer	Abbreviation	Direction	Name	Modem
1	DCD	←	Data Carrier Detect	1
2	RxD	←	Receive Data	2
3	TxD	→	Transmit Data	3
4	DTR	→	Data Terminal Ready	4
5	Gnd	—	Ground	5
6	DSR	←	Data Set Ready	6
7	RTS	→	Request to Send	7
8	CTS	←	Clear to Send	8
9	RI	←	Ring Indicator	9

line called *Ring Indicator* (RI) to tell the computer when an incoming call is being received. If there is no modem and no telephone line, what is the instrument manufacturer to do with the RI line? Another handshaking line, called *Data Carrier Detect* (DCD), is used by the modem to tell the computer when it "hears" the audio tones used to carry the digital data over the analog telephone lines. Again, with no modem and no telephone line, what should an instrument manufacturer do with the DCD line?

While we're on the subject of confusing modem terminology, let's put to rest the definition of **baud rate**. Technically, it only has meaning when used in reference to a modem and refers to the rate at which the analog tones can change on the telephone line. Low-speed modems have a one-to-one correspondence between the rate of the digital serial bit stream on the computer side of the modem and the rate at which the analog tones change on the telephone side of the modem (Fig. 16.2). Because the telephone line has a limited bandwidth and can't tolerate a high switching rate between just one pair of tones, higher-speed modems collect groups of bits together and produce a larger number of possible tones, but they switch between the tones at a much lower rate than the rate of the serial bit stream. This lower switching rate between tones on the telephone side of the modem is called the baud rate. A typical 1200-bps (bits per second) modem has a baud rate of 600 because each pair of bits selects one of four tones (Fig. 16.3). The term *baud rate* was invented precisely to handle this difference between these two rates, but unless you are a modem designer you will probably succumb to the common usage (and so will we!), which is to apply it to the digital side of the modem, especially when using serial instruments where no modems are involved.

One of the ways serial instrument manufacturers can solve the problem of not having a modem is to pretend that there are two modems with a telephone line between them. In this case you use a **null modem**, which is simply a pair of connectors wired as if they were two modems connected by a telephone line (Fig. 16.4). These two connectors can be

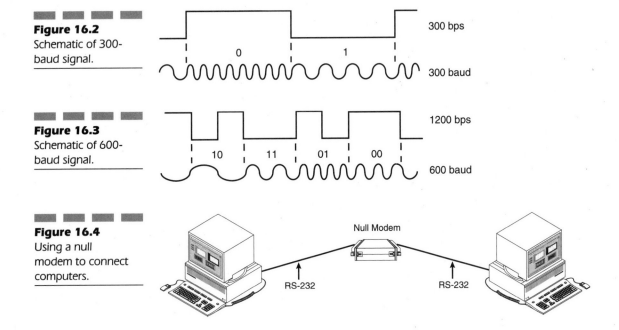

Figure 16.2
Schematic of 300-baud signal.

300 bps

0   1

300 baud

Figure 16.3
Schematic of 600-baud signal.

1200 bps

10   11   01   00

600 baud

Figure 16.4
Using a null modem to connect computers.

Null Modem

RS-232   RS-232

mounted together on a small module barely larger than the connectors themselves, or they can be wired into the connectors on the ends of a cable. Either way, it is a good idea to make sure the module or cable is clearly labeled *null modem*. A null modem is almost always the solution to tying two computers together over their serial ports and works perfectly well for the two data lines (pins 2 and 3 are interchanged). But if any handshaking lines are used, all bets are off. You can buy null modems with different configurations of their handshaking lines, or you can get a module with jumpers so you can customize your own. The DIN-8 cable that connects two Macintosh computers together is wired as if it had a built-in null modem. You will also need a null modem module and/or cable to connect a Macintosh to a PC or other computer.

The more common way serial instrument manufacturers have solved the problem of not having a modem is to pretend that the instrument itself is a modem or has a built-in modem. This means that you do not have to worry about how to wire the cable; it's pin-to-pin (2 to 2, 3 to 3, etc.) as long as the connectors are identical. Although the RS-232 spec does not define a connector type, the DB-25 is considered the de facto standard. There is an abundance of cables, null modems, gender changers, adapters, breakout boxes, and testers based on the DB-25 connector.

In recent years, a new connector, the DB-9, has gained in popularity. It's found almost exclusively on newer PCs and on a great many serial instruments that cater to the PC market. It does not follow the RS-232 convention for pin numbering, but this generally is no problem, especially if you are connecting a nine-pin serial port on a PC to a nine-pin serial instrument. Cables exist that are wired pin to pin and are of the proper gender to make the connection easy, and many manufacturers even provide a cable with their instrument. The challenge comes when you need to interconnect devices with a different type of connector. Most of the time the connection can be made with off-the-shelf adapters, but you may feel as if you are building something out of Lego™ blocks by the time you are done stacking all the adapters together. Just put together whatever adapters it takes to make the connection, but do not use a null modem unless you are connecting two computers together or unless you cannot make the connection work otherwise (Fig. 16.5). If you shop around, especially through mail-order catalogs, you may even find a single cable that meets your needs. Later, we'll go into more detail about making connections when all else fails.

Assuming that you have made a connection from your computer to a remote device (we'll use that term to apply to either another computer or an instrument), it's time to start sending and receiving character strings, which we'll call **messages**. In our examples we use an Advantech ADAM

▬▬ ▬▬ ▬▬ ▬

Figure 16.5
Null modems with
gender changers,
showing 9- and
25-pin types.

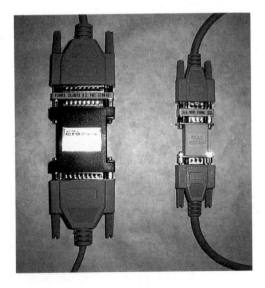

4018M device that has been set up to measure temperature. Even if you do
not have a device to work with, you can always experiment with the serial
ports by connecting one serial port on your computer to another one on
the same computer. Remember to use a null modem module or cable. Or
you can create a *loop-back* on a single serial port by tying the two data
lines together (pins 2 and 3) on a 25-pin or 9-pin port. If you are using a
Macintosh, the easiest way to do this is to buy a *Macintosh modem cable*
with DIN-8 to DB-25 connectors (Fig. 16.6).

There are two ways to use LabVIEW to communicate over the serial
ports. The first, and more convenient, is to use the **serial port VIs** be-

▬▬ ▬▬ ▬▬ ▬

Figure 16.6
Examples of RS-232
adapters and cables.

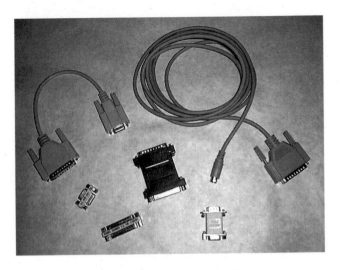

cause you can run them as is. The other way is to use the newer **Virtual Instrument Standard Architecture** (VISA) functions, but you will have to create a VI to exercise them. We'll cover them later.

Using the Serial Port VIs

Start by opening the **Serial Port Init VI**, shown in Fig. 16.7. It's available from the Instrument function menu, or from the serial library located in the labview/vi.lib/instr/serial.llb directory. If you are connected to an instrument, set the parameters the way the instrument requires. If you are not sure about any parameters, leave them alone and they will probably work (9600 baud, 8 bits, and no parity are extremely common settings). On a PC, the port number is one less than the COM port. Use 0 for COM1, 1 for COM2, and so on. On a Macintosh, 0 is the modem port and 1 is the printer port. Run the VI and make sure that the error code is 0. If not, the port is either in use or nonexistent, or a parameter is illegal. If you have a connection between two ports on the same computer, initialize both ports.

After successful initialization you can begin sending and receiving messages. Open the **Serial Port Write**, **Serial Port Read**, and **Bytes At**

Figure 16.7
The Serial Port Init VI. Call this before any other serial VI.

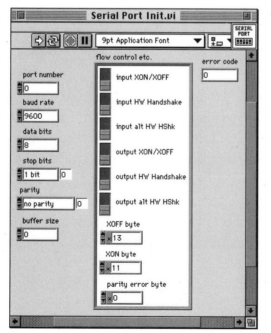

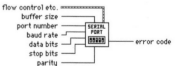

Serial Port VIs. If you have a connection between two ports on the same computer, set the *write* port number to one port and the port numbers on the other two VIs to the other port number. Continuously run the Bytes At Serial Port VI. It should return a byte count of 0. If not, run the Serial Port Read VI once with the requested byte count set to the byte count from the Bytes At Serial Port VI to "flush" the receive buffer.

Now type a valid message into the *string to write* control if you are connected to an instrument (Fig. 16.8) or type anything, such as *Hello World,* if you are not connected to an instrument. Run the Serial Port Write VI. You should immediately see the byte count in the Bytes At Serial Port VI increase by some amount (Fig. 16.9). Enter this amount into the Serial Port Read VI and run it (Fig. 16.10). You should see a valid response (if connected to an instrument) or whatever message you sent (if not connected to an instrument).

If you are connected to an instrument and do not get the expected response, it may be because you are not using the proper termination character(s). It is advisable to turn on (or leave on) the \ Codes Display by

Figure 16.8
The Serial Port Write
VI sends characters to
an instrument.

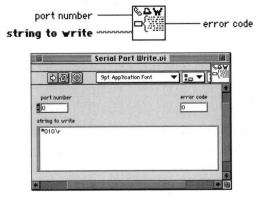

Figure 16.9
The Bytes At Serial
Port VI tells you how
many bytes are wait-
ing in the receive
buffer.

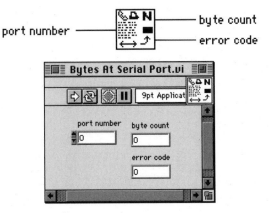

Figure 16.10
The Serial Port Read
VI reads characters
from the receive
buffer.

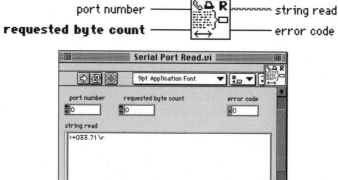

popping up on the string control of the Serial Port Write VI and the string indicator of the Serial Port Read VI so that you can tell exactly what control codes are being sent and received. Some instruments require just a carriage return (\r), while others require a carriage return and line feed (\r\n) or maybe just a line feed (\n). Depending upon the preferences you have set for your copy of LabVIEW, hitting the carriage return key may enter a carriage return as expected, or it may enter a line feed, or it may terminate the string as if you had hit the *enter* key. To be on the safe side, enter the required termination characters as backslash codes.

If you are sometimes getting incomplete responses, this may signify a recurring problem that exists on some PCs that can be solved by using the VISA functions instead of the serial port VIs. The VISA functions are preferred anyway because they better handle the command-response protocol used by most serial instruments, and they offer many more useful features. You will need to close any ports that you have initialized using the serial port VIs before you can use those ports with the VISA functions. Use the **Close Serial Driver VI** (Fig. 16.11) found in _sersup.llb in the same directory that contains the serial library. Or, you can just quit and restart LabVIEW to free the serial ports.

Figure 16.11
The Close Serial Driver VI releases a port for use by other applications. See text for this VI's location.

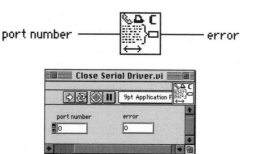

The VISA Functions

As stated earlier, you will need to create a VI to use the VISA functions. Let's begin with a simple VI that will write a string to a serial port and read a string back on the same port. This is exactly the same process used before with the serial port VIs to communicate with an instrument or in a loop-back configuration. It will operate at 9600 baud with eight data bits and no parity, the most common parameters for serial instruments. We'll cover other cases later.

LabVIEW 5 has *easy-level* VISA functions that may simplify the process of writing an instrument driver. In particular, the **Easy VISA Serial Write & Read VI** makes a great starting point for serial I/O development. But, for the purpose of education, we'll build our own version—called VISA Test—and see how the lower-level VISA functions work together.

Start with a new VI and put the following four VISA functions—**VISA Open**, **VISA Write**, **VISA Read**, and **VISA Close**—on the diagram one after the other as shown in Fig. 16.12. The functions are located in the Instrument I/O function palette under VISA. Wire the *VISA session* and *error out* terminals on the right corners of each function to the corresponding inputs on the left corners of each next function. You can pop up on the last error output to create an indicator on the front panel to show if there are any errors. In addition, you should pop up on several other terminals, starting with the *resource name* of the VISA Open VI to create a string constant. For the resource name, you should type ASRL# where # is replaced by the port number. The port number here is one greater than that used with serial port VIs and is the same as the COM port number on a PC. On a Macintosh, use 1 for the modem port and 2 for the printer port. Next, pop up on the *VISA session (for class)* control on the VISA Open VI (upper left corner) and create a control. Note that you cannot create a constant. Pop up on this new VISA session terminal and

Figure 16.12
Diagram for the simple VISA Test VI.

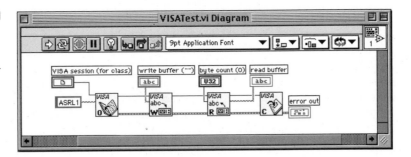

from the pop-up menu choose **Select VISA Class>>Serial Instr**. Next, pop up on the *write buffer* input on the VISA Write function and create a string control. Pop up on the *byte count* input on the VISA Read function and create a numeric control. Finally, pop up on the *read buffer* output on the VISA Read function and create a string indicator.

On the front panel, turn on backslash codes for the string control and indicator and save your VI with a name such as VISATest.vi. On the front panel (Fig. 16.13), type a valid command into the write buffer if you are connected to an instrument or any other text string if you're doing a loop-back test. Set the *byte count* to the expected number of bytes returned. Unlike with the serial port VIs, this number can be larger or smaller than the actual number; it will still work, although if the number is too small, you will not see all the characters, and if it is too large, it will just take longer, based on the *timeout value*, which defaults to 2000 ms. Now you should be able to test your serial port using VISA. If you're lazy, just open the VISA Test 1 VI on the CD-ROM; it's ready to use.

If you have a serial instrument that requires parameters (now called **properties**) other than the VISA default (9600 baud, eight data bits, no parity, etc.), you can set the parameters with a **VISA Property node** (previously called **VISA Attribute node** in LabVIEW 4) inserted between the VISA Open and VISA Write functions (Fig. 16.14). It works very much like the attribute node for controls and indicators except that the top portion of it provides a place for the session and error parameters to be strung together as for the other VISA functions. You can pull down several properties and select which items appear in each terminal individually. In our descriptions we will use the long names for all the properties. Some of the properties are similar to the parameters used in the Serial Port Init VI, but there are a whole lot more. We'll cover all the relevant

**\Serial_
Utilities\VISA
Test 1.VI**

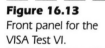

**\Serial_
Utilities\VISA
Test 2.VI**

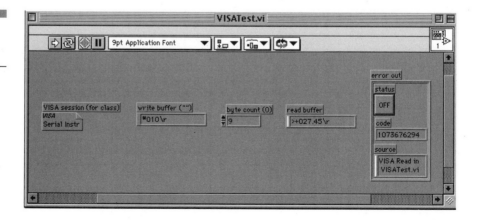

Figure 16.13
Front panel for the VISA Test VI.

Figure 16.14
Diagram for the
Enhanced VISA
Test VI.

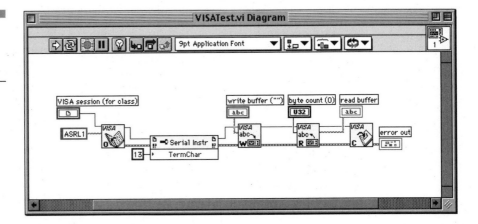

ones shortly. For detailed help on all of the VISA properties, consult the VISA reference manual, available from National Instruments. LabVIEW's Online Reference will give you full information on the LabVIEW VISA functions, but hardly any on the VISA properties.

If you have connected two serial ports together on the same computer, you will need to use the VISA Open and VISA Close functions twice, once for each port. You will also have to put everything in a sequence structure so that both ports are open before you execute the VISA Write function.

In a real serial instrument application, you would more than likely open the VISA session once, do a whole bunch of writes and reads, and only close the VISA session just before quitting. The VISA functions make it very easy to communicate with command-response-type instruments because they eliminate the timeout and hang-up problems to which the traditional serial port VIs are prone, and they offer several significant new features designed specifically for command-response devices.

End Modes for Termination Characters

One of these important new features is called **end mode**. It has to do with determining the end of a response message. As mentioned earlier, most serial instruments use some combination of carriage return (\r) and line feed (\n) to terminate each message. When you are writing a command message to the instrument, you simply include the termination character(s) at the end of the message. But when you want to read the response message back from the instrument, things get really messy, especially when the response can have a variable length. Serial VISA sessions default to looking for a line feed as the termination character and will automatically stop reading whenever a line feed is received. If that is what your instrument uses, then all you have to do is request the maximum expected byte count on the VISA Read function, and the function will quickly return the actual message that the serial instrument sent. This feature alone should induce you to start using VISA functions over serial VIs in case you haven't already been persuaded. If your instrument uses a termination character other than line feed, you can set it with a property node right after you open the VISA session. The code for carriage return is 13; that for line feed is 10. If your instrument uses the CR-LF pair, then of course you do not have to do anything since the line feed is the final termination character and the default case will handle it. Figure 16.15 shows the result of using a carriage return as the end mode termination character with the ADAM 4018M device.

The VISA serial property **Serial End Mode for Reads** determines whether termination characters will be recognized when received. The default value for this property is 2, meaning that end mode is active. If you do not want to have your VISA Reads stop on a termination character, then you need to set this property to 0. This is especially important if you are receiving binary data—it's likely to contain termination character equivalents.

A second type of end mode has a value of 1 and uses the most significant bit (MSB) to signify the last character of a message. When this mode is used, the VISA Read will stop whenever the MSB of any character is set. You always need to provide one more bit for this end flag (therefore, never use parity); for this reason the default eight data bits per character works great for ASCII text, because it uses only 7 bits. You could manually set the MSB of the last character of each command message written, but VISA can do it for you. You need to first change the **Serial End Mode for Writes** property to 1 and then set the **Send End Enable** property to true. You can do both of these operations with one property node.

Figure 16.15
Selected items from the front panel of the Enhanced VISA Test VI, showing results of communications with an ADAM 4018M.

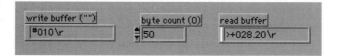

To make VISA Read work in this mode, you only have to set the Serial End Mode for Reads property to 1. The VISA Read function will stop and even clear the MSB of the last character of each response message read.

If, for some strange reason, you want to read a specific number of bytes without regard to the MSB end flag (mode 1) or termination character (mode 2), you can set the **Suppress End Enable** property to true and it will behave like mode 0 (ignore termination characters). In this case, if you are in mode 1, the MSB of every character will still be cleared when read. Setting the Termination Character Enable property to true forces mode 2 operation independent of all other settings. These two enable flags are redundant to the mode settings and their use is not advised. They are described here merely for completeness.

One important factor you must consider when using command-response devices is to make sure that your system never issues a second command before a previous command has received its response; otherwise, garbage happens. This can be handled by creating a generic write-read subVI through which all commands and their responses flow. Doing this with the serial port VIs is quite a challenge, but it's much simpler with VISA because of the available end modes.

One last set of serial VISA properties (beginning with LabVIEW 5) is the ability to individually monitor and control the handshaking lines. Two of these, **Data Terminal Ready** (DTR) and **Ready To Send** (RTS), are outputs; the other four are inputs. Negative voltages correspond to a value of 0 and positive voltages correspond to a value of 1, although the actual switching threshold on most computers is around +1.5 V, so you could use the inputs to monitor digital logic levels. The outputs will return to a negative voltage when you close the VISA session.

More Detail on Making Connections

We return now in greater detail to the subject of making connections to serial ports when all else fails. If, after experimenting with various cables and adapters, you have not found an interface that works, you can use a volmeter to unambiguously determine which pins on your RS-232 device are inputs and which are outputs. When the unconnected RS-232 device is powered on but sending no data, inputs will be within a couple of volts of ground while outputs will have greater (positive or negative) voltages on them. You should also verify which pins (including the connector shell) are actually connected to ground. Some so-called RS-232 cables leave the normal ground pins unconnected and rely on the shells to carry the ground reference—a sure recipe for disaster when you try to use the cable on a device with a plastic housing and no connection to the shell. The ground pins on a DB-25 are 1 and 7. On a DB-9, ground is pin 5, and on a DIN-8, it is the center pin.

Now let's say you are working on a new computer, and you do not even know which connectors on the back of the computer go to which serial ports. An easy solution to this problem is to run the Serial Port Init VI with several different values for the port number to see which ones do not return an error code. Then free-run the Serial Port Write VI with the valid port numbers sending a bunch of uppercase *U*s. This produces a serial bit pattern that approximates a square wave. If you examine the pins on the connectors on the back of the computer, you will eventually find one that reads a large negative DC voltage when you are not sending any characters, but will read near 0 VDC with a large AC voltage when you are sending the characters. If you have an oscilloscope or frequency counter, you will be able to measure a square wave with a frequency of half the baud rate. This identifies which pin on which connector is the transmit line for the corresponding serial port. On a DB-9 it is usually pin 3 and on a DB-25 it is usually pin 2.

Next, you can jumper this pin to other pins on the same connector, one at a time, until you find one that will allow you to send some characters on the Serial Port Write VI (*Hello World* does nicely) and then receive them on the Serial Port Read VI. This is called a loop-back test.

As a preliminary step to this process, you can free-run the Serial Port Write VI sending multiple *U*s and free-run the Bytes At Serial Port VI until you find a pin that causes the byte count to start increasing. Make sure when you are doing these tests that you use the same port number on all VIs.

You can use a voltmeter to determine whether a serial instrument needs a null modem in its cabling to your computer. With the instrument powered on but doing nothing, measure the voltages on pins 2 and 3 with respect to ground (pin 5 for a DB-9, pin 1 or 7 for a DB-25). Only one of these two pins (2 or 3) should have a large negative voltage on it (−3 to −20 V). Add this pin number to the number of pins in the connector. If the result is divisible evenly by 3, you should use a null modem module or cable when connecting the instrument to your computer. For example, say you want to hook your computer to the DB-25 connector on a serial buffer box. Pin 2 measures −11 V and pin 3 measures +0.2 V. Since pin 2 has the larger absolute voltage, you add 2 to 25 and get 27, which is evenly divisible by 3, so you conclude (correctly) that you need a null modem between your computer and your serial buffer box.

RS-232 Waveforms

The serial ports work by sending characters one bit at a time over a single signal line. We use the term *character* rather than *byte* for two reasons. First, the Serial Port Read and Write VIs and VISA functions accept character strings, and second, the characters we send may not be full 8-bit bytes; they can contain as few as 5 bits each.

When no characters are being sent, the signal line rests in an idle state, having a negative voltage in the range of –3 to –20 V for an RS-232 port (Fig. 16.16). Just before a character is sent, the voltage on the signal line switches positive in the range of +3 to +20 V for a specified interval of time. This is called the **start bit**. Then the bits of the character are switched on to the signal line one at a time, starting with the least significant (LS) bit, each bit lasting for the same specified interval of time as was used for the start bit. Each bit with a value of 1 will cause the line to go negative and each bit with a value of 0 will cause the line to go positive. If two or more adjacent bits have the same value, the line remains at the same voltage throughout their bit times.

At the end of the 5 to 8 data bits making up a character, an optional **parity bit** is asserted for one more bit time and finally the line returns to its idle (negative voltage) state for at least one bit time. This is called the **stop bit**. If another character is ready to be sent, its start bit can immediately follow the proceeding character's stop bit, but it doesn't have to—there can be a delay of any length. Once a character string is started, there will usually be a continual fluctuation of voltage on the signal line, making it difficult or impossible to distinguish the start and stop bits from the data and parity bits. For this reason, it is generally required that the serial ports pause periodically, so the receiver can resynchronize on the correct start bits. This form of serial communication, the only one supported by LabVIEW, is called **asynchronous** because it has start and stop bits. The other form, called **synchronous**, runs continuously and will not be discussed here.[2]

---

[2]Those start and stop bits were originally included in the standards because data was transmitted and received by rather sluggish equipment—namely, teletype machines. The various gears and levers required extra time to synchronize to the electrical impulses. Modern electronic equipment can generally do without the extra time, but old standards die hard.

Figure 16.16
Example RS-232 serial waveform with seven data bits, odd parity, and one stop bit.

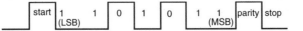

start | 1 (LSB) | 1 | 0 | 1 | 0 | 1 | 1 (MSB) | parity | stop

Serial Port Protocols

As mentioned earlier, there are several parameters (or properties) that must be specified and agreed on by the two devices involved in the serial communication. One of these is the time interval for each bit, specified by its reciprocal, the number of bits per second, or (informally) the baud rate. Common baud rates are multiples of 300 baud (bits per second), but, for historical reasons, 110 baud is also usually allowed. The most common baud rate is 9600 baud, and most computer operating systems will support at least double that rate. VISA and the traditional serial VIs default to 9600 baud.

A second important parameter is the number of **data bits per character**. Most operating systems will allow between five and eight data bits. If fewer than 8 bits are specified, only the LS bits are sent and, when received, are right-justified within the characters returned by the Serial Port Read VI or VISA Read function. Seven data bits are common when parity is used, and eight data bits are common with no parity. VISA and traditional serial VIs default to eight data bits.

The next parameter specifies the optional parity bit. Most operating systems allow *none, odd, even, mark,* and *space* parity. None (code 0) turns the parity bit off, meaning that the stop bit immediately follows the last data bit. Odd (code 1) and even (code 2) insert the parity bit such that the total number of data plus parity bits set to one is odd or even, respectively. Mark (code 3) and space (code 4) insert the parity bit forced to a value of 1 and 0, respectively. No parity is most common, but when parity is used, odd parity is more common. Parity is really not important unless a modem and telephone line are being used or unless you are using long cables at high baud rates. VISA defaults to no parity (code 0).

Most operating systems will allow LabVIEW to report an error if any character is received with the parity bit in the wrong state. You can reserve a character to signify wrong parity in the Serial Port Init VI by setting the parameter **parity error byte** to a value greater than hexadecimal FF. The low byte will be the substituted character. Of course, this feature can only be used when the substituted character will not appear during normal transmissions, such as for ASCII text messages. If you do not want to use this feature, leave the parameter at 0. This feature is not available with the VISA functions. Parity errors are also returned in the error codes of the Serial Port Read VI and VISA function, but you will not be able to determine which characters are in error.

Another parameter that must be specified is the number of stop bits. Most operating systems allow 1, 1.5, or 2 stop bits, although 1.5 may be allowed only under certain situations such as when five data bits are used.

One stop bit is almost always used, except for the practically obsolete 110 baud, where two stop bits are used. VISA uses values multiplied by 10, and because it defaults to one stop bit, it uses the value 10.

All of the above parameters must be correctly specified and agreed on by both the senders and receivers. The manual for any device that you may want to use will tell you the parameters required or how to set them. Most operating systems and LabVIEW require that the same set of parameters apply for both sending and receiving, although different serial ports can have different parameters. You set these parameters, along with others to be discussed shortly, with the Serial Port Init VI or, under VISA, with a property node.

One of these other parameters is the **buffer size**. If you leave the buffer size parameter at 0, it will use the previously allocated value, or a default value (which can be different on different platforms) if you have not previously allocated a buffer size. For this reason, it is advisable to set the buffer size if it needs to be larger than the VISA default of 50. Although there are separate buffers for sending and receiving, they can only be different sizes under VISA. If you attempt to pass characters to the Serial Port Write VI or VISA Write function faster than the serial port can send them, the VI or function merely waits until there is room in the buffer before returning. If the serial port receives characters faster than you retrieve them with the Serial Port Read VI or VISA Read function, some characters will be overwritten in the buffer and lost. The VI or VISA function will report this error.

If a large buffer size is critical to your application, you should run a test to validate that the desired buffer size can actually be achieved on your particular platform. An easy way to do this is to set up a loop-back (connect pins 2 and 3) and continually write bytes out while free-running the Bytes At Serial Port VI until the byte count stops increasing. That will tell you the actual buffer size. Be aware that the buffer size in the Serial Port Init VI is a U16, so if you pass a U32 or I32 value to the buffer that is greater than 65,535, the value will get truncated and will end up much smaller. The special VISA **Set Serial Buffer Size** function has a U32 type for its size, allowing very large buffers.

Handshaking

To accommodate finite buffer sizes, two types of handshaking are provided and must be agreed on by both devices. The first type is **software handshaking** and the second is **hardware handshaking**. The advantage of the software type is that it does not require any additional signal lines and may be used with modems, but unfortunately it limits the kind of data that can be transmitted because a pair of characters must be reserved to start and stop transmission. These characters are called XON (pronounced ex-on) and XOFF (ex-off) and are predefined in ASCII, although most operating systems will allow for any pair of characters to be used. You can set them in the Serial Port Init VI. Under VISA, software handshaking is enabled by setting the **Serial Flow Control** property to 1. VISA does not allow you to change the XON or XOFF characters and requires software handshaking to be used in both directions when enabled. VISA defaults to no handshaking (code 0).

Here's how software handshaking works. Whenever the local serial port receive buffer gets around three-quarters full, an XOFF character is output on the transmit pin (TxD) by the operating system, just as if it were another character, except that it does not pass through the transmit buffer; it cuts to the head of the line. The remote device that receives the XOFF character does not put it into its buffer but instead halts transmission of the characters it is sending to the local device, thus obtaining time to read the characters in its receive buffer. When the local device buffer gets down to about one-quarter full, an XON character is transmitted to the remote device, allowing it to start sending characters again.

In a similar way, whenever the receive pin (RxD) on the local device receives an XON or XOFF character, it does not put that character into its receive buffer but instead starts or stops the sending of characters on its transmit pin (TxD).

Immediately after the Serial Port Init VI or VISA Open function is executed, the buffers are cleared, the transmit port is ready to transmit, and no XON character is sent. Therefore, it is important that a proper start-up sequence be established with any remote device, so that you do not get into a locked-up state where both devices are waiting for an XON to be received. Obviously, using software handshaking where the XOFF character is used as data will also result in a locked-up state.

HARDWARE HANDSHAKING   Hardware handshaking works similarly to software handshaking, except that instead of special characters being sent down the same signal lines used for data, two separate lines are used for this purpose: one coming from the local device driven by the capacity of its receive buffer and one going to the local device to start and stop its transmitter. All operating systems provide at least one pair of handshaking lines. Some provide more, although usually only one in each direction is used. This versatility may save you from having to wire up a special cable. With the serial port VIs (but not under VISA) it is also possible to use hardware handshaking in one direction and not the other.

Hardware handshaking requires correct wiring of the interface cable between your computer and the remote device as well as correct programming of both. You specify which handshaking lines are used with the Serial Port Init VI. The input and output labels in the flow control cluster refer to the direction of the data being controlled, not to the actual direction of the handshaking signals. Under VISA, hardware handshaking (in both directions) is enabled by setting the Serial Flow Control property to 2. VISA outputs handshaking on both the RTS and DTR lines but inputs it only on the Clear To Send (CTS) line. Handshaking is rarely used with command-response instruments because the command-response protocol itself acts as a form of handshaking.

Since there is no standard on hardware handshaking, you may find an RS-232 tester invaluable in figuring out which lines are being used and when they are activated. Some testers even allow you to custom-wire the lines (Fig. 16.17).

SENDING A BREAK One additional function used with serial ports is called the **Send Break VI**. It probably will not be used with any modern device, as it had its origin back in the days of mechanical teletypes operating with current loops rather than voltages and was used to interrupt transmission from a remote device. In effect, Send Break sends a very long start bit, one so long that it violates the stop bit. When this bit is received, it is reported as a **framing error**. You can send a 1-second break under VISA by setting the Serial End Mode for Writes property to 3 and calling the VISA Write function with an empty string. Of course you will want to set the End Mode property back to its previous value before calling the VISA Write function with a nonempty string. LabVIEW 5 includes a convenient **VISA Serial Break VI**.

Figure 16.17
An RS-232 tester helps you figure out which lines are active.

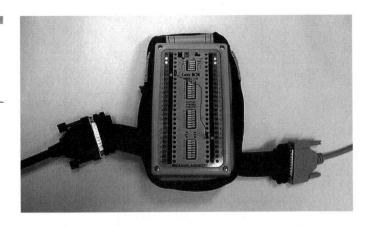

Command-Response Considerations

Most of the serial port devices that are likely to be used with LabVIEW are of the command-response type, which means your LabVIEW program will send a command to the device and wait for a response. Usually these commands and responses consist of strings of less than a dozen or so characters. Sometimes the number of characters received depends on the type of response or is variable for some other reason, such as an error condition.

In any case, you should never execute the Serial Port Read VI until you are sure that the number of bytes you request is actually in the buffer. The reason for this is that some operating systems can *hang* the Serial Port Write VI while the Serial Port Read VI is waiting for characters, and, in a command-response-type system, you would never be able to send a second command if you were expecting more characters from a previous response than were actually sent. Therefore, you should always repeatedly execute the Bytes At Serial Port VI until you get the number of characters you expect or until a specified period of time has elapsed. (This functionality is available in one of the serial utility VIs, described shortly.) You should always read the number of bytes in the receive buffer before issuing another command to the transmit buffer. As mentioned earlier, VISA is immune to this problem and is highly recommended for all command-response-type devices.

Serial Utility VIs

On the CD-ROM, you will find some serial utility VIs that are quite helpful:

\Serial Utilities

- The **Find VISA Resources VI** quickly locates any devices connected to any port on your computer, including serial, GPIB, or VXI instruments. It's useful for obtaining properly formatted VISA resource names and verifying that the expected devices are really there.

- The **Serial Test VI** is a big help when you're trying to establish communications. It lets you type in strings to send and displays the receive characters.

- The **Serial Port Receive Message VI** adds timeouts to the traditional serial port read and adds error I/O.

- The **Serial Port Send Message VI** encapsulates the traditional Serial Port Write VI and adds error I/O.

RS-422

So far our discussion has involved RS-232, which is characterized by bipolar signals on single lines. RS-422 has all the same timing as RS-232 but uses a pair of differential signal lines with complementary voltages. Usually the voltages swing between 0 and 5 V, but they can also swing between +5 and –5 V. One of the lines is labeled + and the other one –. The one labeled – is similar to RS-232 in terms of the shape and polarity of the waveform. RS-232 cannot drive lines longer than a few tens of feet because it is intended to connect directly to modems that allow the telephone lines to handle long distances. RS-422, due to its higher common-mode rejection, can drive lines of a few thousand feet. It is also designed for higher speeds, typically up to 250 Kbaud.

RS-422 is actually what the Macintosh provides on its input and output data lines, but the handshaking lines are singled-ended just like RS-232. The DIN-8 to DB-25 cable has internal wiring to change the differential RS-422 data lines to single-ended RS-232.

RS-485

RS-485 has the same voltage requirements as RS-422 but allows multiple devices to share the same pair of signal lines on a bus. It is quite common for the type of command-response data acquisition devices likely to be used with LabVIEW. Usually the family of devices provides a conversion between RS-485 and RS-232 to make interfacing simple. There are also plug-in boards that provide RS-485 directly. The trick to RS-485 is to provide a mechanism by which all of the devices are in a high-impedance state except whichever one is transmitting.

Simplex and Duplex

Sometimes when using serial ports you will come across the terms **full duplex** or **half duplex**, the latter of which is also called **simplex**. Duplex means that there are separate signal lines for transmitting and receiving. Thus, RS-232 and RS-422 are duplex. RS-485 is simplex because bidirectional signal lines are used for both transmitting and receiving, but at different times. Full duplex means that transmitting and receiving can occur simultaneously. The serial ports in computers are always capable of full duplex operation, but when used with the command-response protocol they operate as half duplex, which means that transmitting and receiving never occur at the same time.

Typical Serial Data Acquisition Devices

There are several brands of serial port data acquisition devices that will be discussed now. They all use an RS-485 converter to allow over 100 individual devices to be hooked up to one serial port and are intended for low-rate analog and digital I/O. Each family has its own advantages and you cannot mix families on the same bus or port.

National Instruments offers the **Analog Devices 6B** series. These physically look very much like the 5B series signal conditioners and plug into a similar backplane, but in addition to offering programmable signal conditioning, they also have a built-in analog-to-digital converter and engineering unit conversion. One model, for example, can be programmed to work with any thermocouple type and to perform linearization. This same model can be programmed to measure voltage. Other models can measure temperature using RTDs or work with 4- to 20-mA transmitters. Another type of backplane provides 24 digital I/O lines. All of these devices require a regulated 5-V power supply. LabVIEW drivers are available from National Instruments.

Another line of devices is **Advantech's ADAM 4000** series. Curiously, these use some of the same commands as the 6B series but the modules do not plug into a backplane. Instead they are intended for industrial applications with each module located near its transducer, although you can also stack the modules. They run on unregulated power between 10 and 30 V. Each module has its own connector, so wiring can be an added chore. One advantage of the ADAM devices over the 6B is that the analog modules have a pair of digital outputs that can be programmed to turn on at particular setpoints so that you can use them in stand-alone alarm or controller applications. There is also a digital module with four mechanical relays, providing one of the easiest ways to drive relays from LabVIEW. Another module has a built-in multiplexer allowing up to eight voltages or thermocouples to be measured. A version of this module has nonvolatile memory built in, and you can program it to be a stand-alone data logger. This is the device used in our examples (Fig. 16.18).

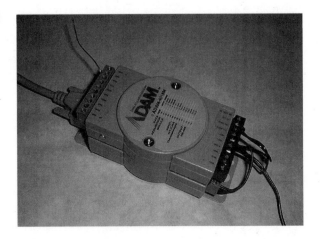

Figure 16.18
Advantech ADAM 4018M module atop a 4520 RS-485 converter module.

A third family of devices is made by **DGH**. Devices in this family can be used as individual modules with their own connectors, like the ADAM, or they can be plugged into a backplane like the 6B. They also run on unregulated power. Unlike the first two families, the DGH modules do not offer programmable ranges or programmable thermocouple types. There is a different module for each range and thermocouple type. DGH has a series of modules that work directly with RS-232, which is a nice feature for very small systems. The company also offers many other unique and interesting stand-alone features.

Conclusion

There are many manufacturers of instruments or controllers that use RS-232, especially in the fields of optics and temperature and motion controllers. Many of the GPIB manufacturers also provide a serial option for their equipment. This oldest of communication protocols seems to be making a resurgence because of its simplicity, availability, and low cost. All you need are the interfacing tricks described here, and your trusty copy of LabVIEW.

Postscript

I wish the need for this postscript did not exist. It concerns the reliability of the PC versus the Macintosh for data acquisition applications. My first exposure to LabVIEW was with version 1.1 when it was only available on the Macintosh. I continued to use only the Macintosh until Windows 95/NT became available. At that time many of my customers expressed a preference for the PC, and it was quite easy to port my LabVIEW programs between the two platforms. However, I had a lot of problems getting the same kind of data acquisition performance out of the PC that I was accustomed to with the Macintosh, despite many people telling me of the superiority of the PC. In particular, I discovered a problem getting any Windows-based PC to accept a continual stream of bytes over its serial port without loss of data. I have finally traced the major culprit in this problem to the *video driver*. Fortunately, in some cases, there is an available fix, but I would like to see the problem addressed by the PC community at large so that Windows-based PCs can attain the same degree of reliable data acquisition performance that we take for granted on the Macintosh.

Here is how to demonstrate the problem so that you can see if the video board on your PC is also a culprit. You will need another computer as a source of a continual stream of serial data. You cannot use the same computer as the source because when the problem occurs, the source stream will be interrupted at the same time the receiver would have lost bytes and thus there will be no bytes to lose. Also, I have found that the problem is worse at the higher screen densities, so choose the highest screen resolution available.

First make sure that you can communicate (with no handshaking) over the serial ports between your two computers at the highest possible baud rate. (If you have read this chapter, you know that you will probably have to use a null modem.) You can use HyperTerminal, LabVIEW, or any other software to make this assessment.

Next, you want to have your source PC repeatedly output a line of text such as *The quick brown fox jumps over the lazy dog*, ending, of course, with a carriage return and line feed. Use HyperTerminal to receive this text stream and observe that the text usually lines up in nice even columns as it scrolls up the screen.

Now resize a window from the desktop by rapidly dragging a corner of it around and over the HyperTerminal window. Watch carefully and see if jagged lines periodically scroll up the window. Shorter lines occur if character bytes from within a line are missing, and longer lines occur if the carriage return byte is missing.

To confirm that this is related to the video driver, resize your screen so that it is the standard VGA mode of 640 by 480 and repeat the test. In my experience, it never happens at that resolution and rarely at 800 by 600. This test is by no means exhaustive—the real test would be your final application. Run your application, move windows around at different screen resolutions, and see if your video driver is to blame.

My guess is that the video driver is disabling interrupts for such a long interval of time (in the milliseconds) that the interrupt routine that is supposed to service the serial port does not get a chance to do so before several more bytes come in and are lost. (The video driver, like any piece of software, can disable interrupts even if it is not itself an interrupt service routine and even if the video hardware that it supports does not have or use an interrupt.)

The solution is, of course, a well-designed video driver. In my case, I was using a Diamond Stealth 2000 video board with the driver supplied by Diamond when I had the problem. This board uses a video chip made by S3, and when I downloaded and installed their driver (at the suggestion of Diamond's excellent technical support) the problem vanished (almost).

I have not been so fortunate with other video boards. In particular, the chip used in Number Nine's Imagine 128 II board is also made by Number Nine, so no alternative driver to fix the problem is available that I am aware of.

Although this problem is demonstrated by use of the serial port, it is not a problem caused by or limited to the serial port. In fact, any interrupt-driven process potentially can be affected in a similar way, and any other software process can create the problem. After the major source of the problem on my PC was fixed, there were two other processes that also generated the problem. The first one was Retrospect Client backup software, which caused the serial port to lose bytes whenever the backup server (running on a Macintosh) interrogated the PC. This was easy for me to spot because the Macintosh was sitting right next to the PC at the time the problem occurred, and I could see on the Mac's screen that it was interrogating the PC.

The second process caused bytes to be lost exactly every 10 seconds and may have been related to a network printing problem. It spontaneously went away days after it started and immediately came back as soon as I generated the same network printing problem, but I could not correlate the solution to anything that I had done the first time it vanished. It did, however, go away after I reloaded Windows NT from the CD-ROM. I have not been motivated to pursue the exact cause of this problem any further.

Again, I want to emphasize that I have never had any problem like this occur on any Macintosh system that I have ever developed, even though these Macintosh systems were doing equivalent serial port processing, had multiple data acquisition boards, and were doing all the usual and some unusual networking activities. And believe me, it is no fun wasting months of time tracking down system-level problems that have no direct relation to the symptoms they cause.

My advice to you if you see unresolved data acquisition performance hits on your PC is to see whether the problem goes away with the standard VGA screen resolution; if it does, see whether you can find a video driver that solves the problem at the higher resolutions. If that fails, get a different video board that has a video driver that does not cause the problem; if *that* fails, use a Macintosh.

Sources

American Advantech Corp.	(408) 245-6678	http://www.advantech.com.tw/
DGH Corp.	(603) 622-0452	http://www.dghcorp.com/
National Instruments, Inc.	(800) IEEE-488	http://www.natinst.com/

APPENDIX

Index to the Accompanying CD-ROM

This is an index to the VIs and other information on the CD-ROM that accompanies this book. It's a multiplatform disk, readable on Macintosh, Windows (3.1/95/NT), and all Unix computers. You can run everything right off the CD-ROM because the files are not compressed. The basic directory structure and file names are the same on all platforms except for Windows 3.1, where shortened file names are required. Windows users can run the setup.exe application to copy all VIs from the CD-ROM to hard disk. That application assures that all the files are not read-only.

VIs on the CD-ROM are flagged in the book with this icon and a path name:
**directory\
file_name.vi**

To locate a particular VI in the book, look up its name in the index.

CD-ROM Contents

The CD-ROM is organized by chapters. Here is a guide to the directories and their associated chapter references. All VIs are compiled in LabVIEW 4 except where noted. Some of the examples have other special requirements, also noted.

ActiveX Chapter 9, "ActiveX and Application Control." Contains three directories of VIs that show you how to view and print reports with and without the SQL Toolkit and how to enter data into a Microsoft Access database using OLE or the SQL Toolkit. **Requires LabVIEW 5.**

ALGORITHMS Chapter 3, "Algorithms." Contains VIs for all of the classical computer algorithms, including sorts, searches, and stacks.

ASYNCH_CIN Chapter 15, "LabVIEW Code Extensions." Contains sample C code for an asynchronous Code Interface Node and its associated calling VI. *Note:* The CIN was compiled for Windows 95/NT only. Users of other platforms will have to compile and load the code resource.

BOOLEAN_ARCH   Chapter 4, "Boolean Machine Architectures." Contains VIs for the basic elements of Boolean machines, such as shifters, adders, flip-flops, and a simple CPU.

CRYPTOGRAPHY   Chapter 5, "Cryptography." Contains VIs that implement various encryption and decryption algorithms.

DATA_STRUCTURES   Chapter 2, "Data Structures." VIs in this directory include queues, trees, and linked lists.

LV9000   Chapter 14, "LabVIEW Software Quality Assurance Guide and Toolkit." The LV9000 toolkit includes documents and VIs for setting up an ISO 9000 quality program. Documents are in Microsoft Word 6 format.

MATH   Chapter 6, "LabVIEW and Mathematics." Features the superlong math library.

   Chapter 8, "Digital Signal Processing." A general-purpose function generator VI, based on the G Math Toolkit. *Note:* You must purchase the G Math Toolkit from National Instruments to use this VI.

SERIAL_UTILITIES   Chapter 16, "LabVIEW and Serial Interfaces." Contains VIs for accessing the serial port with VISA and traditional serial functions.

TCP   Chapter 10, "Networking with TCP/IP." Contains two libraries of VIs that implement a bidirectional TCP/IP client/server architecture, and a fast unidirectional example. **Requires LabVIEW 5.**

Index

ABOUT THE AUTHORS

Ed C. Baroth conceived, developed, and is the Technical Manager of the Measurement Technology Center (MTC) at the Jet Propulsion Laboratory in Pasadena, CA. He holds a bachelor's degree in mechanical engineering from City College of New York, and master's and doctorate degrees in mechanical engineering from the University of California, Berkeley. He has been at JPL since 1981. For recreation he plays electric bass in a straight-ahead jazz band and builds model airplanes. He can be reached at (818) 354-8339 or by e-mail at ebaroth@jpl.nasa.gov.

Joseph P. Damico is a Senior Member of the Technical Staff at Sandia National Laboratories in Livermore, CA. He holds an A.A.S. degree in laser electro-optics from the Texas State Technical College. He also holds B.S. and M.S. degrees in computer science from the California State University, Hayward. At Sandia, he uses LabVIEW to develop instrumentation and control systems for extreme environments including high pressure, high temperature, high energy, and ultrahigh vacuum. He is currently responsible for the design and implementation of an Internet-based global remote monitoring system. He enjoys travel, mountain biking, and cooking. When he is not on the road, he lives in Livermore. He can be reached by e-mail at damico@sandia.gov.

Gregg Fowler is a software engineer with the LabVIEW development team at National Instruments in Austin, TX. His current focus is on developing toolkits to extend LabVIEW's functionality and simplify LabVIEW for various markets. In addition, he has written material for many of the manuals used in the LabVIEW distribution and its associated toolkits. He graduated from Rice University in Houston, TX in 1990 with degrees in computer science and electrical engineering.

Chris Hartsough has been building systems and thinking about how to build them for over 20 years. He has worked on diverse projects from a payroll system to command, control, and communications; from systems management of the engineering data processing for a spacecraft to managing audits; from document preparation with a formal database to testing large-scale flight instruments. He holds a Master of Computer

Science degree from West Coast University. As a volunteer, Chris is assisting the Los Angeles Police department in the design of a crime lab management system. He is also the vice president of his homeowners' association (739 units worth), which was hit hard by the Northridge earthquake. The subjects of his publications range from methodology to software evaluation.

Brad Hedstrom is a senior systems engineer with Advanced Measurements, Inc., Calgary, Alberta, Canada and one of the founding members of the National Instruments Alliance program. He started using LabVIEW 2.0 on a Macintosh in 1991 after spending several frustrating and fruitless weeks with a non-NI DSP/DAQ board with only C and assembler support. He quickly realized that G was much more efficient and, more importantly, much more fun than C, and has been on the LabVIEW bandwagon ever since. Brad currently lives in Victoria, British Columbia, managing AMI's West Coast operations. His e-mail address is brad.h@advmeas.com.

Gary W. Johnson is an instrumentation engineer in the Chemistry and Materials Science Department at the Lawrence Livermore National Laboratory in Livermore, CA. He has a B.S. degree in electrical engineering/bioengineering from the University of Illinois and holds commercial radiotelephone and amateur radio licenses. His professional interests include physics diagnostics, material characterization, measurement and control systems, transducers, analog circuit design, and of course, LabVIEW programming. In his spare time, he enjoys woodworking, bicycling, and audio. He and his wife Katharine, a scientific illustrator, live in Livermore. His e-mail address is johnsong@llnl.gov.

Brian Paquette works as a Senior Systems Engineer with SensArray Corporation.

George Wells graduated from Cal Poly, Pomona, CA, in 1969 with a B.S. in electronic engineering and has worked ever since in the Instrumentation Section at JPL doing analog and digital design for instrumentation systems. For the first 20 years, most of George's work involved building custom data acquisition and control systems, in the early years with discrete ICs and later with microprocessor chips. But since the MTC was established seven years ago, all of his work has been based on off-the-shelf computers, plug-in boards, and external signal conditioners, using LabVIEW to customize applications. These applications range from simple testers that take only a couple days to assemble to full-blown data acquisition and control systems sampling a hundred analog channels plus miscellaneous digital inputs, with real-time engineering unit conversion and display, automatic and manual control, data logging, postprocessing and analysis, and file manipulation.

Lothar Wenzel is a senior software engineer in National Instruments. He received his Ph.D., habilitation, and M.S. in mathematics and computer science from universities in Germany. In his spare time, he likes to think about quantum computers.